Fire
at the
Stymie
Club

Fire at the Stymie Club
Stories from the Mississippi to Chesapeake Bay

by Sandra Olivetti Martin

Editor
William Lambrecht
New Bay Books
Fairhaven, Maryland
NewBayBooks@gmail.com
Cover design and photo collage by Suzanne Shelden

Interior design by Suzanne Shelden
Shelden Studios
Prince Frederick, Maryland
sheldenstudios@comcast.net

A note on type: Cover and section heads are set in
American Typewriter; text is Garamond Premier Pro.

Library of Congress
Cataloging-in-Publication Data

ISBN 979-8-9853477-7-7
Printed in the United States of America
First Edition

For my husband William Ray Lambrecht,
who has been there from beginning to end,
ever the champion for me and for these stories.

Sandra Olivetti Martin

CONTENTS

INTRODUCTION

Sandra Olivetti Martin is best known as founding editor and publisher of *Bay Weekly*, which started in Chesapeake Country thirty years ago as *New Bay Times*. Running a newspaper and writing columns and features for some 50,000 readers was a natural progression of a lifelong obsession with stories. She counts herself lucky to have lived in the heyday of weekly newspapers that invited writers and readers to discover their regions and themselves in print in deeply connected local stories. Writing first for *Illinois Times* and then for her own paper, she discovered the abundance of stories popping and sizzling around her—and those hidden like truffles waiting to be sniffed out.

She lived and wrote in the capital city of Springfield, Illinois, and later in Maryland's Chesapeake Country, at a time when the old ways—be they shoeshine artistry, cultivating tobacco, or home-birthing—boldly stayed relevant in the arrival of the digital age. These are the stories she has told during a writing career that peaked in Maryland, with her column on people's lives and regional culture.

After a lifetime telling the stories of others, in this book she also tells her own. She will be happiest if some of those recollected moments spark your own memories into stories you enjoy again and share with your children and grandchildren.

Sandra grew up far from Maryland, in St. Louis, where she was a bookish girl surrounded by stories above a supper club operated by her father, a charming bookmaker, and her mother, the glamorous daughter of Italian immigrants. Sandra mines her memories from those years in stories throughout the ten sections of this book.

She burrows deepest into family history in the section Past Tense, creating stories from long-lost World War I correspondence in one and in another embarking on a sleuthing mission into the mysterious death of a cousin along the Mississippi River more than a century ago.

Her family's Stymie Club, a supper club and cocktail lounge, offers an enticing setting for the first story, Fire at the Stymie Club, with its extralegal doings and the perfumy sensuality of female clientele and waitresses alike, who look out for precocious little Sandy. Men in ties play cards in the afternoon and women, Sandra's mother among them, eat diet pills so those shimmery dresses that come out nightly grip just so.

Sandra didn't begin her career in journalism; she was a college teacher by trade, of writing and literature, in St. Louis and in Illinois. In the late 1970s in Springfield, Illinois, after long teaching the stories of others, her own writing began to pour forth in *Illinois Times*, a long-lived weekly of repute. In those years she traveled up and down Illinois, which stretches 390 miles from its top to its bottom, where it is closer to Mississippi than to Chicago. Prospecting for stories, she discovered them abundantly, often forgotten, in plain sight. Notebook in hand, she'd talk a story out of anybody, from legendary politicians to persecuted women to an elephant.

Often she embarked in the company of photographer Sue Eslinger, whose photographs adorn this book, and about whom Sandra writes in the Farewells.

While still in the Midwest, Sandra began her trek into long-form writing in the lively style that was a staple of bold weekly newspapers in that era. Pieces in this collection include The Lawrenceville Peephole Incident, a case of perverse sexual harassment, and on-the-scene reporting of a spectacular skyjacking in southern Illinois.

Journalism for Sandra became full time in Washington where she was dragged by me, her husband, and where she took on the post as managing editor of the *Hill Rag*, a walk-to-work distance from our Capitol Hill residence. Soon, her writing would be shaped by a powerful discipline: owning her own newspaper, a fateful plunge after her family moved to the western shore of Chesapeake Bay.

Columns and stories she produced for start-up *New Bay Times*—renamed *Bay Weekly* at the millennium—reflect the curiosity and joy of a writer making her stand along a storied shore. They chronicle the stresses and joys of unfailingly putting out a paper, which grew more difficult amid changing reader habits and predatory Big Tech. Many writers have sprung from the region; H.L. Mencken, Edgar Allen Poe and Dashiell Hammett, to name just a few, and in the modern era, Tom Clancy, Tom Horton and Laura Lippman. Sandra was proud to join their ranks, making *New Bay Times* a weekly anthology of and for Chesapeake Country. Regular in the paper were her own columns and features offering cultural touchstones for Chesapeake Country residents and guideposts for people moving to a mid-Atlantic boating and fishing playground. Stories in the Learning to Live in Chesapeake Country section delve into challenges for women boaters and fishers and profile legendary Marylanders, among them Bernie Fowler, the aging senator and conservationist whose practice of gauging water health by peering down at his white sneakers made him an icon beyond the political realm.

With the title of editor and publisher, Sandra also molded dozens of the young reporters and creative writers who went on to writing and journalism careers.

While editing the paper, she branched out to memoir, beginning the family and personal history stories sampled throughout this book. For some, she found hooks that allowed her to share them with an audience of 50,000 along a 60-mile stretch of the Chesapeake.

Births of grandchildren sent the author on ancestral forays in print, backward and forward. Grandmothering at births in Maryland and California, she explores "lineaments of lineage," pinpoints advances in a newborn's brainstem and confesses that her birthing reading taste evolved from Sartre's *No Exit* when she had kids to J. K. Rowling's Harry Potter series when grandchildren arrived.

In Farewells, a selection of elegantly written appreciations for those who have passed, she honors family, animals and people of her communities. These stories resemble the elegiac styles in *New York Times Magazine's* annual The Lives They Lived, featuring pieces that convey the sadness in the passing of people not widely known while crediting them for what they achieved.

Among her subjects are the eccentric Vera Freeman, the *grande dame* who created a South Pacific-styled restaurant and marina after landing in rural Maryland from Hollywood. In From Triple Trouble Blueberry Farm to Composting Immortality, Sandra recounts the career of Frank Gouin, a renowned academic, composting pioneer and in retirement the *Bay Weekly's* highly regarded weekly Bay Gardener columnist. She returns at book's end to where it began, with salutes to her parents.

Versions of some stories appeared in *New Bay Times/Bay Weekly* and in *Illinois Times*. Finding My Roots in Italy was first published in the *St. Louis Post-Dispatch*. Am Liking This Life Fine ran in *Kentucky Monthly* magazine. She has also written for the *Washington Post, Illinois Issues* and *Planning* magazine. Fire at the Stymie Club, from which this book's title is drawn, and The Untimely Death of James Smith highlight Sandra Olivetti Martin's previously unpublished work.

—William Lambrecht

Fire at the Stymie Club

STORIES FROM THE MISSISSIPPI RIVER TO CHESAPEAKE BAY

SANDRA OLIVETTI MARTIN

PART I

Fire at the Stymie Club

*stymie (v.) to prevent advancement. From stymie (n.) in golf, 1857, "condition in which an opponent's ball blocks the hole" (1834); of uncertain origin, perhaps from Scottish stymie "person who sees poorly"

PRELUDE

I was born into a world that seemed newly created, like me, by amnesiac parents. Past and future converged in the crystalline droplet of the present. History was made up day by day in our lives.

Headlong as they were, Gene and Elsa Olivetti Martin gave our history a place in time and space. Our place had a name: the Stymie Club. Roadhouse, restaurant or tavern—whatever it was when they bought it, they classed it up into a supper club and cocktail lounge.

My parents had not known that place with its inherited name was where we were going. If my father were to rise from his grave to tell me his—hence our, my mother's and mine—life had a plan, I'd say, "Are you kidding me?"

Plan or no plan, our life in the Stymie Club played out like destiny. With such a name, how could it not? We were stuck in place and purpose.

Before the Stymie Club, we lived in Eden. Primal memories take me back to the surrounding warm oceans and big skies of Key West, where blimps played tag with clouds. My father's improbable Navy career put us in an island paradise where the most obeyed rule was seize the day. In 1943, as World War II blew on, life played out in the present. Midway between harm's way and the lives they had lived, my parents were having too much fun to think about the future.

A small sandy girl, I fed on sun-warmed images: giant, leathery leaves of the impatient jungle; coconuts falling from trees; lizards regenerating lost limbs; conch shells walking off before you could hold them to your ear to hear the ocean; flotillas of Japanese men o' war, renamed for the enemy; grown-ups playing like children. Those are my first memories, and they still keep me warm. But consciousness dawned in a small, post-World War II house in the developing suburbs of St. Louis.

My father, no longer a sailor in crisp Key West whites, is mostly absent from those memories, though he too lived in that small house on Echo Lane, Overland. Even my mother, the center of my life, is tangential.

My grandmother guides my days. She and I set fire to the kitchen curtains lighting our Halloween pumpkin. Between the little front yard and street, I splash in open storm channels instead of the ocean. Was my other companion a wirehaired mutt named Pal? If so, he was ephemeral, like his memory.

Mother, the force of law and order, gallops in like the Lone Ranger to put out our fires and rush me to the hospital when I have fallen down the cellar steps. For our transgressions, she holds her mother-in-law to blame. At three and four, I watch and listen, a spy on the divisions of my elders. Thus begins my training for a career in journalism.

Mother: Elsa Olivetti Martin. Grandmother: Florence Bunting Martin. Father: Gene Martin. They were my only elders. Plus me, that was our family: tiny and insular and seemingly dropped out of time to a new quickly erected bungalow in a new place in an old city. Out of the giant dislocations of Depression and war and the loss of all others dear to them, they abandoned our Key West Eden to resettle in their point of last departure, St. Louis.

READJUSTMENT

Now I understand that Echo Lane was a waypoint as my parents plotted their course. The Servicemen's Readjustment Act of 1944 made the low-interest loan that let them buy the bungalow, hastily assembled for just their sort of post-war refugees. It offered shelter on the run as they figured out what might come next.

My father could have used the G.I. Bill to go to school. "Become an undertaker," my mother urged. "There are always customers," she reasoned, and Gene Martin was suited to the work. "He has no conscience," she explained. "He doesn't care what he does to people."

Food and drink—plus in my father's case, gambling—were what they knew. Wartime Key West, Dad's luck-of-the-draw naval station, had let the good times roll. They'd come back to St. Louis—a decision both regretted in later life—but they weren't going to let the party end.

By 1948, they'd found their place. Stymie Club, Supper Club and Cocktail Lounge proclaimed neon lettering on the twin disks—were they stymied golf balls?—topping the tall sign at the road.

Back then, this stretch of Olive Street Road in the first west St. Louis suburb of University City still had a small-town feel. Our block had two grocery stores, a Kroger and an A&P; a hardware store; a second-floor bowling alley; a five-and-ten-cent store; a pharmacy, Millburg's, that sold comic books and cigars; a movie theater, the Beverly; and the workshop of a stonemason who specialized in tombstones and displayed his work outdoors. Location was on his side. Across Olive Street, behind a Missouri limestone-block wall supporting an iron fence, Chesed Shel Emeth Cemetery buried the Jewish dead of the region.

Exploring the stonemason's lot, I discovered sparkling pieces of quartz, discarded as if they were worthless. Walking atop the rise and fall of the limestone wall brought me close as I dared to the cemetery. I hadn't yet felt the presence of the past, so no ghosts of its complex history rose up to haunt me.

Our place in this mid-century neighborhood of low brick-front buildings was a throwback to when the land had been country. The Stymie occupied a big old two-story house, set in an old-fashioned green yard where a pair of pear trees aged and snowball bushes bloomed blizzards. The house was a long rectangle running east and west, parallel to the street, fronted by a full-length open porch with a floor of clay tiles. Nobody walked up the porch stairs to the front door. Everybody drove up the crushed-rock—later asphalt— driveway to the parking lot and entered by unassuming back doors. One door led to the main dining room; the other to the bar and cocktail lounge. Indoors, the rooms met at a central staircase. It climbed straight upstairs to our second-floor home.

The Stymie Club's originators had failed, for one reason or another, to stymie enough customers, and the place had closed, awaiting a future. Along came Gene, who had not only the G.I. Bill but also a small inheritance from a relation back along his Martin line. And he had Elsa, who believed she could do anything, and just about could.

Elsa lived by the gospel of work. She took the shuttered place they bought in hand. She scrubbed floors, knocked out walls then replastered and painted them, washed windows (there were many) and sewed curtains. As they set up to paint the staircase wall Indian red, Mother established their labor contract. "Gene," she said, after his first clumsy dabs. "You're so good at stories. Tell me stories to make the time pass, and I'll do the painting."

In those years, 1948 or 1949, we were at the cusp of eras. Until the ramped-up industrialization of World War II, for many Americans home and work were one place, whether farms or rooms above their small business, market, shoe repair shop or tavern. Post-war, home and work quickly and broadly distanced.

When mother abandoned her immigrant mother's subsistence boarding house, with its home garden and winery, cow shed and chicken yard, for wage-work in St. Louis, she had jumped from the old economy to the new. My father's family had made the transition a generation earlier. Elmer, my grandfather, had abandoned his family's migrant way of life to hook his wagon to his era's dominant industry, coal.

Now, with all our family's money flowing into the Stymie, we followed the old tradition. Sometime in the whirl of preparation, we all moved upstairs. We had a bathroom shared with women customers and a foursquare of big rooms divided by the staircase, but we lived mostly on one side. Mother and Dad shared a bedroom. The other, plus a side-hall play space, was mine.

Where was grandmother? I say we moved, but she did not come with us. With our occupation of the Stymie Club, she must have begun her life on her own, setting up with few belongings in a series of apartments that diminished over the years to rooms. I was still in her charge, but she came and went, and some charmed times I stayed with her.

Those sleepovers seemed like visits to other planets. Grandmother's rooms and ways were quiet, without flash or striving. Days with her were sufficient unto themselves. More alien were excursions to friends' houses and school, where families were all of the new era. Mothers stayed home while fathers went to work in a small business or for big business. How I wished my father sold cars, as did fathers of my classmates. We were not like these people. Their worlds were not ours.

The Stymie Club was my world. Like a potter handling wet clay, the Stymie and its people molded my consciousness. And forever after, it furnishes the rooms of my unconscious. In dreams decades later, I have pushed enemies down the foot-worn wooden stairs into the scary abyss of our club's basement.

AWAKENING
–SEVEN A.M.–

I awaken in my upstairs bedroom before the morning is very old.

But not before the Stymie's business begins. First to arrive is Leon Williams, the porter. His day begins in the cavernous basement, casing empty beer bottles before the distribution truck arrives and its driver unloads new cases of longneck Budweiser, Michelob, Falstaff, Stag, Schlitz and Griesedieck and loads up the empties from the previous day.

Those empties follow a path I find captivating. I have watched and imitated part of the journey, sortieing into the bar in silent early morning when the dankness of yesterday's beer and cigarettes hangs heavily in the air. Collecting empties from the bar and tables, I copy the bartender's smooth, thoughtless insertion of the spent bottles into the chute. Through the hole they go, clattering down a flexible tube a whole story to bounce on the slanted top shelf of a chicken-wire bottle cage, then descend four shelves unharmed to the bottom. There Leon finds them the next morning.

He is a steady man, conscientious in dress, demeanor and movements; erect, trim and well muscled in a self-effacing way. His uniform—checked pants and white, short-sleeved button-up shirt—is fresh starch-pressed every morning and stays so despite the dirty job that starts his day.

Bottles are never fully empty. Stale beer, sticky as honey, runs everywhere. Worse, drinkers in these cigarette-smoking days are likely to snuff their butts into spent bottles. Bottle-washing, I learn later, is a line of its own at 1950s' breweries.

Next Leon assures the Stymie's customers—many of the same men who drained last night's empties—do not go thirsty this new day. He carries in a day's worth of full heavy cardboard cases, precisely apportioned by brand, to be buried in crushed ice in the behind-the-bar cooler.

In the back scullery, he scoops the hollow-center cubes from the icemaker's whirling maw to feed the crusher. Pouring the shining cubes into the machine's cornucopia, he pushes the mass through with the metal plunger. Sparkling crystals rush from the blades into his galvanized bucket. Into the cooler they cascade around the bottles to be served, cold and damp, to the day's thirsty customers.

Upstairs, the sounds of Leon's work are part of my early morning. Otherwise, all the noise has gone out of the Stymie. In the quiet, Leon's footsteps and the noise of the grinder are reminders of another waking person.

I do not rush the morning. There is awakening, sifting through dreams to come back to the daylight. Then, in my nightgown, I read comics and books about heroic dogs and noble horses. I read in bed or sitting in my kid-sized red leather armchair. At my little roll-top desk I draw crayon pictures of trees with the hair and faces of women. I have a china cabinet of dishes to prepare parties and a growing collection of horse statues to bring to life. One is a foot-tall plastic Palomino saddled Western style. We reimagine the cowboy movies I have seen down the street at the Beverly Theater.

I am allowed to walk that block and cross Olive Street Road on my own. My Uncle Maxie insists on holding my hand, diminishing my independence, when he lives with us. In those months, he sleeps in the cross-hall oversize closet and dressing room where Mother kept her clothes. He is trying to take care of me, and she is trying to take care of her slow big brother, Massimo with a string of middle names Olivetti. Thoughts play in my mind as I move from the musings of my bedroom into my playroom.

KITCHEN PREP
–EIGHT TO TEN-THIRTY A.M.–

Downstairs, Lovie Mitchell opens up the kitchen. The lights go on, banishing the emptiness of a place meant to hold people. Now coming down will be safe rather than a raid into alien territory. Lovie is beautifully, glistening black with a rosiness echoing her red lipstick. Her breasts and bottom bulge out her starched white dress and apron, but her calves and ankles are thin. From bottom to top, she is shapely.

Lovie brings the kitchen to life. Supersized aluminum pots that had hung quietly from the overhead rack clatter into action on an eight-burner stove. Ovens, broilers, grills, and steam tables fire up. Refrigerators yield provisions. As her minions, kitchen boys and salad girls, appear, Lovie sets them spinning.

Meat is carried up from the basement walk-in box, a chill tomb where a side of beef hangs among crates of oysters, live, wiggling lobsters and brown waxed boxes of pre-cut filet, sirloin, T-bone steaks and thick pork and lamb chops. Freezers supply hamburger patties and bags of cut potatoes for our short, stocky French fries.

Hands fly making the salad station ready, grating carrots, chopping celery, slicing radishes, washing cherry tomatoes and boiling eggs. Soups begun by the night chef are perfected, at least one new one every day. Lovie oversees creation of daily specials: Salisbury steak; beef tenderloin tips with noodles; chicken and dumplings; spaghetti with meatballs; calves liver with onions and bacon;

macaroni and cheese crisp on top and gooey in the center. Coffee is brewed in the giant three-tube urn with sections for regular, decaf and hot water.

The warming kitchen throbs with energy, a handful of people working full out at a couple of dozen jobs in sync to please dozens of customers with fat portions of appetizing treats. Having absorbed synchronicity with the kitchen steam, I recognized it years later in the newsroom where I, imitating Lovie, cooked up each week's stories.

Mother comes downstairs while the kitchen is heating up. If help is needed, she pitches in, maybe grinding up a couple of gallons of chicken for salad. I like it when she does that and follow her down into the basement, which must be the only workspace left, to watch as she pulls the meat off stewed chicken carcasses and thrusts it into the whirring machine.

Mother doesn't drink coffee or eat breakfast—women of her class live on alcohol and diet pills—but what I want, perhaps a quick sauté of chicken livers, she or Lovie will make for me. I eat as I watch from the end of the sprawling kitchen work table the orderly rush toward lunch: stirring and sampling of soup; the downward blow that cores iceberg heads; pounds of bacon sizzling in the deep fryer for club sandwiches, BLTs, and orders of livers; the slicing of hard-boiled eggs, one by one through an egg harp, for salads.

As the lunch hour nears, Mother climbs the stairs to shower and change. Her preparations are simple. Hairdressing amounts to washing her short, curly hair in the shower, toweling it dry and running a comb through it. She wears little makeup, only mascara, eyebrow pencil and red lipstick. Over her matching, silky underwear and girdle, she pulls on a belted dress or suit sporting a little peplum shirt and smart lapels. She clips on showy earrings and, on three-inch heels, she walks down the stairs into the rising buzz.

The waitresses now arrayed are all nearly as pretty as my mother. Ethel and Lorraine, Margaret, Jeannie, Irma, June and Lou—three or four each lunch—dress in black skirts, white blouses and starched white aprons. No, perhaps that is their evening wear. A photo reminds me that their daytime uniform is a dress of some pale pastel, perhaps yellow. Reserved Lorraine, who always wears her hair pulled into a bun the size of a lunch plate at the back of her head, has a tomboy daughter, Patty, who is my friend. Ethel, who I call Pretty Bird, has a talking parakeet she brings to my birthday party as guest and entertainment. We are confidants.

I am the background, taken for granted as I watch the women at work and listen as they talk with their customers, with each other, and with my mother. I collect the stories behind the faces they show to the customers. Most are mothers, with children some- times far in the background. They take care of themselves; the few husbands are invalids or men on the edge, where some of the kids are, too. Like my mother, each has troubles in her story. Broken hearts figure in them all.

But they do not show it—except June, who wears her hard times on her face and in the posture of her long, thin body. They take Mother's advice: "When you come to work, leave your troubles outside. Nobody wants to hear them."

Stymie waitresses laugh and joke and know their customers by name and habit. To one and all in the Stymie's democracy, they serve cocktails, club and prosperity sandwiches, hot lunch specials, steaks and affectionate banter. Affairs, even marriages, rise from their companionship. Margaret Hertzog marries Red Pritchard, who does not get along with her tough son, Johnny Nero. Lorraine Gibson—mother of Patty and a boy dead crossing a street—eventually disentangles from the manipulative union-organizer Gib to marry high school coach Bat Masterson, whose real name has been subsumed by his TV-borrowed nickname.

Some affairs end badly. Ethel loves and loves again, but never for long—at least apparently, for my big ears have picked up whispers of a secret love, a priest. Irma—who Mother has stolen from the Chinese restaurant where we eat chop suey—dies after a back-alley abortion. Mother's lost loves—in combinations I am still understanding—push her more than once to swallow bottles of sleeping pills.

Whatever their story, the waitresses wear smiles and work like poets, with succinct, elegant accuracy. These are not educated women, many may not have gone to high school, but they have polish and secret, refined skills like fileting a fish off the bone or setting a dessert aflame without burning down the restaurant. They are complex, deep women with laughing faces.

These stories unfold over the years, until finally they seem foreordained, as if they have been true forever.

THE FELLOWSHIP OF MEN
–TEN-THIRTY A.M. TO TWO P.M.–

When my father descends the staircase, the barroom stirs to life. Leon has polished a shine to the wood-topped bar, to the black-topped tables, to the stainless-steel cooler doors. The stage is set for another day and night as Dad steps behind the bar to see that all is as it should be, the coolers full, the bottles rows deep, the glasses ranged like by like: shot, cocktail, martini, old-fashioned, after-dinner. Out of sight behind the bar are the tools of the trade: worn wooden mallets, long spoons, sharp, short knives, cutting boards, shakers, strainers.

Beneath the bar at the tight turn of its closed end, away from the bins of ice and double sinks for washing and rinsing glasses, are well-handled leather dice cups with red plastic dice inside. Shelved next to them are stacks of unopened Ace playing cards. A black telephone hangs on the wall at that same end of the bar. Those, plus a memorandum pad for recording bets, are tools of the backstory of the Stymie bar. Bookmaking and gaming are open secrets, practiced in plain view, an everyday part of life.

In early years, a pinball machine lights up the room, collecting the small change that keeps the club's lights on and rewarding small victories with bells and whistles. There's even a game of shuffleboard, with a sprinkling of sand on its polished deck. A showy nickel-a-play jukebox adds music, light and color. As the Stymie gets classier, only the jukebox remains. It and the cigarette machine with so many brands to choose from. I am allowed to slide in the quarter to buy Chesterfields for my mother. It's almost like playing a game.

Year in and out, Gene Martin starts the day on the phone, calling in his orders, checking the day's odds, doing the morning business. Then, while the morning is still quiet, he sits at his bar, resting his short, hairy forearms on its bolster, to read the morning newspaper, the *St. Louis Globe-Democrat*. He's casually dressed in cuffed, belted slacks, tailored to be loose fitting, and a dress shirt open at the collar. For a bite to eat, he asks Lovie for an egg sandwich or an onion sandwich with mustard, opens a can of sardines or devours a glass of milk thickened with saltine crackers.

About 11:30, the drinking day begins, as my father mixes himself a Bloody Mary and takes the first shift behind the bar. Over a long lunch hour the bar fills up with regulars—Big Dog, Harvey Wheeler, Shelby Curley, Irv Kress the jukebox man, Texaco Eddy—who are self-employed, little employed or able to leave their business to their crews for most of the workday. In some redecorating, Mother has papered a back bar wall with a comic scene of card-playing dogs. Big Dog is named for the heavy-jowled great Dane, in honor of their resemblance.

At or behind the bar might be any of a buff trio of football players who are off-season regulars. Washington Redskin fullback Ed Quirk, six-foot-one and 231 pounds, welcomed the Stymie to the neighborhood where he grew up. Hanging out with him are fellow St. Louisans Bob Steuber and Jim Kekeris. All three played for the University of Missouri, and all three went to the pros.

By 1948, when the Stymie opened, Steuber was out of the game with a broken bone in his back, but the pain in his legs is what I hear him talking about. My father, a sporting man, has the score on all of their careers. He reads about their exploits in the newspaper where, from their high school days, they have been regularly featured. He knows that Ed is a strong man, not only a punishing runner through the line of scrimmage but also an Olympic-class shot putter who set records in world competition. He enjoys their company, and it is good business for customers to mingle with sports celebrities.

15

At some invisible signal, perhaps it is a quorum, Dad glides out from behind the bar—he is a short, stocky man smooth in his gate—and action gathers at the tables lining the window wall. Fresh packs of cards come out for an afternoon of gin rummy. My father presides, blunt fingers shuffling gracefully—no fanfare—the two stacks merging seamlessly, the crisp cards clicking as they fall into place. As the men play, they eat and drink, smoke and joke. Money changes hands. The waitresses serve more rounds.

The afternoon Stymie bar is a men's club, aromatic with cigar smoke, deep with men's voices, devoted to sport, expectant with the flow of the game and heady with the testosterone of big-armed, solid-thighed football players.

STYMIE GIRL
-THE AGE OF INNOCENCE-

Sometimes there is a job for me. I am dispatched from the barroom to the drugstore for a new box of cards or a new supply of—always— Robert Burns Panatela cigars. Returning with the box of cigars, I may get another assignment: Play the jukebox, feeding it the handful of quarters the bartender takes from the register. As I open my palm for them, the bartender may tease me, throwing a block as if I were a defensive back to be hurled aside. I may cuddle up to a waitress, running my hand down her slick shirt as she waits for her order of drinks.

I have the run of the place. I have explored from basement to roof. The basement is a dungeon of dangers. The stairs are dim, treads worn with footfalls and risers open into dark space. Corners hold more than shadows, boxes and crates. Ghosts are stuffed behind the cases of whiskey locked in the storeroom. The walk-in box, where meat hangs in still-recognizable body parts, is a cold tomb whose door will seal closed if not watched from the corner of an exploring eye. I venture to the basement to test my bravery. The roof is an aerial adventure. When no one is watching, I have crawled around it from porch to turret. Built on a rise, the Stymie stands so high that I can see all the way to the University City city hall two miles away. Maybe all the way to the Chase-Park Plaza Hotel. If this were two decades into the future, I could see the riverfront St. Louis Arch.

The empty rooms of early morning are mine to reconnoiter, among the leftovers from the eating, drinking and smoking of the night before. Wet beer and tobacco hang in an acrid funk before they are overtaken by chemical pine, sweeping compound and open windows. I examine the remains of the night before as if I were Dick Tracy from the *Sunday Post-Dispatch* color comics, seeing what can be made from what can no longer be seen. I am the ghost haunting the Stymie—until I am not.

I have been seen. Peter Switzer's hair is the color of the red liquorish of his family's famous St. Louis candy business. He is a class bully, and I am a favorite victim. I see him first, an enemy invader, sitting down for dinner with his family in a booth in my family's dining room. I make myself invisible to cover my slinking, head-down retreat up stairs to safety. But he sees me.

"She's in my class," he tells Ethel, their waitress, and my dearest Pretty-Bird betrays me, dragging me to their booth. "Restaurant girl," he whispers at me under his breath. To him—and to all my schoolmates, with whom he'll share his discovery—I am of a different, lesser tribe.

My pride has become my stigma, his taunt.

THE LIMITS OF INVISIBILITY

In this world of our own making, we only think we are safe. We are who we are—only until our shield of invisibility fails.

Visible, we are vulnerable. I feel the shame in being seen, publicly identified. It burns like the stigmata that blesses the saints. Even Wonder Woman has her tender spot, and so does my Amazonian mother, who is watched by enemy spies. My father, who has no conscience, is harder to touch. He has also given thought to protection, as Mother and I carelessly have not. The sheriff is my father's friend. Lunch is always on the house for policemen, in uniform or not, and my father's handshake may include the passage of a fold of bills.

But other eyes are watching. The part of our story they see explodes as news. The afternoon paper—where my husband will work decades later—hires good reporters who tell the story well. Six decades later, I am the latest of tens of thousand to read damning page-one paragraphs, including quotes from an ambitious deputy sheriff to a *St. Louis Post-Dispatch* reporter:

"Numerous telephone calls were received, and the person answering the calls would discuss the placing of bets on horses in certain races and write down notes on a memorandum pad, which he retained in his pocket."

Patrons spoke of "bets on horses and betting on results of certain baseball games," the deputy told the reporter, recounting his undercover surveillance.

What the sheriff's gambling squad saw was against the law. But the day his posse raided the joint, they found more, and less, than they expected: They interrupted their sheriff's lunch. How that went down made good telling for both the reporter and the editorial writer who later took up the story.

"There was the sheriff, waiting for a sandwich in the club room, when in bursts his own gambling squad, looking for something besides lunch. What a surprise," the droll editorialist commented,

18

lambasting St. Louis County Sheriff Arthur C. Mosley. But not my father.

The raiding party had not expected to see the sheriff, and the sheriff had not expected to see his squad. But the sheriff rose to the occasion.

"I see you fellows are here for the same purpose I am," he said.

"Let's combine forces," he added, big-footing the investigation.

Here's what happened next, reported in his own words—

Said the sheriff, "I asked Martin: 'What have you got upstairs?'"

"He answered, 'Let's go look.'"

"The three of us went upstairs," the sheriff said, including the deputy, on the journey to the second floor. There, he reported, "We found a desk. In it were records of the club's business. We looked through these carefully. We searched the entire upstairs. And there isn't even a telephone or a telephone jack up there. Then we searched the downstairs. There's a pay telephone booth on the porch and one private telephone behind the bar. We found no evidence of gambling."

"I'm convinced there is no gambling there," the sheriff added.

He got a second from a "member of a recent grand jury" who happened to be on the scene.

"I asked him if he had heard rumors of gambling there," the sheriff recounted. "He said the tavern was anything but a gambling establishment."

That was the end of it—for my father, if not for the sheriff, at least for a time. For when trouble came knocking, my father had a knack of sliding out of its way. No arrests were made in that raid.

As far as arrests, my father was not always so lucky, *Post-Dispatch* readers learned from the unnamed reporter, who knew the police blotter. "Martin has been convicted 55 times by St. Louis police, mostly in connection with gambling investigations," he reported.

That count was generous, according to an earlier *Post-Dispatch* story. That 1940 story put his arrest record at 113—"with no convictions."

THE FLOW OF TIME
–TWO O'CLOCK TO FIVE PM–

Before beginning a new shift on the Stymie's cyclic clock, my parents step back from their working roles. Perhaps they rest, though neither seems to need much sleep. Dad can nap like a cat, then snap to alertness. Sleep makes Mother vulnerable, so she enters it briefly and cautiously, with the help of pills.

Often they have an afternoon out, on their own. My parents spend their free time with other partners. That is one of the many things people do that they don't talk about in our world. We see but we do not say. Not to outsiders. Not even to each other.

My mother and girlfriends Virginia and Kay dress up for lunches out, or cocktails, at other friends' restaurants. Tony Henschel is another friend. He is a golf pro, and Mother is improving her game. Often, I get to come along on their outings. Tony says I could be a Babe Zaharias with my strength, but I complain that golf is toooo hard. I'm happier just seeing what I can see.

I am driving with them, feeling the 115-degree-heat blast through the wing window of Tony's Ford Sunliner convertible on St. Louis' hottest-ever summer day, July 14, 1954. When we visit his mother, I play with an antique bisque-headed doll.

When we don't see Tony anymore, Mother is sad.

"What's wrong?" I ask her, desperate to help.

"You're too young to understand," she says, swallowing her tears.

On the night she carries out her threat to swallow a bottle of sleeping pills, she is rushed to the hospital to have her stomach pumped. I remember the hospital, the stranger, a Black woman who comforted a shrieking child.

My father's companions become regulars at the Stymie, and they join him on afternoon and evening outings. Some of those afternoons, in my early teens, he takes me along speed-boating on the Mississippi River.

I often sit in the back seat on our rides to the river. My father drives with his shirt off, exposing his sloping belly and broad, hairy back and arms to the sun. He is provisioned with a gallon thermos of icy Salty Dogs. Still, he might have a "sinking spell," so we stop at roadhouses along the way.

There's always a full cup and a case of beer in my father's Cadillac convertibles and in his Chris-Craft. He drives the boat as smoothly as he does the auto. His vessel has no name, but it has water skis, and I get one lesson on land before he drops me in the big brown river. Eventually I rise out of the frothing wake, exhilarated. When I fall, he circles back for me. I never see him in the river, but he has had to swim for it.

A storyteller who cultivated a streak of derring-do, he told this story on himself. It was a good one, and made its way into the *St. Louis Post-Dispatch's* gossipy boating column in August of 1959: "Martin and an unidentified companion swam to shore after their 18-foot-speedboat struck a log in Dardenne slough at 1 a.m. and sank in 20 feet of water."

Dad would have told it over a game of cards, with more detail than the columnist reported it. My mother must not have heard it, and she didn't read newspapers, for if she had, she'd have put an end to my trips to the Mississippi.

However the afternoon passes, it ends the same way. My parents dress for dinner. My father upgrades to a full sharp-creased suit with a Countess Mara tie. Advancing in her glamor over the years,

Mother slinks into deep-cut cocktail dresses and three-inch heels, plastic Springolators in summer. I watch from her chaise lounge, hypnotized by the transformations of womanhood.

When my parents appear, brushed and glamorized, the Stymie Club's nightly party begins again.

THE HIVE
–EIGHT P.M. UNTIL ONE A.M.–

A dream has roused me from bed and sent me from the loneliness of my bedroom down the stairs into the throb of life below. As I sit shivering, perhaps sniveling, in my nightgown on the third stair from ground level—the intersection of large and small dining rooms, then to the buzzing cocktail lounge—a customer notices the grieving child. "What's wrong, sweetie?" she asks, and I hold my arms out to her wailing "Mama!"

She hoists me on her hip and carries me into the crowded barroom. "Look what I found," she says, from a position that assures that everyone in the demi-octagon room will hear her. My mother unbuttons herself from the good-time throng and unpeels me from the other woman. "I've got her," she says, and her look says don't plan on making much hay from this. I've also got your number.

Sleepy, sad, and five or six, I understand none of this. But all of it seeps into me so that even now, when I am older than my mother ever lived to be, I can read the meaning of her silent telegraphy.

Reassured in my true mother's arms, afloat in her signature smell of White Shoulders perfume, I grip my sturdy legs around her. She carries me upstairs, scratches my back with her short, red fingernails and calms me with sweet nothings. I vanish into sleep, and she descends back down the stairs, into her hive, where she is queen bee.

Everyone in the hive recognizes her position. Sexual authority sizzles off her in her walk, her confidence, her huge diamond ring. Around her, the crowd swirls like a swarm, each bee eager to make honey. She and my father—*Elsa and Gene* as their pink matchbooks say—glide among them, working the crowd. He is hail-fellow-well-met; she—don't you wish she was yours. All the men do. She plays by this rule: Never say yes, never say no.

The only criterion for entrance to the Stymie Club's nighttime scene is money to drink at the bar. Come often, and you'll feel like a member. Novelty is not unwelcome, but regularity is the norm.

I watch and memorize the nightly pageant. The women are fascinating; I get to share their spell, though it is not cast for me. Women with names like Lucille, Jo-Bob and Dru have dressed to sweeten the night ahead. Their preparation is a sacred ritual. They lift from their chests of drawers matching lace-trimmed lingerie—bras, panties or girdles and half-slips—to glide or struggle into. Half dressed before the mirrors of their dressing tables, they do their hair, make up their faces and choose their jewelry. From their closets they pick party dresses, pinched waist and off the shoulder or with a bit of plunge in the neckline. Except in summer, when they go bare legged, they roll up nylon stockings and fix them in the hooks of their girdles or garter belts. They plunge their feet into three-inch high heels. In the species of humans, the females dress to be chosen.

Tame-plumaged men allow themselves a bit of flash. The era of casual wear is dawning, but suits are evening standard, though in the heat of the hour a man may strip down to his dress shirt. Some will dare an open collar, but most choose neckties, and those may be as flamboyant as the draperies my mother has chosen, and likely sewed and hung. Their jewelry is cufflinks, a tie pin or tie bar and often a heavy diamond pinky ring like my father wears. Like him, some of the men have manicured nails, buffed to a shine in hotel barbershops.

By day, the men are sheet-metal dealers, plumbing contractors, appliance salesmen and dentists plus the occasional star—the golf pro or pro football player—drawn in by fellowship and female attractions. The night transforms the men. Drink by drink, small tradesmen brighten into more eligible suitors. By night, they are part of a scintillating company, and the women may allow them to stage a flirtation.

Early comers fill the bar stools, leaning in against the leather bolster. As the crowd swells, people cluster two and three deep, mingling together so familiarly that they are as much with everybody as anybody.

Their numbers are doubled by reflections in the wall of mirrors behind the bottles along the back of the bar. Sometimes a woman steals a look at herself, pats her hair, considers how she exhales her cigarette. The tables that ring the outer wall, deuces and fours, are full with a changing cast as the players shift from one pod to another.

People lean in very close to one another, and there is lots of touching, man to man and man and woman to each other: the arm around the shoulder, the pat on the behind, the cheek stroked with a fingertip.

The steady flow of alcohol fuels the buzz. Bills, glasses and bottles slide across the polished wood surface of the bar, amid ashtrays fuming with cigars and cigarettes. The bartender works fast and efficiently, pouring liquor into a jigger, adding soda, seltzer or water from the soda gun, popping the tops off beer bottles, making change. He wears a white shirt and starched, long white apron tied high around his waist. His hands are big, the hands of a lumberjack. He can slide a handful of highballs across the bar in one swoop. His eyes cover the whole bar, all the customers and the waitresses who come and go with little round trays of drinks and empties. He knows everybody, and he jokes as he works.

The cash register rings. The jukebox plays. Laughter explodes amidst the barrage of words and song.

The Stymie Club hosts a nightly party, through every night and into the next morning. I have fallen into a deep dream sleep when my parents come up to bed in the small hours.

THE ETERNAL PRESENT OF MEMORY

In the eternal present of memory, my girlhood Stymie years are all one day. I am not yet initiated into clocks and calendars. I must beg to have the color funny pages of the *Sunday Post-Dispatch* read to me. Yet, mysteriously, I can suddenly read books. School does not exist to trouble my world. Yet I go to school, enduring the daily repression of life on another planet. I am five, six, seven, eight or nine; it makes no difference. The Stymie Club's umbilical stretches a quarter mile away to the just-built ranch-style house at 7756 Burr Oak Lane, a street with nary a burr oak and few grown trees. Even after Mother and I have moved into that house, as I metamorphose into a pre-teen, a teen, a high schooler, I am the Stymie girl.

FIRE

Even as a college girl exploring the maze of who I will become, I am still the Stymie girl.

My mother will not have me going away to college; she will miss me too much. So I live at home with her and stepfather Gene Schaper (my mother has a thing for Genes), a Burt Lancaster looka-like in face and Marine physique. To placate me, she has given me the third bedroom of our ranch house as my study to decorate as I chose. Of course there is a wall of board bookshelves that should have been supported by bricks except that this Gene is talented in all kinds of handwork and installs a frame of vertical channels of metal perfo-rated so that shelf brackets can be fitted in at any height.

I chose a Danish modern desk so simple that it mystifies my grandmother. "Where are all the drawers and crannies?" she wants to know. Nowadays the customary weekends my grandmother and I share together at Mother's house are less frequent, as I have my own life to live. Now, when Grandmother comes, I am the one doing the driving, picking her up from the ancient high-rise where she lives in a single room.

I relish the mobility of my own car, bought for me by my parents. The two-tone green Chevrolet Corvair sedan on which my father gets,

I think, the short end of some kind of a deal, is not nearly my dream. An Austin-Healey convertible is the style to which I hope to become accustomed. But Dad doesn't drink with an Austin-Healey dealer.

My parents do not understand me, now less than ever. No more than I understand them. But the way I figure, understanding them is not my job. I am the child. They are the parents, and understanding me is their job. I take it for granted that I am smarter than everybody in their generation and mine—a few exceptions allowed. In matters from taste to morality, I know better than they. I am setting a course different from theirs.

A June Sunday breaks so full of promise that, I decide, this will be the day I begin my career as a writer.

With my portable typewriter and a blanket, I set out on the 75-mile trip to my godmother Kay King's place on the St. Francois River outside Farmington, Missouri. Kay lives in the country retreat she shared with her last husband, Bill King, when he retired from the tavern business. He raised pheasants and turkeys and made wonderful bowls and chests of cedar. After he dies of a stroke, Kay says she raises hell on the 500 stony acres.

I have grown up traveling to Kay's in raucous multi-car gatherings of increasingly intoxicated adults with Michael 'Butch' Dalton and me, the only kids. Virginia, Michael's mother, Kay and my mother have been best friends since they were teens making their own way. Virginia strums the ukulele, singing about being "fat, fair and 40." She is fair at 40 but she is not fat. None of my mother's friends are fat, for they gobble diet pills along with their cocktails.

Assuming I am ever welcome, I tell Kay I have come to visit her river. Lugging my blanket and my typewriter in its grip, I set out on the bare remains of a path through the woods.

The free-moving river has cut its way through granite cliffs. On the lichen-sprinkled bluffs above the river, I plan to get inspired. I know I want to be a writer, but I don't know what I want to write about.

Instead of the muse this green day, I am visited by ticks. Legions of the eight-legged bloodsuckers crawl toward me in slow, encircling assault. I rocket to my feet, slam shut the lid on my typewriter and the still-empty sheet of paper in its roller, shake my blanket ferociously and get out of there.

"Thanks, Auntie Kay," I holler as I flee.

My muse has fled, too.

With one thing or another—the hour-and-a-half drive and likely a stop at Parkmoor for a Premium Frank—toasted bun, bacon, cheese and relish—or Howard Johnson's for a peach shake, summer's favorite—it is early dusk by the time I pull into the empty driveway at home. Sunday the Stymie is closed, so I expect to find Mother home. She might have tanned by the pool earlier in the day, but by now she will have cooked dinner and will be lounging in the living room with Gene the stepfather, having a drink and half watching television.

All the lights in the house are on, just as I expect, and so is the television, flashing pictures in black and white. Dishes sit on TV trays, dinner still on them. I hunt for Mother in all the rooms of the house—the breezeway and the pool, the two bedrooms and my study, even the bathrooms. No Mother and no Gene, only the two dogs, Mother's poodle Cina and my Fuddy Duddy, anxiously following me.

They must be downstairs, I imagine, not stopping to fabricate why—a washing machine gone wild?—that might be. The paneled rec room is as bright as upstairs. It, too, is recently empty. Six or eight men must have suddenly stepped away from the big round table, where cocktail glasses and beer bottles are still sweating. Chairs are pushed back, askew. In the moment of their disappearance, the card players have thrown down their hands, many face up, and they lie where they fell. The gamblers haven't stopped to pick up their money, and each place has a strew of bills, plus the center pot.

Has my whole family—my father downstairs with his card-playing friends, my mother and stepfather upstairs—been snatched by aliens, beamed up into a UFO—leaving the dogs behind?

Now I am panicking, hyperventilating as I run for a phone and dial the Stymie: Parkview 77552. The dogs crowd my legs as I listen, ring by ring, for a phone that never answers.

The drive to the Stymie is fast, three minutes, less with tonight's heavy foot on the gas. Two blocks out of my neighborhood, six blocks down North and South Road, one right turn—and that's when I smell the lung-clogging burning plastic and see that the darkening June sky is blackened by swirling smoke and pierced by circling red lights. Noise fills my ears, though the sirens have long since silenced.

Fire trucks block the driveway, and cars are parked all askew, like dropped Pick-up-Stix.

At about 7:50 p.m., neighbors saw smoke "pouring from the restaurant," the *Post-Dispatch* will report the next day. Three local fire departments—with five pumpers and two hook-and-ladder trucks—staunch the blaze in 10 minutes, but not before the interior of our Stymie Club was "destroyed."

There's more drama as firemen search for both my father and a janitor—Leon, our porter—believed to be working late. In fact, neither is at the scene and both are safe.

I know none of that as I run into the smoldering aftermath, calling for my mother. I never find her that night.

Only hours later, after I've cried myself to sleep, will she come to my bed, wild-eyed and reeking.

On the scene, it is my father I see. Luciferian, he is caught in an engine's revolving spotlight against the scorched front door as the life Gene and Elsa Martin built—the Stymie Club that defined us all—swirls to the red sky in sooty smoke. As I watch, his future walks to him through the funk, climbs the short, wide flight of stairs and takes his hand. From here on out, it is Gene and Violet, the woman for whom he would do anything.

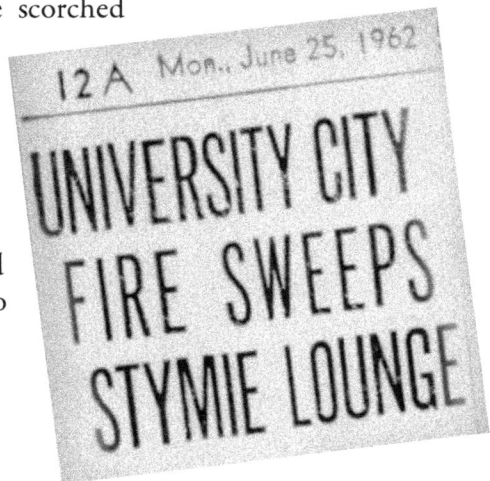

12A Mon., June 25, 1962

UNIVERSITY CITY FIRE SWEEPS STYMIE LOUNGE

Sandra Olivetti Martin

PART II

Past Tense

In these stories, Sandra ferrets out family history that preceded the Stymie Club. She ventures with her mother on a roots quest to an Italian village near the French Alps, investigates the mysterious death of a young cousin and finds a story in the enduring relationship between a teacher and her student in a set of World War I letters, discovered in whiskey boxes of a family legacy.—Editor's Note

Finding My Roots in Italy

Our search was for family we had never known.
They did not know we were coming.
Perhaps they had forgotten we existed.

TRAVES, Italy—Leaving the suburbs of Turin behind, the electric train rattled into the mountains. Urban grime and country dirt streaked the half-opened windows of the second-class coach. Morning pressed in, cool and damp.

The train was filled with shoppers from the open air mercado that occupies the city's Piazza della Repubblica on Saturdays. Plastic bags of cantaloupes, cabbage, fish, fennel and fresh tomatoes sat on laps and empty seats. Across the aisle, a family argued in stinging Italian about the fare of the youngest. The conductor triumphed, but not before he had retreated for reinforcements. Lire changed hands.

Cirie, Germangnano, Lanzo—each stop took us farther from the monumental sights of Italy that draw more than 40 million tourists yearly. We had encountered antiquity in Rome, the Middle Ages in Siena, the Renaissance in Florence—and glimpses of ourselves in the fire and ice of the Italian temperament.

But this out-of-the-way journey roused anticipation sharper than we had felt for the Colosseum, castle or cathedral.

Now we were bound for home.

My mother and I had traveled 5,000 miles from St. Louis, Missouri and Springfield, Illinois to the village of Pessinetto, midway between Turin and the French border in the Italian Alps, to search for family we had never known. They did not know we were coming. Perhaps they had forgotten we existed.

33

An old family photo was our only guide As the train approached Pessinetto, mother stroked the creased photo. Here, posed forever as they'd looked in 1921, were her Italian people—her peasant grandparents, three comely aunts, and two dandified uncles, stiff in knickers, tight collars and tall pompadours.

In the center place of honor sat a third uncle, his shoulders squared with the responsibilities of family and manhood. His infant daughter, Lidia, wiggled on his lap. Lidia and my mother were first cousins, born in the same year.

Only Catherine was missing from the Bergamino family portrait. Catherine, the daughter who had gone to America, was my grandmother; my mother's mother.

Some 125,000 Italians came to the United States in 1920. Like the three million who immigrated before World War I, most were unskilled laborers seeking work in mines and factories. Catherine Bergamino and her husband, Sylvester, were two of the immigrants. They settled in southern Illinois, among the coal mines of Franklin County. Their daughter, Elsa, conceived in Italy, was born in America. Other dreams failed. Worn down by poverty and three bad marriages, Catherine took her own life twenty-one years after immigration.

The first generation corresponded but the second did not. Elsa moved to St. Louis, married into an American family and worked her way out of poverty. After her mother's death, she never again spoke Italian. A jumble of memories and photographs were all she had left of her past.

I was the third generation *mezza Italiana.* Growing up in St. Louis I knew of The Hill, a famed Italian community that had produced the likes of Yogi Berra. Southern Illinois was an alien land of slag heaps and old men whose ears indulged terrible tufts of hair. I scorned Marco Polo and Christopher Columbus for sophisticated-sounding French heroes. In high school, the Donnas and Marias of Italian surnames were unknowable, dark-skinned others.

When at 16 my Bohemian best friend christened me "the Amorous Italian," I felt a thrill of private pride, but I still hated pizza. I toured Europe on my honeymoon but skipped Italy. At 30 I divorced and added my mother's name to fill the void. At 40, I wanted a past.

Armed with the photograph and the Bergamino name, mother and I were going home. We'd come 5,000 miles. *But could we cross sixty years?* I wondered, as the train slowed for Pessinetto.

We left the platform at Pessinetto with a few other people and the delivery of a bundle of afternoon newspapers. The main street was a fast highway banked against the mountains. On either side, haphazard rows of houses, their sienna-colored stucco soft with age, curved into the mountain's steep sides. Jagged slate roofs tumbled into the crease of the valley. A wide river flowed from the hills, its currents cold enough for trout.

"My grandfather made electricity for the town from that river," mother said, awed by the connection.

The street was quiet. Except for an occasional car speeding deeper into the mountains, the village had gone indoors for lunch and siesta. We surrendered ourselves to the magic of where we had arrived, wanting to collect every sensation: the cool day's shadow and light; the river's sounds; and the smell of espresso escaping a loosely shuttered door. As a child I had laughed at mother's old world superstitions. Here, I could believe in ghosts.

We peered into the windows of the first of Pessinetto's two restaurants, a tiny trattoria. Its sidewalk tables stood empty, but working men lunched inside. Alertness sharpened our hunger. But we walked on.

At the *albergo*, the hotel, we could wait no longer. For 8,000 lire ($5.25 at the day's exchange) we welcomed ourselves home. Ravioli in tomato sauce touched with fennel, warm rolls whose crusts cracked like eggshells to reveal hollow centers smelling of yeast, mild and creamy Gorgonzola, homemade white wine, and a whole trout fresh from that river were the offerings of the house.

Flies buzzed through open windows in the light dining room. The darker bar crackled with static as Italian kids played American video games.

The town was still resting when we reached the church. We had come to ask for records of our cousin Lidia's marriage, for a name to help us trace her from tiny Pessinetto to Turin, Italy's fourth largest city.

Memory intruded like an omen as we tried the door. Was it here that mother's paternal grandmother, reputed to be a witch, prayed hour after hour while her children cried outside for bread?

A voice from the walled garden above the church demanded what we wanted. We wanted the priest. We found him, and he asked what we wanted with a coldness that chilled our hopes. Mother tried to explain, but her Italian stumbled against the man's hostility. Like so many officials in that crowded land, this priest wore his position like armor, hoarding any information. He knew no Bergaminos, had no marriage records and cared nothing for cousins from America.

We had come so far, but our plan for reunion crumbled beneath the priest's stone wall. I cursed him. I cursed officialdom as a damned

Italian invention. I cursed myself for lacking the power to withstand the shriveling power of the Italian insult.

My mother was undaunted. I had guided our travels by map, choosing marked routes to planned destinations. Mother preferred to stand at the roadside, asking advice of passers-by. She did that now.

A man old enough to be a village elder had heard our troubles. He didn't know our family, but he was too hospitable to let us go. Our story had roused his sympathy and he embraced our quest. A young mechanic repairing his motorcycle on the sidewalk stopped to listen. Americans? he asked, wiping grease from his hands. He spoke English poorly; he apologized, though it sounded as good as the king's own to us. He knew Bergaminos; they owned the little market at the top of the hill. Like a foursome from Oz, we climbed the road together.

The second half of the working day had begun. Signora Bergamino stood, arms folded across ample breasts, framed in a doorway hung with braids of garlic. She listened politely, but shook her head regretfully. Pessinetto was the wrong place. If we really wanted Bergaminos, we should go to Traves, two stops up the line. Travis was full of Bergaminos, he said.

Traves was too small even for the few maps that show Pessinetto. But trains arrived every hour, linking the tiny village to the world. The station was a stone cottage lined in ivy. The station mistress, aproned in the style of women who have kept their country ways, waited on the train. We were her only arrivals, the news of the day.

"*Cugine dal America*—American cousins!" she exclaimed as mother told our story.

The women conferred in cascades of words too fast for me to begin to catch. I felt confused, lost, hopeless. Bits of understanding pieced together from her flying gestures depressed me more. Though the station was in the valley, the village was in the mountains. There were no taxis, and I felt crushed. Mother was dressed for visiting. How could she climb mountains in fancy Florentine shoes? And why? We'd find nothing but frustration when we arrived.

I had not yet learned the measure of Italian generosity. Whatever lay in the mountains, we needed to see.

"She says her husband will drive us. She says it's an honor." Mother translated, suddenly at home in the Piedmontese dialect of her early years.

In a tiny Fiat, we sped around second-gear mountain cutbacks for fifteen minutes or so and slid into the village piazza, beneath the tower of St. Ignatio's church. From the porch of the first house on the square, three matrons oversaw the town's business. Chickens scratched at the hardscrabble side garden and a hen drowsed beneath ripening tomatoes. The women sat, snapping beans. Our guide invoked the Bergamino name, and that interested them. The youngest of the trio set aside her beans.

In the family vein, we were about to strike it rich. At 4 o'clock, the Bergaminos would be presenting an infant at church. It was 3:50. Was this woman a magician? As she spoke, cars drew up in the piazza, disgorging loads of Bergaminos. All of them are relatives. Here were the living daughters and sons of the images in our photos.

Excitement crackled like pulses from telegraph wires as cousins surrounded us, identifying their parents in the old picture. As the hour of the christening rang from the bell tower, mother asked for Lidia.

"Si, Lidia, she is at her summer home," came the triumphant reply. Hands pointed back across the valley toward a distant green range.

Down one mountainside in the Fiat, past the train station and up another in a feat of supercharged motoring, we halted in a spray of gravel on the shoulder of a blind curve.

"This is the house of your cousin Lidia," trumpeted our guide, charging ahead on foot.

Broken flagstones made an uncertain path. We huffed after him. Half steadying, half pushing my mother, I feared catastrophe—cardiac arrest at homecoming.

Still, we climbed. "Your cousins are coming. Your cousins from America—they are here!" our guide shouted.

Up the scythed slope, we caught a breathless image of an Italian afternoon idyll: a family reposing beneath a grape arbor, roses as the backdrop, fat russet hens feeding in the garden, a bottle of wine on the table.

Then, "ELSA!" We heard my mother's name with the same shock you feel at catching your reflection in an unexpected mirror.

"LIDIA!" she answered. In racing to embrace, the cousins forgot those sixty years.

Half-century old ties held. Cousins half a world apart cherished one another. Like distance in space, distance in time could be crossed. We were not strangers. Out of all logic, we had been expected. Out of all coincidence, the uncreased double of our old photo stood on Lidia's mantel, enshrined in a silver frame. We had come home.

"Even the most common among us have a chance of surviving our deaths in the great democracy of record-keeping."

The Untimely Death of James Smith

*My cousin died on the Mississippi River
125 years ago. His letters told me how he lived
the last months of his life. How he died
was a lost story for me to discover.*

James Smith, an American everyboy, arrived in St Louis, Missouri on St. Patrick's Day, 1894. A twenty-year-old seeking his future, he bumped right into death. "I saw a man killed last Sunday night, just beat to death," he wrote his mother, on his third day in the city. "I run in and made him quit and he drew a revolver on me. I tell you I was scared."

Six months later, James, too, would be dead—victim of a sudden, unanticipated fate all his own. Over a century, the story of his death—so final for him, so consequential for his generation—got lost in the sad, nearly forgotten history of a family with fraying connections.

Most everything about this story goes a long way back.

It starts a century and a half ago in James' home in Calhoun County, Illinois, a little country place marooned between big rivers, with the Illinois to the east running down to the Mississippi, just before "Big Muddy," the Missouri, which rolls in from its 2,350-mile journey from Montana. Follow that conjoined river a dozen miles from the confluence, and it will take you to St. Louis, as it did Lewis and Clark's Corps of Discovery on the return from crossing the continent. As it did James Smith, who lived and died at the gathering of the rivers.

James' death was 75-year-old news by the time I learned of it. "I lost my only brother to the river," his long-lived youngest sister told me when I was a young woman. Cora, my grandmother's first cousin, was by then an old woman. James, had he lived, would have been past 90.

It was Memorial Day in the mid-1960s, and we were visiting Wilson Cemetery, in Batchtown, Illinois, a hilly, blackberry-ringed burial ground overlooking a Mississippi backwater. It was home territory to Miss Cora Smith, who was born and lived much of her life only a mile or so down that stone road, which became a dirt track near the cemetery. Much of Cora's family awaited her in Wilson Cemetery, where her gravestone, ready engraved with her name and birth year, presumed her arrival.

As we wandered through the old graves, watching our footing on the uneven ground, Cora talked about her mother and sisters, her aunt and cousin, my grandmother and great-grandmother. Truer to say, she was talking to them; I was only overhearing. All but her mother I had known in life. Her brother was the only stranger, mentioned now for the first time.

James Andrew Smith was not among the family awaiting Cora in Wilson Cemetery. He had no tombstone here. No mention in family correspondence. No citation in findagrave.com, no record in Latter Day Saints' populous genealogy sites.

He had disappeared from Earth and record. Perhaps his body sank into the cold and snaggy depths of the mighty Mississippi. Perhaps he washed far downstream, tumbling in the turbulence of current and riverboats past Chester, Cairo, even into Memphis. He could have fed the giant catfish that slug in the river's silt.

Cora joined the family in Wilson Cemetery in 1971. Her estate went to auction, carried out piecemeal to bidders on the sagging porch and little lawn of her rustic frame home. To me came my frugal cousin's savings and her papers, including a collection of letters spanning a hundred years.

I expected I'd do something with them...eventually. But then I was a very young woman. I had a family to raise, a career to nourish, life to live.

For decades my cousin's century of letters moldered in whisky boxes in basements and closets, following me from Illinois to Maryland.

In the mid 1990s, I rediscovered them. Reading and sifting, I found a history of middle-America told through the life of a family and a village. Letters hopped from the mundanity of daily living—sometimes tiresome, other times so familiar—to stark drama. I read them like a novel. Amid notes detailing the quality of peaches, twice daily reports of mileage gained on car trips to Florida, or negotiations for plowing a garden, letters like this, written on a Monday evening in March, 1938, rose up to shock me:

"Just a few lines to let you know how we are making it.

"Last night Chas. got out of bed after they had retired, went in the bath-room and shot himself in the heart—they rushed him to the Hospital and tried to save him but he passed away about 1:30. Lily is here and just almost crazy."

Cousin Lily's second husband, and second Charlie, Charlie Briggs was dispatched by a single gunshot and a single letter. I wanted to know more. But I had more pressing business. By then my family and I were raising a newspaper, supported in its toddler years by the legacy of Cousin Cora.

Another twenty years brushed by me. Then, after almost forty years as a journalist writing other people's stories, a demand rose up from the grave—or from the river. Cora's stories were mine to tell—and I had better hurry, the ghosts insisted, to give them their last chance at life. James Smith is one of those ghosts. Long-dead, he speaks to me in words written in his own hand, transcribing his own voice. He wants his story told.

James wrote the first chapter of his final story. The brittle letters I hold form a chain of human touch. We hold hands, from me to Cora—for she surely read them; Cora to her mother; she to James, who wrote long letters to his mother between December, 1893, and August, 1894.

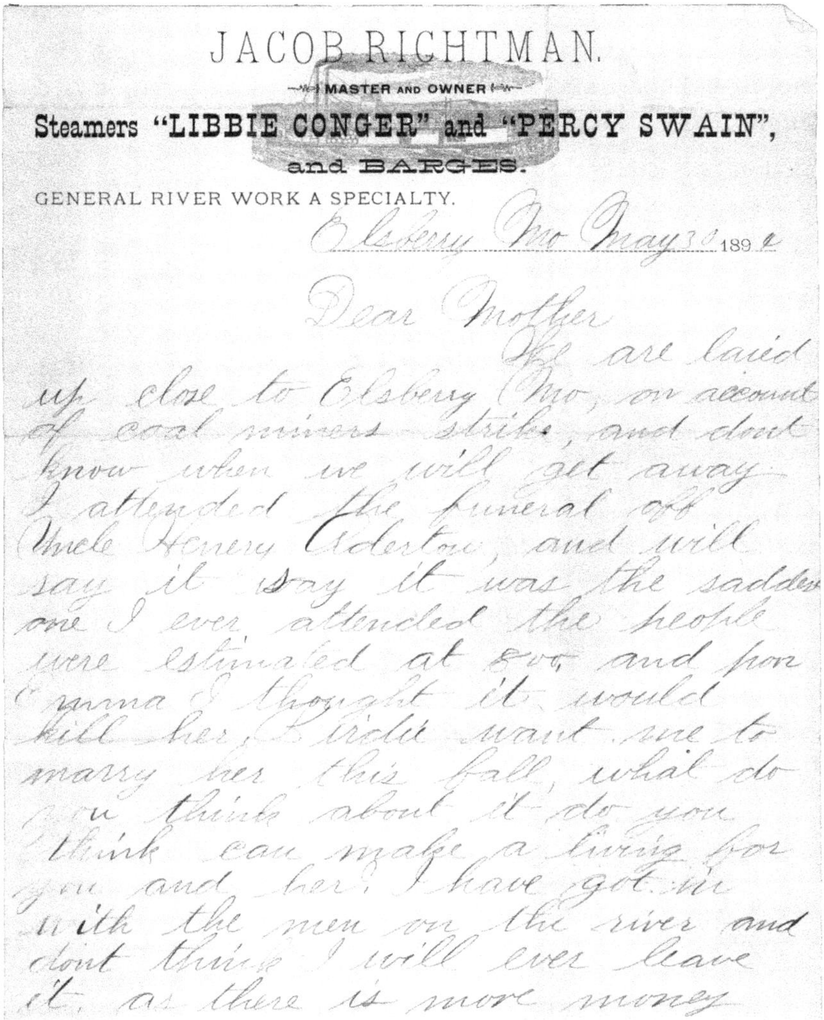

JACOB RICHTMAN.
MASTER AND OWNER
Steamers "LIBBIE CONGER" and "PERCY SWAIN",
and BARGES.
GENERAL RIVER WORK A SPECIALTY.

[Handwritten letter:]

Elsberry Mo May 30 189 2

Dear Mother

We are laied up close to Elsberry Mo, on account of coal miners strike, and dont know when we will get away. I attended the funeral off Uncle Henery Alderton, and will say it Say it was the saddest one I ever attended the people were estimated at 800 and poor Emma I thought it would kill her. Eckle want me to marry her this fall, what do you think about it, do you think can make a living for you and her? I have got in with the men on the river and dont think I will ever leave it, as there is more money

James addresses all his letters to Mrs. Katherine—her middle name—Smith. He must not have cared for his mother's first name, Sophronia.

In them, he confides his falling and rising hopes as he seeks to make his way in the world. He is "scared," he is "lonesome and homesick," he is "disheartened."

By August 30, six months after his arrival in St. Louis, he is "fine as a fiddle." His hopes have risen. Anticipating a new job—"$30 a month and board and only eight hours aday"—he looks forward to supporting both his widowed mother and a bride.

Then his letters abruptly stop.

I knew what that meant.

My inquest to learn when, where, how and why began in St. Louis.

ST. LOUIS IN ROUGH TIMES

The Panic of 1893 sent St. Louis, and the nation, reeling into recession. Times were hard, and a country boy away from home earned no special dispensation.

A hub of rivers and railroads, St. Louis was America's fifth most populous city, having mushroomed to 452,000 in the ninety years since Lewis and Clark's Corps of Discovery followed the Missouri River into the great open west from the trading village of 1,200 frontier folk. St. Louis of 1894 was a working city, a making city, a dirty, coal-fired engine alchemizing into wealth all that came to hand—from the rank carcasses of slaughtered animals to millions of bricks kilned above clay pits.

"St. Louis is getting to be an awful tough place," the country boy wrote. *"Just last night there was two prize fights."*

James likely had reached St. Louis by steamboat, traveling downriver. He apprised his mother of the basics.

"I arrived safe and sound and have the promise of work the first of next week in the same shop I worked in before," he wrote on his St. Patrick's Day arrival. *"I rented me a room at 1019 Pine St."*

But the promise of work fizzled.

"There is about 100 painters, loafing, they can't get anything to do. I never saw this place as dull as it is now."

Work was scarce; trouble was not. James feared he'll be the next victim of the murderer he'd witnessed beating the life out of a man.

"I want to get a way from here."

Like American dreamers of every century, he looked west for a better future. Aunt Rue Bunting, his mother's younger sister, lived in Kansas City, where "times are a little better." Rue was prospecting work for her nephew with a "street car man." But no promises had been made. James would have to take a risk, as the boss "wouldn't hire any body without seeing them first." Aunt Rue had said, "come on."

Come on is what James planned to do—if his working widowed mother could fund the cross-state trip. Urgency rings in his words, as he tells his mother—

"Send me some money for I have not got only enough to take me to K.C, And get it here by Friday morning for that is when I want to start."

That morning, the first day of spring, James Smith came close to boarding a packet boat steaming up the many-curved Missouri first west, then northwest, all the way across the state to that other frontier city.

But fortune seemed to turn in his favor, and his westward plans were abandoned.

"I have got work at last. "Mr. Hopkins told me work as steady as he could, and that he would pay $2.50 a day."

If James indeed worked as a painter, his boss would have been Samuel Hopkins, though he might also have worked as a varnishers with Harry Hopkins. Hopkinses practiced both trades around the corner from James Pine Street digs at 406. N 11th Street, according to the 1894 Gould's St. Louis directory.

With a little money coming in, James was of easier mind.

I can tell you I feel much better for I was getting disheartened.

But murder—"the most cruel thing I ever saw"—was still hanging over him.

That poor man that got such a beating died Monday morning. He was a good honest fellow. He was a fore-man in a livery stable just across the street from where I room, but he would fight when he was imposed upon. He had whipped this man twice previous to this scrap which he lost his life in. The fellow is held for murder in the first degree. I had to appear at the four-courts at the inquest.

The inquest would have been serious business: a judge interrogating witnesses, the court reporter documenting the proceedings, a full transcript typed with carbon copies. Still more civic duty loomed; James wrote that he'd be a witness at the trial.

BRIGHT PROSPECTS ON THE RIVER

The echoes of murder seem to have quieted over the next weeks, as James made the fateful decision to leave the mean streets for one of the two great rivers embracing St. Louis: the Mississippi.

I have got in with the men on the river and don't think I will ever leave it as there is more money in that than any thing else.

Fortune was coaxing James Smith. He warmed with optimism under the spell of her smile. Finally, he'd gotten a good job.

Among the river men James got in with, Jacob Richtman was likely at the top. Richtman was secure enough to advertise himself on letterhead that proclaimed him

JACOB RICHTMAN

—MASTER AND OWNER—

STEAMERS "LIBBIE CONGER" AND "PERCY SWAIN".

AND BARGES

GENERAL RIVER WORK A SPECIALTY

One or another in Capt. Richtman's fleet—James never says which—was his address in the third quarter of 1894. He received his mail in care of Richtman, wherever they were tied up. Starting in May, that was Elsberry, Missouri, a name I'd see again as this mystery unraveled.

Along with the job, James was about to get the girl.

Birdie, whose hometown Batchtown family had invited him to Thanksgiving dinner, was the one.

"Birdie wants me to marry her this fall," James wrote his mother.

Working on the river, James could be both dutiful son and husband. "What do you think about it?" He asked his mother. "Do you think I can make a living for you and her?"

Swept by the mighty currents of his times, James made his way.

But just as he had found a path in life, on April 26, commerce along the river and much of the nation seized up in the great coal miners' strike of 1894.

Bituminous coal—the black gold that powered the burgeoning industrial economy—also fueled the rise of America's labor movement. Complaining of starvation wages, three-fourths of the United Mine Workers from Pennsylvania and Ohio, and stretching to American Indian territory laid down their tools.

Just across the Mississippi, the coalfields of southern Illinois, in Centralia, Edwardsville and Mt. Olive—where Mary 'Mother Jones' Harris is buried in the Union Miners Cemetery—erupted in violent clashes. By May 6, only six of the dozens of mines in the region were working. The strike all but shut off the coal that powered manufacturing—and Jacob Richtman's vessels.

With his success suddenly seeming short-lived, James started looking elsewhere for work.

"I'm still on the boat," he wrote. "Am thinking of changing and go[ing] on a government boat that is working near Alton Ill. I am only getting $20.00 a month with board, while the other boat offers me $30. a month and board and only eight hours a day. I think that is better don't you?"

James' government boat was likely under the command of the Army Corps of Engineers. During the heyday of inland river navigation, the Corps controlled more boats than the Navy.

Taming the big rivers of America's heartland was government business throughout the 19th century. Rivers were wild, temperamental forces of nature. Fickle as they wanted to be, they jumped their beds for new territory, roaring out of their banks to flood towns, wipe out farmers and rob graveyards. Downriver, just eighteen years before, the Mississippi suddenly changed course in Tennessee, turning folks in Tipton County into Arkansans.

The rivers meandered, stretched out and fooled navigators with sandbars and currents. They were snaggle-toothed, attacking passing vessels with flood-propelled flotsam, limbs, and entire uprooted trees.

The Mississippi River Commission had been organized fifteen years before to "execute a comprehensive flood control and navigation plan on the Lower Mississippi." Congress appropriated piles of money for the ambitious task of making waterways navigable and keeping them so. The Army Corps of Engineers, James' likely employer, usually got even more than budgets called for.

Projects aplenty ranged from removing snags to stabilizing banks to building wing dams. (In the 20th century, the Corps would bring out the big guns, constructing massive locks and dams.)

For much of that work, the Corps hired labor directly off the street. One of those laborers could have been James. He might well have heard tell of opportunities through the waterways grapevine. He could have been lured by a newspaper ad. Every town had at least paper in James' day. Trade papers, like the *Waterways Journal*, added more news and opportunity to the mix.

James might have signed onto a Corps boat that September...

Or—and this is just as possible—weather, a delaying Congress or any of so many—who can count them?—other forces could have kept him working with Captain Richtman.

He doesn't tell us. He was thinking of his today—never imagining that history would one day hold him accountable for questions he never thought to answer. In his present, into his future, fortune—in a guise much resembling Birdie—was calling come-hither.

Reverse of the envelope James used for one of his letters from St. Louis advertises the scope of offerings at the Famous department store.

'WHAT DO YOU THINK OF YOUR BOY'?

Over the Fourth of July holiday, neither coal nor strikes nor threats to navigation were on James' mind as he hitched a ride across the Mississippi from Elsberry, Missouri, home to Batchtown for a holiday weekend with his girl. Over the holiday, he splurged on a cabinet card portrait shot by itinerant photographer Frank Woodard, of Golden Eagle, Illinois.

"The next time you hear from me you will be surprised, for when at home Birdie and I had my pictures taken," he wrote his mother. "But I haven't got them yet, will send you one as soon as they come."

Back then people were at least as photo crazed as we are now, as entranced by scarcity as we are by excess. James was delighted with his newly made photograph. In its sepia tones, a fresh-faced youth—clean-shaven with light hair freshly barbered high and tight—stares into the future. He is dressed in the formal fashion of the time: white, spread-collared shirt, Windsor-knotted tie and—despite the steam of the humid Mississippi River valley—heavy wool vest and coat. I imagine his complexion peaches and cream and seem to see the blush of high color on his cheeks.

He was looking good, and he wanted to hear his mother say just that.

I forwarded one of my pictures, he wrote. *I want you to answer, as soon as you get this and tell me what you think of your boy, and if you don't think he is the best looking child you got.*

From your boy, he wrote, signing himself James A. Smith Esq.

That letter, dated August 30, 1894, would be his last.

What he did in the days that followed made all the difference in his world. For the boat he would board would become his passage to death.

That September, James Andrew Smith, 20 years and 11 months old, lost his life on the river.

With the turning of autumn, widow Sophronia Katherine had no son on whose love and support to depend.

Birdie mourned before she married.

Cora lost her "dear brother."

And I, 125 years later, inherited an untold story.

SEARCHING FOR JAMES: BY RIVERS

What was the fateful path he chose? What boat did he crew? Did he stay on with Master Richtman? Did he jump ship to a government boat? From that nameless boat, did he tumble? Was he thrown? By light of day or dark of night? Was he caught underwater? Or did his body rise? Did his family have a corpse to mourn? Or did James disappear?

Does every family have a disappearance? That is all you have, a disappearance, when a person steps into that hole. Water is often a conspirator. At twilight, a brother-in-law falls from the bow of a bass boat into a deep Canadian lake. An Atlantic shelf fisherman is pulled from his boat by a tuna when line entraps his hand. Mountains will take you, too. A second DUI, a dead-end job, a fed-up wife, failed expectations—and a husband walks into the Georgia mountains and doesn't come out. Searchers find no sight of him. Dogs catch no scent. Not even a bone turns up. A desert could also do the job. City streets do it all the time. A brother stumbles out of a bar. That's all. Then all you have is a disappearance—and a memory of all that was lost. Forever and ever. For James, it was the river.

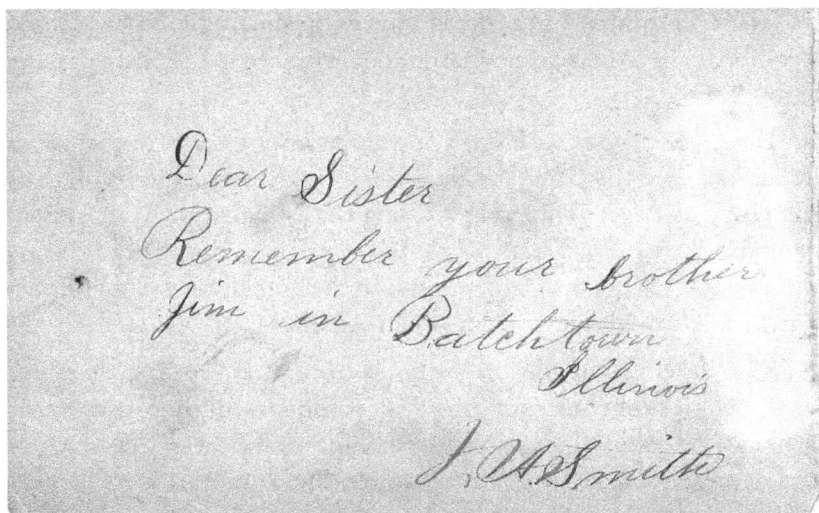

James' words, inscribed on the autograph book that was his 1892 Christmas gift to Cora, must have been her lifelong promise to keep.

Yet beyond noting the month and year of his death on an envelope, sister Cora left no clues to his fate.

So I followed brother Jim to the river.

Rivers were the way you got from here to there in much of America's 19th century. The Mississippi, along with the Ohio, Missouri and Illinois, tied the expanding nation together. Fleets of barges loaded with grain moved on the rivers, so many that Chicago, up the Illinois, supplanted Odessa, in Russia, as the self-proclaimed grain capital of the world.

By James' day, even as industry moved onto rails, rivers still floated America's restless populace and its ever-growing wish list of wares. Railroads never bothered with James' out-of-the-way home, 70 miles upriver in Calhoun County, Illinois. Steamers served both sides of that narrow sliver of Illinois, paddling both the Mississippi on the west and the Illinois on the east.

James Smith might have worked on any of those rivers. His last mailing address, Elsberry, Missouri, puts him finally on the Mississippi. But on what boat?

Jacob Richtman's letterhead makes a starting point. Named steamboats like the two he mastered leave a record of their passage through time.

The *Libbie Conger* and *Percy Swain* are among 6,000 packet boats documented in the Way's Packet Directory, an encyclopedia of boats carrying passengers and freight along the Mississippi River system from 1848 to 1994. Those boats, Way explains, "dominated during the first forty years of steam, providing the quickest passenger transportation throughout mid-continent America."

As well as their pedigree—rig, class, engines, boilers, the shipyard, the years of construction—Way chronicles all those boats' use, mishaps, frequent changes of ownership, modification, conversion and demise. A steamboat's life was often short and full of mishaps.

Libbie Conger was, like many packets, a hodgepodge of sunken boats. The stern-wheeler's three-deck, 168-foot wooden hull was hewn, fitted and caulked in 1878 in Metropolis, Illinois, on the Ohio River. Her working parts had propelled three boats before her: *Fannie Harris, City of Keithsburg* and *Josie*. Reconditioned, they were configured in the new hull in Dubuque, Iowa. *Libbie Conger* steamed a thousand miles up the Missouri River to Bismark, North Dakota as, her company advertised, a "fine and fast passenger packet of the Diamond Jo steamboat line."

Libbie Conger had many masters before settling down with Richtman out of St Louis as a regular carrier of all work. She had a long life, eighteen years, before fate downed her.

"Wrecked at St. Louis during the tornado," wrote the reporter who got to tell the world about

DEATH IN A CYCLONE'S AWFUL PATH.
Hundreds of People Perish, and Many Buildings Are Destroyed in St. Louis.

TRAINS WRECKED AND STEAMERS FOUNDERED BY THE TERRIFIC STORM.

Houses Are Unroofed and Electric Wires Snap, While the Rain Pours Down in a Drowning Deluge

ST. LOUIS, May 27—The most disastrous cyclone in the history of the city visited this section to-day. Hundreds of people perished and property valued at millions of dollars was destroyed. The city is in a state of panic. Nearly all electric wires are down, and the city is in darkness. To add to the confusion the tornado was followed by a deluge of rain and vivid flashes of lightning, which still continue. Telephonic wires are useless, and livery men refuse requests for conveyances on account of prostrate electric wires. The situation In East St. Louis is appalling. The tornado struck that city with terrible effect, and it is now estimated that 300 persons are dead as a result of the wind, flood and flames. The tornado was followed by an outbreak of fire caused by lightning...Among the dead on both sides of the Mississippi River are Captain Seaman and wife and three of the crew of the steamer Libbie Conger.

The reporter got no byline, but his story went round the country. I found it in the Sacramento Record-Union.

James missed that disaster. He died two years earlier. Perhaps— so far it's just perhaps—he was an earlier casualty of the ill-fated *Libbie Conger.*

Percy Swain also qualifies. Another steamboat risen from many old parts, she was, "a rafter until sold to river contractors, who used her building wing dams, etc."

Steamer Percy Swain, Henderson, Ky.

Just such a boat could have been hired as the Army Corps of Engineers tried to bend the Mississippi to America's will. Boats were poised for action in James' very territory, near the busy river port of Alton. The *Waterways Journal* reported that—

"Lieut. Judson, who has charge of the government river improvements between Alton and Grafton, says that he expects to begin active operations in the vicinity of the Piasa (just upriver from Alton) within eight or ten days. The long delay has been due to the failure of Congress to dispose of the River and Harbor bill, but as soon as this receives the President's signature he will give the word to go ahead with the work there."

Percy Swain could have been on the job. James could have been aboard. I can't place either of them at the site nor at the site together.

But I can see how James would have looked on that boat, photographed in a single image collected at the St. Louis Mercantile Library at the University of Missouri at St. Louis.

From each of *Percy Swain's* three decks, people look at the camera. "Grandfather Kirchner stands on the upper deck," a caption writer recorded, with a pair of the girls. One is "the cook's daughter." On the middle deck are a woman—perhaps the cook?—with another girl. On the lower deck, four rivermen pose. Their faces—known so well to mother, sisters and lovers—are nobody anybody living recognizes. Perhaps a blowup will bring James' features into focus...

Old riverboats make good stories. But they have not carried me to the end of James Smith's story.

SEARCHING FOR JAMES: BY NAME

My next strategy was to search for James Smith by name.

How to track a long dead boy—a boy of no standing, a boy so commonly named, one James Smith among thousands? James' middle name, Andrew, reversing his father's Andrew James, gave him distinction in life but not much in death.

Yet even the most common among us have a chance of surviving our deaths in the great democracy of recordkeepers.

Recordkeepers are institution builders. They publish newspapers, collect libraries and archives, found historical societies, organizing our comings, goings and transactions along the way according to the terms of our social contracts.

Successions of factualists, one after another, have dedicated themselves to recording, preserving, publishing and translating their knowledge into ever-changing technologies. When their time was ended, they handed along their records to new keepers in the by-no-means-certain hope that this generation would keep faith with the old.

Author's note: James Smith surely passed by the Piasa
Bird [pie-ah-SAW], an air-and-water monster with
supernatural powers painted on the limestone bluffs
overlooking the Mississippi River. Dodging rocks in
1673, Father Jacques Marquette came upon an earlier
version "which at first made us afraid, and upon which
the boldest savages dare not long rest their eyes."
I imagined a wizened riverman telling James as he came
upon the iconography for the first time how a wise chief
coaxed the beast from a cave, at which point the tribe's
most intrepid warriors equipped with poison arrows
dispatched the Piasa Bird to the netherworld of lore.

All that information and all those people are linked in a great web. Multi-dimensional and -directional, the web is spun of parallel and perpendicular strands. Every strand leads to intersections with many others. Each strand of a quest holds clues, if not answers, and opens new questions.

I am a fly in that complex web: caught up in any strand I bump into, entangled in an expanding web of information, inspired by glimmers of revelation.

I searched for James on trips back home to the Midwest, from the tiny Calhoun County Historical Society to the Abraham Lincoln Presidential Library in Springfield, Illinois, to the Missouri Historical Society, the State Historical Society of Missouri and the splendid St. Louis Mercantile Library. I hunted in person, often guided by patient experts who might have been simply doing their job—or might have themselves been momentarily caught in the web of curiosity.

On a summer Friday afternoon, Curator Eric Reinert of the Corps Office of History in Arlington, Virginia, picked up the phone, listened patiently to the story told by a stranger on the other end of the line, and left the work he had been doing to dig up what the Corps was doing in a small Mississippi River town a century ago. "I enjoy the challenge of questions like this," he told me.

At the Abraham Lincoln Presidential Library, I spun the Calhoun County Herald through a microfilm reader, searching the last months of James' life. The papers of September 20 and 27 had been lost. About James, I learned nothing. But the Oct. 4 paper recorded that "Mrs. Andrew Smith, of Jacksonville, is visiting at Tim Stone's."

James' mother's return home as September, 1894, turned to October would have been no social visit. It would have been a journey of grief. By then and forever after, her every step would be shadowed by James' death.

For most of that weekly paper's readers, the news that mattered was the river's rise, returning life, and supplies, to their accustomed level. Finally, the water level was high enough to allow the steamboat

"Odil to complete her trip to Kampsville Thursday. It had been so long since we had seen a real steamboat that she looked as majestic and palatial as a Cunarder."

The rivers would rise high enough, I would learn over two years searching, to float James' body.

§

If the public record did not track James through life, perhaps it tracked him in death.

In 1877, Illinois decided to keep track of its births and deaths. But not much record-keeping was done until 1916, when it all got systematized by the brand-new office of Vital Records in the Illinois Department of Public Health.

Neither Illinois' pre-1916 Death Index or its Western Regional Depository Archive—one of a system of seven that collect and organize the records of Illinois' 102 counties—turned up my James Smith.

So I narrowed my search to James Smith territory, starting with his home county, at the county clerk and recorder's offices, in the town of Hardin. Small though it is among Illinois' 102 counties—100th by population and 93rd by area—Calhoun had its 19th century records. But among all its losses, James Smith's was not recorded. One more dead end.

The Mississippi hugs two more Illinois counties before bending to St. Louis: Jersey County, where the river slides by Grafton, and Madison County, where the 19th century Corps worked out of Alton, the clerk advised. Neither recorded James' ending. Would Missouri, the Mississippi's western shore?

Elsberry, in Missouri's Lincoln County, was James' on-shore mailing address for the last three months of his life. That search dead-ended at the Lincoln County Health Department, where records go no farther back than 1980. Nor would I find James in state records in Jefferson City, for Missouri was slower than Illinois to resolve to keep track of its living and its dead.

I was down to the last dime in my roll of ideas. So I took the advice of the Lincoln County Registrar and called George Giles, who everybody knew as the local historian of Lincoln County, Missouri.

I told my story to a message machine and was about to hang up when Mr. Giles himself came on the line. He didn't offer much hope; his interest was his hometown, Troy, the county seat. The river town of Elsberry, some 20 miles away, was not his territory. But one thing or another—his own love of local history or the mystery of a young man so long lost—drew him in. He'd look in the local newspaper morgue, he promised.

Stymied, I turned to reading the 30-odd page record of the inquest into the death of another James Smith, in St. Louis in September, 1894. This James Smith, a junior, was a 12-year-old who'd spent his pocket money—and then his buddy's—on candy. So to get home he hopped a ride on the city Lindell Railway only to fall between the train's two cars. Another rider, Mrs. M. D. Heltzell, held young James in her arms as he died.

I was mourning this James Smith's early death when George Giles phoned to announce he'd found my James.

The *Troy Free Press* of Friday, October 5, 1894, reprinted on page 5 the *Elsberry Advance's* report of the week before noting that—

> *James Smith of near Batchtown Illinois fell from a boat at Sterling [Island] on Friday afternoon and drowned. His body was recovered Sunday near Turners Landing and he was buried Monday at Hardin.*
>
> *Smith was a watchman on the boat and said to have been a most exemplary young man. He was to be married to a young lady and she is almost prostrated at the sad event."*

That would have been Birdie.

Instead of a wedding, James had a funeral. Instead of walking down the aisle, he was carried into the Calhoun County cemetery where his father had lain for twelve years. Both their graves have disappeared into the ages.

SYNCHRONICITY

Now young James Smith's body had risen from the deep. There it was, my mystery solved in a newspaper, the medium to which my family has devoted our fortunes, even to founding our own paper, in part through Cousin Cora's financial legacy.

Solved through the help of many strangers, ultimately by George Giles, who followed a path I might never have seen, asking nothing but a copy of my story to enrich his local archives.

The *Elsberry* story was likely a week old when it was picked up by the *Free Press* in its October 5 edition. If the *Advance* story ran on September 28, the Friday of James' death was likely September 21. That was the day, add 125 years, I finished his story.

Epilogue: *Reading "The Untimely Death of James Smith," Emerson Retzer, president of the Calhoun County (Illinois) Historical Society, had an epiphany. The line "he was carried into a Calhoun County cemetery where his father had lain for twelve years" rang a bell. Obvious, Retzer said, slapping his forehead at what he, the expert on who was who in county cemeteries, had overlooked.*

Among the graves in the little Smith family cemetery south of the county seat, Hardin, was that of Smith, Andrew J. 1850-May 9, 1882. Andrew James was the name of James' father. The date was twelve years before the death of James Andrew Smith. Retzer also found the overturned, aged tombstone of Augustus Smith, father to Andrew and grandfather to James, in the little cemetery. "Witching" led him to shifted bones from other burials, but no tombstone confirmed James' burial in the time-ravaged cemetery.

Does young James lie with his ancestors? Retzer, and through him I, believe so.

As for the fiancée "almost prostrated with grief," Birdie G. Heffington eventually, twelve years later, married Robert H. Cockrell.

Hello: am liking
this life find—
now writt-for
it helps us
soldiers in our
new work.
F. L. D

Miss Cora Smith
Batchtown
Ill
Cal Co.

POST CARD

THIS SPACE FOR WRITING

THIS SIDE IS FOR THE ADDRESS

LOUISVILLE
OCT 19
4 PM
1917
KY.

Am Liking This Life Fine

A WWI soldier writes home

The War to End All Wars had raged for three years when the United States entered the conflict on April 6, 1917. Immediately, the war effort went into overdrive. Registration of fighting-age men began June 5 and the draft itself July 26, eventually making soldiers of 2.8 million men. A.L. Dixon's turn came on October 4.

By the summer of 1918, 10,000 Americans shipped out to fight in France every single day. Dix never got the anticipated call. He served his country in Camp Taylor, Kentucky, supporting the waves of new soldiers training for the trenches.

The war that debuted aerial bombing and poison gas was in other ways an old-fashioned war, dependent on the hauling force of millions of horses and mules.

At Camp Taylor, 29-year-old Dix was "boss of" 22 of those mules, plus "30 men & 25 wagons."

His was an easy war, with loneliness the enemy.

December 13, 1917

> *Dear Friend:*
>
> *When you want to know how good home made candy tastes, why just join the army for the candy was sure good, a sergt here stoled some of it and when I bawled him for it he said that I should be satisfied to know a girl that could make good candy.*

Calhoun County, Dix's Illinois home, was a little country place marooned between big rivers, with the Illinois to the east running down to the Mississippi just before the Missouri caught up. Of the best count of 323 Calhoun men drafted, many, Dix among them, were sent to Camp Taylor, Kentucky, built to receive Illinois boys like them—plus Kentuckians and Indianans, according to Ken Maguire, founder and curator of the Camp Zachary Taylor Historical Society.

For Kentucky, Camp Taylor was an economic engine revving in farmlands just outside Louisville. It brought uncounted but appreciated thousands of wartime dollars to a city of 235,000. One hundred and fifty thousand soldiers trained there, many on their way to fight the Hun in France. Others stayed to keep the camp running—with the working help of over 10,000 horses and mules

In the newly risen war city, Dix found himself in his element.

I am making good here nowdays and I am acting Sergt' seems with good luck I will have my stripe some day but don't tell this for one is never sure of a thing here and I may get fooled, he wrote three months into his war on December 13, 1917.

I have had charge of the QMC wagon train for over three weeks...and you should see my head swell when I line these men up and yell 'tention' squadron right boys march, am such a bear on that & they can hear me all over the camp.

Dix's only complaint was the weather.

When anyone trys to tell you that Ky is a warm state you tell em that its all wrong for we have about one foot of snow here and some cold.

For all his jaunty tone, the young man knew he was caught in a life-stakes game.

Me thinks we will soon see France and I hope so, just to get this over with. I have taken out $5000 insurance and Mother may find herself rich some day soon...

For Dix, as for so many soldiers, letters from home were lifelines in a sea of homesickness and uncertainty.

Between October, 1917 and April, 1919, Dix's pen pal was Miss Cora Smith.

DIX AND CORA

"Friend Cora" was 37 years old when their World War I correspondence began; Dix 28. They'd met a decade earlier when Miss Cora Smith was teaching and boarding in his hometown, Hardin, the Calhoun County seat.

Perhaps she was his teacher. Perhaps she had seen his schoolwork at a shared kitchen table.

> *I know you have a hard time making out my writing and you know how hard I worked in school, gee—but we never thot them days that all of this war would spring up and get some of us shot.*

Dix is playing the schoolboy to Miss Cora's marm. His handwriting is clear, sometimes even lovely, and his grammar not half bad—though he has little use for punctuation and refuses the second o in too. His thoughts pour from his pen as he describes his experiences in regular letters that hop from teasing to reflecting on life and death. Dix's 12 surviving letters from Fort Taylor amount to 6,000 words. Most fully fill four pages, often back and front.

Many were written on YMCA stationery, advising wartime thrift at the bottom of every page—

TO THE WRITER:
–save by writing on both sides of this paper

TO THE FOLKS AT HOME:
–save food, buy Liberty Bonds and war savings stamps

I am able to tell you Dix's story at Camp Taylor because the never-married schoolteacher Miss Cora kept his letters, along with hundreds of other letters, post and greeting cards she received over seventy years. She was my grandmother's first cousin. The letters are part of her legacy to me.

Their relationship is...well, that's a good question. Miss Cora clearly has top billing. But in his aspiring manhood, Dix is climbing up.

Some how I have been afraid of you ever since you called me a 2 face and laughed at me when I took that hard fall at the barn gate remember how you laughed at me? he writes in his first letter.

By January, he's gaining confidence—

Friend Cora–Darned if I am going to call you Miss any more for I am learning to save nowadays, I suppose you would make me stand on the floor for doing this but if you just have to be called Miss why say so for I am in the habit of doing just as I am told these days.

As their relationship finds new footing, Dix tucks tales of escapades and girls into his long letters.

I am going in town Sunday to meet a girl and I am most afraid to for I wont know how to act so pray for me ha ha

Often he signs himself Mike, scratched in rough printing if his left-handed alter ego had taken the pen. But beneath the bravado, Dix is a lonely boy, and Friend Cora is his confidant.

Last Sunday, he wrote in a letter dated March 10, 1918, *was my birthday (29 yrs), say but I'm getting old, there never will be a chance for me when I get out of this army but its best to get old for one learns lots and time flys here.*

> *I know you are sick of all this junk. But I have to bother some one and it may as well be you*

> *And please write again soon and tell me all the news; we're going to have a swell camp hotel here for visitors and you had better come and see us poor fish.*

Life at Camp Taylor

Camp Taylor was a fast-growing city of men. The first draft recruited young men, 21 to 31 years old. So the place must have been full of testosterone. There was gambling...

A big crap game is going on and those boys should be at church or somewhere, Dix wrote on March 10, 1918.

There was tough talk and cursing.

> *No we don't go to the guard house for all our meanness, they just bawl us out till the guard house would look like a palace to us, for some of these birds here can think of some mean things to say, and about things that make one want to cuss why I can't tell you.*

Many of the Camp Taylor's soldiers were country boys like Dix. But not all, as he wrote on December 13, 1917.

> *In this barracks we have lawyers – Drs – artist – school supts – and most any kind of trade but all are soldiers now.*

In that same letter, he recognized their diversity and skill: We hear better singing here than at a show. Plays were regular fare, he wrote to lure Friend Cora to visit.

> *Come down and I will take you to a show at our new theater its some play house and will seat 4000 of us boys and we have the best of shows here.*

Dix was a fan. *They have been giving us some good shows and I try to see them all*, he wrote.

Stop – Look – Listen was on the bill in March, 1918. In June, *It Pays to Advertise*.

As well as live theater, movies played the camp. In July, he cried over D.W. Griffith's propaganda movie *Hearts of the World*.

> *I saw it last night and it was great of course I had to be a boob and bawl but one cant help it, if you ever get the chance be sure and see this play for its real war – it takes three hours to play it but don't seem that long.*

Dix was so starstruck that in the summer of 1918 he took a part-time theater job.

> *I worked at our camp theater about a week, I helpt on the curtains, they were playing a Bit of Broadway, those were good girls but to blame careless about their dress they (or one) almost caused me to fall off a ladder so I quit the job, it paid 50c a night to but to much risk.*

About girls, Dix was always of two minds—at least when writing to Friend Cora.

Actresses so distracted him that he had to flee. Kentucky girls were too fashionable for his budget

> *If those French girls dress any worse than these Ky girls do, why I sure want to marry one of them for it wont cost me much to buy their duds.*

Nurses were distracting, and—was he sizing up their wifely potential?—not very good cooks.

> *Two nurses sat near me and that is why the show seemed better some of these nurses are real dolls, but they dont go with no one except a com' officer, but the privates sneak out with them quite often, I don't fool with them for I am sore at them I bummed a lunch from them while making them a tennis court and I am sure that nurse knows horrible drugs for that sandwitch she gave me almost caused my death.*

Kidding aside, girls' home cooking was one of the wartime comforts for the boys.

We are about to have a party here at the Y...the girls said they would bring ice-cream & cake so they will find me here waiting for the eats, he wrote on July 17, 1918.

In a nation mobilized in support of the war effort, The YMCA was one of many charities helping the "boys," as Dix styled the soldiers At training centers like Camp Taylor, the Y was home away from home for the soldiers. As well as supplying letter paper, it became Party Central, drawing Kentucky girls to keep the soldiers company.

From any source, sweets were always well received.

Thank you for the cake, he wrote to Friend Cora, *it was all in good shape when it landed here, and I never tasted angel-food cake that was a good as that.*

Not always so well received were the socks hand-knitted for the soldiers.

> *It's good of your Mother to knit all those socks for us boys, would like to see them that you made but wont say that I would want to wear them for we have some of them here that wont' fit any one or any thing.*

Gifts of all sorts brought comfort from home to men whose fate was out of their hands. The first Christmas of the War, Dix wrote—

> *found the most of us broke here but we all got gifts of some kind from the Red Cross—my old Arkansas sweetheart sent me a dandy air-filled pillow made of rubber and silk and it sure came in nice—for the pillow I was making use of was made out of two suits of heavy underwear rolled up in the side of my shirt arm—and it was a good way to use this under wear for its wool and I would rather fall against a barb-wire fence than to put it on.*

THREE TIME LUCKY

Camp Taylor's distance from German firepower did not protect it from all the ills of war. By April, 1918, the city of men had swelled to its capacity of 47,500. It was a transient place mixing men from distant places. Disease liked those conditions. First came spinal meningitis.

I have lots of time to write you now as the whole works is under a quarantine, Dix wrote on April 18. *Now don't be afraid of this letter for there are no danger or germs.*

Next came influenza, which would travel round the world, even above the Arctic Circle, and prove more deadly than the war.

The flu was sure bad here and some few of our boys 'kicked off' I had it two days & felt punk, was so darn sick could hardly stick in the saddle, he wrote on November 4.

Flu took about 1,000 lives Camp Taylor historian Ken Maguire estimates.

Dix's luck held.

The flu failed to land me this time so you and others will still have to keep on sending letters to Camp Taylor and trust the Huns to get me when I go across, he wrote.

About that seeming inevitability, Dix couldn't manage a joke.

There are lots of the over sea boys here in camp all wounded and all quartered at the base hospital, they most make me bawl every time I see them for some are in bad shape and one can see just what war means, he wrote on the eve of 1919.

GOING HOME

Dix's November 4, 1918 letter to Friend Cora speculated, uncensored, that war would soon be over.

Don't the war news look fine now days this can't last much longer for the Germans are in their last stand, he wrote.

The rumors were true; the Armistice was signed on November 11, the day we now celebrate Veterans Day.

Reflecting on his imminent freedom, Dix opened his heart to Friend Cora:

I guess that is why I never cared to stay here or leave for there was no one cared what happened to me and I thot the same about my self, he wrote.

Among no one who cared seemed one in particular.

In a melancholy mood, he wrote:

One of the boys is playing 'The Long Trail,' and it always makes me think of the dark nights I walked that path thru the woods to the Metz home, them days I was young & tender me thinks Amy would see a great change in the old boy now.

On a six-day furlough near the war's end, Dix "had the bestest time" with his brothers but no luck with the girl on his mind.

I tried to talk her into the notion of returning to Louisville with me & be Mrs. Dixon, but, he wrote Friend Cora, *she thot it best to stay with Dad where she was sure of her three squares a day.*

By April 4—"just 18 months [since] my last night as a civie"— Dix expected to be mustered out in two weeks.

He evaluated his army time as well spent. *I am not sore on the army life, and I am leaving it a better man that I was when I came here,* he wrote.

The qualities made Dix a better man did not include money.

There aint a chance in the world for Amy & I to marry, he confessed to Cora. *I might ask her, but when I leave this army I am flat broke and I haven't the nerve to use her money.*

About what came next, he had no idea.

I dont know what I am going to do think I will hobo all summer.

Thus Dix's letters from Camp Taylor end.

WHAT NEXT?

Where in the world might Dix have gone, I wondered as I read his letters a century after he penned them. In all my cousin Cora's hundreds of crisp and fading letters, no more showed his flowing hand. Then, in the centennial of the season of his discharge, I came on a Christmas card postmarked Kansas City, 1937. On the back of its parchment paper, I read these words–

Dear Miss Cora,

Albert wishes me to tell you he's using the Bible you gave him in 1907. Many years have been lost but on Oct. 19 he was gloriously saved and you never could imagine how changed he is.

Paragraphs of family news later, the message is signed by Amy, writing and signing on behalf of both of them, her big news, that Albert had been gloriously saved. Between the lines, Cora reads, her old friend finally got his girl.

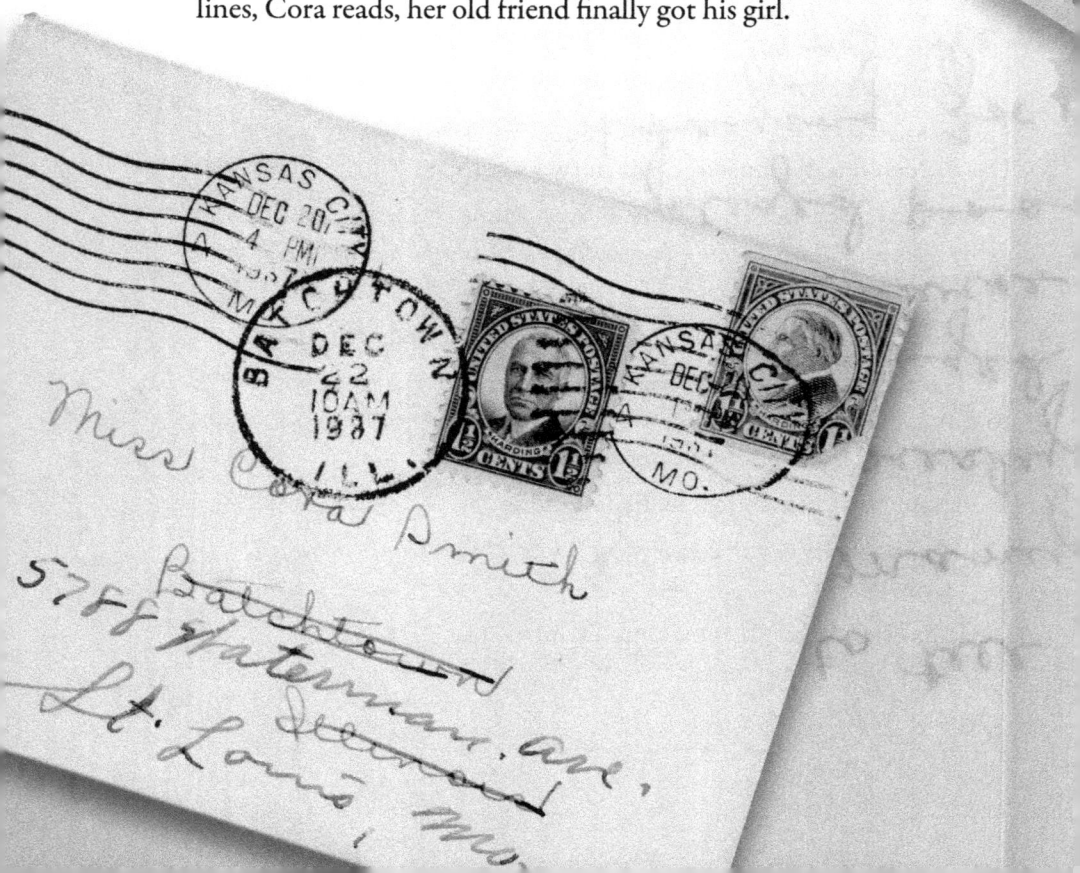

Dear Miss Cora,

Albert wishes me to tell you he's using the Bible you gave him in 1907—many years here [have] been lost but on Oct. 9—he was gloriously saved and you never could imagine how changed he is. He goes to a Bible class on Mon. nights and twice on Sunday to church and hopes to see he's baptized soon for his mother.

Curtis & Pissy going for his mother.

Albert was as [Hardin] in Oct. — he works nights for J.W.W. — he not [get] this last night. Please was robbed & clothing & money — [Sobbley] took his one and only [freedom] gets out this paper states, that so I had been [glued] up 250 last night, & [speeling] & foods against them & big [police] & to Amanda's and [mama's] & bought — used fine yourgetter. [dad's] daughter is [pushing] his gift on money & I was planning [I carrying] check books against with him Xmas & asked me to send his gift on mother with him "here's [up] "No matter yet mothers' hair turns gray "here's [beautiful] yet I saw you but they told me you [tried] since. Christmas smiles to you & your mother Bertha [Riffer Papa] is in business.

Love [Aunt Amy]

bring [you]

and the New [Year]

joyful and bright.

your mother included—
Albert my Amy.

PART III

Getting Personal

Sandra's writing shifts in this second set of recollections to memorable moments including, apparently, a decision she made in utero. We've all had a best friend, but perhaps not too many women have found theirs through baseball. There's a shortstop in these stories, and a football star at the Stymie Club who comes to Sandra's rescue one spooky night. Her sons, Alex and Nat, get stories of their own, and she searches in Italy for both her long-lost family and a perfect melon and in Ireland for Cork County cooking secrets—Editor's Note

My Birthday

*Seeking harmonic balance in the auspicious days
marking the fullness of the solstice*

Back when I was born, babies chose their own birthdays. Everybody waited on us to make up our minds, and when we did, we always got our way. Not so good a time? Too bad. This is when I intend to be born.

I chose June 30. Though I do not remember making that decision, I've always approved of it. Of all the year, June is No. 1 on my list of favorite months.

"The month of the roses. The most beautiful—and the shortest," my grandmother Florence Martin always said, with a sigh.

That's my only objection to June 30. To celebrate my birthday, I have to let go my favorite month. Fortunately, July—when my husband celebrates his birthday—is No. 2.

June 30 it had to be. I don't exactly mean by conception. That, almost, was none of my business. But I do believe that I was seeking my harmonic balance in the auspicious days marking the fullness of the solstice.

Grandmother Florence Bunting married grandfather Elmer Martin on June 27. Mother Elsa Olivetti married father Gene Martin on June 29.

I could have chosen June 28, the usual day of the year's latest sunset. But, as became apparent over the years, June 30 was my date with destiny.

My mother came into this world on January 1. (Unless we are mistaken, but that's another story.) Together, we halved the year, sharing its axis points.

In sequence, my first son, John Alexander Knoll, chose March 31 for his birthday.

When Nathaniel Martin Knoll came along, no date would do but October 1—though he'd been expected since late August.

They, too, halved the year, at its quarter days.

When the four of us packed all that prime energy into a single space, it often exploded.

The symmetry of our Earthly union over three generations was not on Mother's mind in the early hours of June 30, 1943.

Contractions are a racking surprise. Neither knowledge nor experience prepares you. Even midwives are slammed by their own contractions. Those seismic shudders told Mother, a primapera, she was in labor.

She lay on her side in the warm predawn, wet with sweat, though a breeze blew the light curtain away from the screened window. Contractions rippled her taut belly, demanding her full attention before they subsided, but always returned. She attended to them quietly until she knew them well. Then she touched my father's hairy shoulder.

"Gene," she said, "I'm in labor. You'd better call the doctor."

"You can't wake the man in the middle of the night," my father snorted, peering at his watch with one half-opened eye.

So we waited, mother and I.

For me, it was an awakening. I'd rolled and stretched, kicked and squirmed in utero. Now I was churning like the sea in a hurricane.

Mother lifted us out of bed and assessed her circumstances. With time to kill, she'd better get some ironing done. She had a long day ahead of her. I was born at 9:08 p.m. in St. Mary's Hospital, St. Louis, Missouri.

For the rest of her life, sometime in the early hours of June 30, Mother would tell me the story of my birth. While I lived at home, she tiptoed into my room after our restaurant's closing to sit on the edge of my bed and whisper. Later, she'd phone, often about 2 a.m. Acculturated to late hours and loneliness, she was used to getting up for a cigarette and maybe another vodka. Me, I slept long and heavily. So I groaned at being woken up for her mushy story.

Mother didn't focus on her long hours of labor or its pains, so I've never known how hard a time I gave her. Maybe we had an easy labor.

"She never caused me a minute's trouble," she'd say later, to her girlfriends or mine or to my suitor, "until she was 16 and talked back to me." I'd tuck my head beneath my wing, just as I did on those birthday calls.

"I wanted you so much," she'd tell me year after year. From there it was all downhill.

"All through it, I'd be hoping we'd make a baby," she'd tell me. "Afterward, I'd lie with my legs up in the air to help it take."

Awwww, Mother…

All the love Catharine Olivetti had been too burdened to share, Elsa Olivetti Martin saved up for motherhood. She said she wanted a dozen kids. She had me—and her poor second daughter, Gina, the half-sister of my teen years, who lived only thirty-six hours. Luckily for only me, Mother was often distracted by work and her own human story, including her search for a man who would love her for herself alone.

> *I heard an old religious man*
> *But yesternight declare*
> *That he had found a text to prove*
> *That only God, my dear,*
> *Could love you for yourself alone*
> *And not your yellow hair.*

Mother's hair was so dark it seemed black, but she shared the fate of yellow-haired Anne Gregory of William Butler Yates' poem.

Too much love for a teen seeking independence was just the right amount for babies. Babies—and later, small dogs—were bottomless pits into which her geyser could flow.

Good smelling with big soft breasts, the most beautiful woman in the world put me in the world's safest place in her embrace. I go back there every time my yoga teacher calls for the Happy Baby asana.

My sons got their own bountiful shares of their grandmother's boundless baby love and all the good food that went with it.

Alex, born March 31, was still mastering sitting up when I interrupted his dinner with mother on an early autumn evening. This was before babies traveled fully furnished. Mother sat him on phone books and tied him into a kitchen chair with a towel. Pulled up to the table across from her, he was gumming a chicken leg while waving an ear of corn. His face—and the table before him—was smeared with mashed potatoes mangled with lettuce. Mother's salads were legendary.

"A full-course dinner for a baby?" I asked.

"The boy's got to eat."

Half a dozen years later, when I was nursing Nat, she reminded me of the perfection of tucking my finger into my baby's waving hand.

I go back there, too.

Mother didn't call me early this morning, though I woke up about the time the phone would have rung. She hasn't called in twenty-seven years, death having called for her in her sixty-seventh year, in 1988.

So on the night of June 30, 2017, I told myself this story.

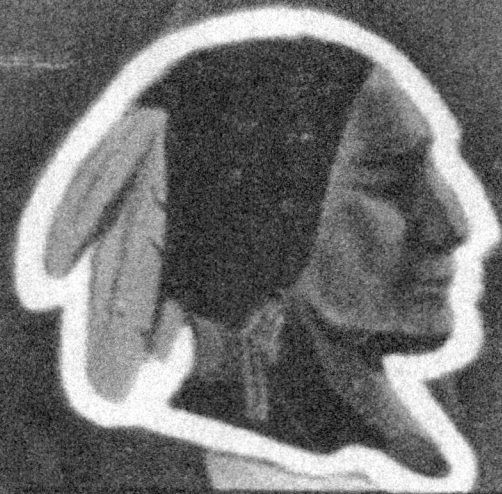

ED QUIRK

Intruders

Voices from the night still send shivers.

The house breathed noisily around the sleeping girl and dog. This house was too new for ghosts to have gathered, but floors creaked and walls settled in stealthy metabolism. Blown by the whirring fan, summer-light white eyelet curtains sucked the screens.

Outside in the big dark beyond the open windows, cicadas shrilled. When a breeze stirred, enclosing junipers ran their green fingers down the screens' outer skin.

Inside, the bedroom was hung with the humidity of St. Louis August. The water glass sweated the bed table. Limp sheets stuck to limbs. The dogs, Fuddy Duddy and Cina, were noisy too, with exhalations bigger than their pint-sized bodies, twitching and sighing in dog dreams.

The girl slept through the noises, and through the heat. The pressure of her open book—it might have been *Lad: A Dog*—imprinting on her cheek, did not disturb. She had fallen asleep mid-chapter, but enough consciousness had lingered for her to switch off the lamp.

The room was dark, as dark as could be in a mid-century suburban street blooming with streetlights and search-lighted, now and again, by the headlights of returning cars.

It would be hours before the headlights of her mother's convertible Ford Fairlane tracked up their drive and into her window. Then, still in her high heels from her night at the family restaurant— The Stymie Supper Club and Cocktail Lounge they called it—her mother would turn on the hall light and come into her room.

Sitting on the bed, she would slip off her shoes and caress the girl's damp forehead. 'Sandra, are you awake?' she would ask, and the girl would half-waken to her voice and aura. Her perfume, White Shoulders, mixed with smells of tobacco, liquor and food. The girl and probably scruffy white Fuddy Duddy would smile and fall back to sleep before their mother had gotten three words into the story of her evening.

That was the surety of the night, and girl and dogs slept well.

The dogs heard it first, the sound that did not belong in the symphony of their sleep. Fuddy Duddy's pointed ears pricked up, tingling with blood surging in veinways beneath pink, fine-haired inner skin. Her bearded muzzle rose to alertness.

The girl gasped awake when she heard it, and adrenalin flushed her cheeks and arms.

The sleeping house was full of human voices. Voices that were not her mother's.

They gripped like a nightmare. Echoing and laughing, they grew enormous and pressed around her until all she knew were their sound and her fear.

Fuddy Duddy and Cina quivered in suspense, snuggling closer to the girl and licking her face. They were together in bed but maybe not alone in the house.

The loudness of the voices filled the darkness. Surely the people full of these voices were here, in the house—though she had not seen the headlights of their car. Nor heard the turning of the door-knob or their footfalls on the thick orange carpet. Were they in the living room?

She listened; she did not breathe. Her only sense was sound.

The voices cracked and burbled and soared.

She and the dogs listened, so tight in their skins with fear they must burst and the explosions give them away.

Were the intruders' faces—stacked one atop the other—peering now from the doorway? Had they turned the hallway corner, headed in her direction. She was frozen in fear. The dogs leapt under the bed, growling.

The voices surged. Now, she knew for certain, they'd be bursting into her room, and she would die of fear when she would see from whom the calls and bellows came. She understood now that they were demons, burst up from hell through the drain in the laundry room. They had crept through the paneled basement, but they could not keep their glee silent. They had laughed up the stairs, chortled through the kitchen, advanced down the hall, giggling.

And now they had her.

Fuddy Duddy produced a howl that could have come from Lad, a dog six times her size. The girl closed her eyes and signed herself with the cross of the God who she was sure did not believe in her.

Nothing.

Nothing, though minutes pulsed through her veins in heavy-blooded anguish. Nothing but the voices.

The dogs scooted out from under the eyelet bed skirt matching the curtains and leaped up beside her.

When finally she was too afraid to endure any longer, she crept out of bed, snaked down the hall, pulled the black phone off its hall table and into her lap.

She nearly shrieked when Fuddy Duddy leapt atop her. Instead, she bit her lip so thoroughly that blood ran metallic into her mouth.

Then she dialed PA77552.

When the bartender, her secret love, answered, she could hear the loud chatter of people—they'd be perched on high stools, and standing, arms draped over one another, or sitting at shiny black bar tables—loosened by drink and living fast. Frankie Lane crooned over the jukebox. Bartender Ed's big voice tried to get her to tell him what was the matter.

She blubbered, and the dog licked her tears.

When he finally understood her, he shouted for her mother to take the phone. While the long cord was still dangling—this she did not see—the young Washington Redskins fullback vaulted over the bar, ran to his Mercury as if he were on the field in season instead of bartending this off-season, and raced the six blocks to her invaded home.

The girl sobbed as her mother told her surely this is a nightmare. It was not, she bawled, it was real and people—or devils—were there. Tears slickening the receiver, she had some hope now of rescue but doubtful it would come in time.

No nightmare was this. The intruders—two men and two women—had left the Stymie drunk, hot and in the mood for a swim. They'd driven, weaving, to the owners' house, where the men had visited for games of poker. They'd climbed the redwood fence with a couple six-packs of beer, stripped to their underwear and leapt into the pool.

That's how Ed found them in the moments before he ran them off in a display of gridiron ferocity. When he went to her room, the girl was in the arms of her mother, who also had raced home.

Ed Quirk was the girl's hero that night, and she would love him forever more. She cried hard when death caught him nine years later, an after-hours heart attack in the parking lot of his own bar, opened in Clayton, Missouri, after his football career ended. Her hero she never did forget. Nor did she forget the fear of fright.

Best Friends Bonded Over Baseball

*...and a St. Louis Cardinals shortstop
who was both cute and a good fielder*

Before I ever laid eyes on her, my best friend called me on the telephone. We talked for an hour and a half, long after my mother—I bet her mother, too—lost patience. Until Mother, well frosted, stormed down the hall to demand *Sandra! Put down that phone!*

Of course Linda called first. Of the two of us, she was the bolder. Way bolder. We both got in trouble, but in different ways. I was so shy, and such a good girl, that I couldn't imagine that trouble would come looking for me. It did. Often in the habit of nuns.

In elementary school, at Our Lady of the Pillar, Sister Alfonso would spy me—out of our class of fifty—and glide down the row to loom over me, ruler in her hand. There she'd stand, the best image I had for our school's odd name, looking like a melting pillar candle, puddling at its bottom. I'd be lost in innocent ignorance, reading ahead in our book. Or, worse yet, reading a comic book hidden underneath. There, Sister would stand tapping her ruler. I'd eventually look up into her Medusa eye, and the sin of eye contact would make my trouble way worse. Even now, this is not a good memory.

In high school, I fell again into the hands of the nuns.

Seventh and eighth grade in public school had not worked out so well. I had big hopes when I'd defied the old nuns by daring to leave that good Catholic school for the heathens. I was going to hell in a handbag. By today's standards, it was like signing on

91

with Al Qaeda. But I'd held to my plan of escape to the new Brittany Junior High about six blocks away. I cajoled Mother—I could walk and she wouldn't have the long drive to take and pick me up every day—until she gave in. She didn't know about schools, and I begged hard.

In public school, I still felt as far out as the girl in the moon. September 1957, I started my freshman year at St. Joseph's Academy, back with the nuns and even farther from home than Our Lady of the Pillar.

Cowering in my tweedy wool green jumper and hunter green blazer, I made my high school entrance by dropping my armload of books on the first stair of the school bus. The upperclassmen had found their victim; the other raw freshman found temporary escape. I found ignominy, and knew it well. For the fourth time in my four-teen-year life, I was starting a new school where I didn't know a soul. Already, I was burning with shame. Again, I was alien as green cheese. Until I met Linda.

Sooner or later, in a class of just over 100, you'd bump into every-body. But Linda and I had a little help from a friend. We were, in the term of the age, set up. We met by the design of a pale redhead with more spunk than I imagined. Anne Pembroke McCauley sat behind Sandra Mary Martin in homeroom.

Anne was a nice girl and a smart one. Smart enough to read my character better than I could, for what I was or might become was to me, and I imagined to the world, so inchoate as to be unintelligible. Linda, I would find, was much more put together. She was determined while I was wishy-washy. She was decisive while I was wool-gathering. A decade and a half later, my type would be called "lost in the ozone."

Linked together by the alphabet, Anne Pembroke McCauley and I were friendly acquaintances. We got along, but we made no click. She was as cool as I was warm.

"You need to meet Linda Kulla," Anne told me in the general gossip before we stood for the Pledge of Allegiance and prayers.

Linda Claire Kulla, a K, was in another homeroom. She and Anne had come to St. Joe's from one of the right parish schools, Mary Queen of Peace in South St. Louis County. They'd both been popular achievers before puberty turned Linda hot in a whole new way. Why Linda and I were a sure pair, Anne didn't say. Giddy with the thrill of being singled out for friendship, I believed her. Apparently Linda did too. So that late winter night I'd been anticipating Linda's call.

In 1957, every house had one telephone. They weren't rationed. You could have more, but why—unless you were very rich or your house very big? A few years later, teens across America lobbied for their own bedroom telephones. That night, I talked on the family phone, a black rotary-dial portable plastic box centrally placed on the hall table, with phone books underneath and a chair beside. Our phone, like most, was black. Soon mother would upgrade to white, though never trendy 1950s' mustard orange or olive green. (If she could have bought orange or turquoise, I bet she would have.)

Long coils of cord that stretched into your own room came later; this cord was about four feet long—about as long as a MacBook Air charging cord. I wrapped the receiver coils around my arms as we talked. Ten feet down the hall in one direction, Mother and my stepfather, Gene Shaper, watched television in the living room. A few feet the other way down the hall, doors opened into the three bedrooms of our mid-century rancher. That night I rose above suburban St. Louis, Missouri. I was levitating, rising like the Virgin Mary ascending to heaven.

Looping in and out, round and round, like the coiled receiver cord that linked us, Linda and I rounded the bases of acquaintance: animals (cats, dogs, horses)...books (still lots of dogs and horses)... family (she with parents, an older sister, grandmother, and lots of uncles, aunts and cousins; me, my mother and I with the unspeakable addition of a stepfather, plus a father and my grandmother)...

fun (horseback riding for us both, books, movies, summertime, our pets, eating)...school (not much good to say there)...

Eventually we landed on baseball.

"Do you like the Cardinals?"

"Sure! I go with my father and sometimes we sit in front-row seats. And I listen on the radio."

"I've been listening since I was a little girl. My grandmother and I listen together on the screened porch, in the dark, and drink cream soda."

St. Louis cream soda, we both knew, is shocking pink.

"Who's your favorite player?"

"Don Blasingame!"

"The Blazer!"

"He's cute! And a good shortstop. He and Joe Cunningham. They're short-to-first magic," my father says.

"I'm starting the Don Blasingame Fan Club," I bragged. Though what that meant, I had no idea.

Linda, it would turn out, had a better idea of fandom. She had a curvy sashay that drew men to her, and she used direct eye contact to better effect that I had with the sidling Sister Mary Alfonso, who I should never have looked in the eye. My front-row seats brought young baseball players to the fence. Over the years, many a player—even non-Cardinals—joined Linda's fan club. All that was yet to happen.

That night we talked baseball. Horses, too, for we both were riders. Books we liked, certainly The *Diary of Anne Frank* for both of us, as well as all the Lad books and all Walter Farley's black stallion books. The terror that was Mother Theresa Martin, our principal. Flavors of ice cream. Our cats, both Siamese. Hers Ming Ling Fu. Mine Prince Si-Am, a copycat name from *Lady and the Tramp*, where we'd both first seen Siamese cats.

That night—when we talked until my mother put her foot down—my best friend and I hadn't yet met. I didn't know about her tight curls. She didn't know about my crooked little fingers. But we each knew we'd found our partner. Getting to know what we'd get up to together would be fun.

The Great St. Louis Snowstorm

When neither nuns nor school buses coped

When I was a kid, we'd walk miles to school in the worst weather winter could throw at us. Okay, I'm exaggerating a generation or two. The only time I walked miles in the worst weather winter could summon was to get away from school.

That escape and its occasion—the great snowfall of Friday, January 31, 1958—came close to disappearing in the whiteout of long-ago memory. Except for the fire that ignites in my fingers and toes whenever temperatures drop below 38 degrees, I might have lost the part played in my life by the seventh heaviest midnight-to-midnight downing in St. Louis history.

Instead, as the numbness returns, memory stirs. I must have gotten frostbite as a kid, I announce, more to myself than to anybody who might be listening.

Had there been such a snow as I remembered? Or had I reconstituted it from the stuff of dreams and stories? An inquiry or two led me to Weather Underground, where I found my storm.

It would have had to have hit in my first two years of high school, before I became a driver rather than a rider of buses. I calculated. Counting way back, I began my day-by-day storm search the winter of my freshman year at St. Joseph's Academy, 1957–1958.

Regular light snow fell that winter, with the big drop—11.2-inches—on January 31. Which was a school day, a Friday.

The scene was set. But could the drama really have played out as I imagined?

Calls to my alma mater yielded nothing. No surprise there. Curiosity scored few points in my time in high school.

So I called my oldest friend, who was the great gift of my four years at St. Joseph's Academy

That snowy day Linda Kulla and I hadn't yet met. Our alliance was made in March, shortly before the beginning of the baseball season, the occasion of our first shared interest. But we'd lived that snowy day in parallel time.

"The biggest snow I remember," Linda told me, "hit during the school day. By the time our principal, Mother Teresa Martin, put out the call, the buses couldn't get through. We had to stay at school into the night, until the roads were plowed. The nuns had to feed us dinner, which they didn't like, and I remember dancing to records in the lounge."

My memory was different. Linda's story rang true, but that wasn't the way I spent the afternoon of Friday, January 31, 1958.

She and I lived in different directions from the school, she south, I north, at about twice her distance. My home, Google maps tells me, was 6.4 miles from my school. That's exactly the distance I traveled that day, though my journey didn't take me to my home.

Perhaps my bus had gotten through. A school bus figures in my hazy memory. I'd gotten on it, probably with the other girls bound for the suburb of University City, Lindbergh Boulevard to Olive Street Road. Someplace along the route, the bus stalled in the snow. Rather than wait for rescue, Carol Clasquin and I set out on foot into the snowstorm.

Our school uniforms were woolly green jumpers over short-sleeved white blouses with Peter Pan collars and topped with green blazers piped in white. We wore brogues and white cotton ankle-high socks. Slacks were forbidden, and if we had tights, we'd have been breaking the rules. Overcoats were wool and long.

Carol—who I've not seen since graduation—was smart, short and seemed to be cut to the pattern of Mary Mother of God. I was smart, short and painfully unconventional. We were neither adventurers, yet we plunged into the wind-driven snow.

Carol's home was closer, and her people would have been home. Both my mother and father would have been at our family restaurant, a warm oasis in the snow for regulars who played gin and drank Scotch every afternoon. That restaurant, The Stymie Club, was my destination. I still go there in dreams. Whether I made it there that night, I can't recall.

For the rest of our journey is murky. We were cold, I know, and we stopped along Olive Street Road into any store we found open, as we trudged through deepening snow from the open spaces of rich Frontenac to our more-developed, working-class area of University City.

No cell phones, of course; no one knew where we were. Certainly not what we were doing. We'd been out on our own for hours. Yet no scolding for our folly met us at Carol's house. Red-cheeked and shivering, we were welcomed like heroes.

More than cold, we were rapturous.

Because of the tingling of frost-nip in my fingers, that much I still remember. Otherwise, I'd only believe it happened in the fictional soft focus of dreams.

At Piazza della Repubblica

A sunset melon

The song rippled through the streets like a sunset resounding from the mountains. It came at the end of a warm Sunday, when walks were ending, attractions closing, buses slowing—leaving few reasons not to go home. There was reprieve in it. Would we savor this June Sunday just a little longer? Come a little closer? Stay a little later? I have brought summer to you, it coaxed.

In the many turnings off Turin's Piazza della Repubblica, people halted and listened. Purposefulness ebbed as it can when, touched by the intimate pink of a summer sunset, you laugh at the earnestness of your comings and goings.

A family forgot its way home. A matron of dark southern complexion unstiffened in her black clothes and smiled as she remembered—perhaps—other June evenings. A child leading a dog twice his size looked in the dog's eye, and the dog in his, and the two took off running. At the streetcar stop, a mother and grown daughter—Americans seeking their roots—shared a stirring.

The great god Pan had come from the south to this gritty Piedmont city. He came as the watermelon man.

"You've never tasted melon so sweet as this," he called. "Come here for a taste of the sun."

At the end of a Sunday afternoon, the market square should have been emptying. Brandishing the shining blade of a butcher knife above the enormous belly of the green fruit, Pan was a day late. Saturday is market day in the Piazza della Repubblica.

Saturday before dawn, a convoy of trucks had smoked into the square. By first light, the harvest of early summer shone on their open beds: orange bells of pepper, giant heads of cabbage, feathery plumes of fennel, nests of tart red cherries. Piedmontese thronged and jostled in the teeming square, eyeing, touching, haggling, searching for the perfect fruit. Their northern gardens—tiny plots as tidy as company parlors—were still barely green. City dwellers, suburbanites, mountain villagers,—after the long winter, all were hungry for summer. By dusk all that remained of the day's market were mountains of rubbish. In Saturday's twilight, bulldozers with open shovels devoured the litter of discarded vegetables.

Sunday's setting sun burnished Pan's single truck. So shiningly ferociously black was that semi that it might have been polished in Hades. Fiery charms were painted on its fenders. Idols dangled behind its smoky windshield. Ripped free, its black tarp revealed a full load of black-green melons.

One had been selected for sacrifice.

"Such sweet fruit. It's been a long time since you tasted melon this sweet!" he sang, and plunged his knife.

His second cut made a V with the first.

Pan withdrew the blade in a single stroke, all the while chanting the mantra of this dark Spanish melon still warm from the southern sun. Enchanted, passersby pressed around the makeshift stage thrown up against a black truck on a lonely square. Appetite and imagination roused with his words.

Pan wiped the blade on his dungareed thigh. He caressed the knife, testing its sharpness on a finger. But he did not raise it for the third cut that would complete the plug. He was in no hurry to expose the sweet flesh. "So sweet, so crisp, so juicy," he crooned.

All who listened mixed their own memories into the spell.

My memories cross an ocean and half a continent, reaching back into childhood summer evenings past the sunbaked hours into a secret adult time. At the point of summer in the center of St. Louis night, a child waited with grownups at Sam the Watermelon Man's outdoor tables for a crisp, chilled crescent.

Memories of grown-up days sweetened with watermelon sugar.

Gathering stories and adventures along the Mississippi River, photographer Sue Eslinger and I had purchased a melon on the outskirts of Memphis. We traveled with it in my Gremlin with no air-conditioning, as far as Louisiana. There, in the full oppression of mid-afternoon, we parked under a tree and broke into the melon's red center, eating thirstily. No parks waited for travelers along these back roads, and in passing cars, the locals turned back to watch two white women sitting at the side of the road eating watermelon, the sticky juices running down their arms.

Tapping makes no promise of a melon's ripeness. The ring that seems to say that here enough sweetness is stored to satisfy all the longings suppressed over winter may be only the echo of the tapper's hopes. Only plugging tells the truth.

Those memories whetted my hunger as Pan sang of his melons on Turin's Piazza della Repubblica. They made a bridge to mother and me that found footing in the *paese* where she had been conceived sixty years before. Her longings and mine were drawn together in the spell woven by a gypsy watermelon man, drawn together with the summer-freshened hopes of a score of Italians who lived at the foot of the Alps.

There, taut in our skins, we waited for Pan's knife to fall the third time. It descended and rose, piercing, lifting, exposing a green shell, a translucent inch of rind, a thick red wedge of earth-summer-rain-made melon. Pan held it high in triumph In every mouth, saliva flowed.

Now the knife danced, carving the melon. Pan fed the multitudes, proffering the multiplying wedges on knife point. Mouths full of fruit and juice, our hands reached into pockets or unsnapped purses. Lira changed hands. Melon by melon, the pile diminished.

Tomorrow Mother and I would go together to the mountains to seek the place—and what more?—from which we had come.

Tonight we had supped with a god.

At Ballymaloe, a Feast-Filled Journey to Ireland

Ireland is even greener than we thought.

America goes green on St. Patrick's Day. From beer to dress to hair (and once upon a time, the Chicago River), green is the color of choice.

In putting on the green, we're not alone. St. Patrick's stomping grounds is doing its own greening, returning to its roots to recapture a way of life and economy rising from the Old Sod.

With weeds and locally adapted seeds, with Atlantic salmon and tidepool cockles and mussels, with heritage cattle and mountain-browsing sheep, Ireland is raising the green flag of food independence. In supermarkets and trendy restaurants, Irish origin is the motto. Eat out, and you'll have such choices as roast rib of Irish beef, tenderly cooked collar of Irish bacon from Crowes Farm, Jane Russell pork sausages, tender roast leg of Irish spring lamb, Dublin Bay prawns, honey-baked Limerick ham, Irish brie and Irish cabbage.

"Getting food as locally sourced as possible is the aim of every restaurant that takes itself seriously—and at least a decent percent of locals," says John McKenna, author of the McKenna's Guides.

It's enough to turn America's locavores green with envy.

To see Ireland's greening, I traveled into the countryside of the Irish village of Baltimore, a distance about the same as from our own Baltimore, Maryland, to Solomons. We'll make three stops, then have a drink in Dublin.

AT BALLYMALOE,
LEARNING TO EAT WEEDS

At Ballymaloe Cooking School, Darina Allen is leading a roots search. An international flock has paid a pretty price—$270 a head—to forage in the company of the fast-walking empress of Ireland's greening. Shod in rubber boots and carrying baskets on their arms, the gaggle is learning to eat weeds. Their heads and baskets fill with bittercress and comfrey, spruce and borage, perennial leek and tansy, chickweed, sweet Cecily and sorrel. Each weed has a distinction and many values.

"The queen had bittercress in a salad for her 90th birthday," Allen declares. "Feverfew has a terrible taste but helps with migraines," while chickweed—the scourge of Maryland gardens—"is sold in the markets at a high price."

Even nettles—the stinging plant for which our nasty Chesapeake jellyfish are named—have value. "Eat four times in the month of May to keep rheumatism away," says Allen, quoting an old rhyme. Even invasive kudzu: Read on and see.

If hunger is driving Allen's students, it's not of the Irish potato famine variety. This well-fed gathering is hungry for lore. Our grandparents knew all these weeds, Allen tells her followers. After World War II, Ireland—just like America—got out of touch with farm and field. Packaged and processed foods swept in on a wave of advertising. The next couple of generations ate out of boxes, bags, cans and aluminum trays.

Now the tide is turning.

"A few pioneers—among them Allen's mother-in-law, Myrtle Allen—decided Irish food could be spectacular," McKenna told me over scones with Irish cream. "Since then, there's been a sea change."

"We don't want the commodity viewpoint," Allen declares.

A garda—an Irish cop—agrees. Newly married, he's returned from Dublin to his nearby hometown, Cobh, his roots, and he's foraging with Allen for the day. A Methodist minister from Oregon is at Ballymaloe for the 12-week cooking school. Sponsored by a $50,000 Refreshment Grant from the Lilly Foundation, she sees divinity in "the grounded table."

It's a nice image, the table spread in green with legs rooted in the earth like potatoes or beets. For us whose mother tongue descends from Anglo-Saxon, it's also easier to say than the French terroir.

Philosophy is guiding the Irish back to food close to home. The reasons are many: energy costs of long-distance transportation; loss of freshness, nutrients and taste; and the knowledge that, with chemicals, hormones, additives, and much that is unnatural, including GMOs—which worry the Irish far more than they do Americans— strange food can be strange indeed.

In a country as small as Ireland, close can be very close: "within a few miles," McKenna says. In your own backyard, Allen demonstrates to her spring foraging class.

Economic potential is another part of Ireland's greening.

"A good economy starts from agriculture, as we've realized since our economy imploded in 2008," Allen told me. "So we take the language of the supermarket—USP, Unique Selling Point—and make ours as local as possible."

In her restaurant and cooking school—and in her books and the long-running television cookery program that's made Allen Ireland's Julia Child—Allen has proved locality a profitable USP.

Profitable and tasty.

The foraging morning leads to an afternoon of feasting. In Ballymaloe Cooking School's teaching kitchen, Allen and an assistant transform weeds—including seaweed plus shellfish, cockles, mussels, limpets and periwinkles foraged from the seashore—into persuasion. Stinging nettles are roasted on a white pizza. Cecily sweetens a rhubarb compote. Chickweed, cress, dandelion, sorrel, wildflowers and wild garlic get tossed together with stove-top smoked salmon in a flavor-filled salad. More salmon is served with horseradish cream, scraped from a freshly dug root. Tiny steamed periwinkles are released from their shells with a pin and dipped in mayonnaise beaten with oil and hen-fresh eggs. Dandelion flowers are dipped in batter, deep fried and sprinkled with vanilla sugar. Sweet elderflower water washes it down. Only the steamed kudzu tastes like a weed.

St. Patrick would approve. You can't get any greener than eating your own weeds. Though to add variety, Ballymaloe also raises 80 crops on an 100-acre organic farm and in greenhouses—plus chickens and pigs.

BROWN ENVELOPE SEEDS

A short drive from Baltimore, near the town of Skibbereen, Madeline McKeever and Mike Sweeney grow Ireland's future from seed. Their company—Brown Envelope Seeds—is small; its range is larger than "a few miles," but not much bigger than southern Ireland. Their field is a backyard garden of an acre or so, plus a greenhouse. The help is a pair of donkeys, a couple of dogs and humans as needed.

In that space, McKeever grows some 200 plants for seed. Tomatoes are her biggest crop. As they—like all the seeds she grows—are chosen for a narrow geographic, geological and climate range, of most you've never heard, like Tommy Toe. A few, like Brandywine, are familiar. Others, like Zapotec pink ribbed, are not likely native to Ireland. Beets, beans, cabbage, carrots, cereals, chiles, cucumbers, eggplants, various greens, herbs, leeks, melons, onions, oil seeds, parsnips, peas, quinoa, radishes, spinach and turnips fill out the list.

All seeds are open-pollinated—as opposed to selectively inbred—to increase their genetic diversity. Genetic diversity, McKeever tells me as a donkey looks on, "means seeds that are sensitive to the environment and capable of adaptation to diverse soil types, climates, diseases and other environmental factors."

McKeever's garden is the testing ground. "Growing through the worst summer on record has been a great way to select seeds for the Irish climate," she says. She trialed seven varieties of quinoa, for example, before finding the right one.

For regular gardeners, going to seed ends the harvest. For McKeever, seeds are the point. The cabbage she wants is bloated big as a beach ball and hairy with seed sprouts. After seed plants are selected, the others go to the family table or freezer.

When a plant's seeds are ripe, McKeever covers some plants above and spreads out a tarp below to catch falling seeds. Other plants are shaken in bags. Seeds are sifted for chafe, packaged in brown envelopes and sold at the Skibbereen Farmers Market and by mail. Envelopes are about $3.25.

McKeever's part of Ireland's greening is creating a Grow-It-Yourself network from seed.

CLARE WATSON
AND QUENTIN GARGAN

Up the coast in Bantry, County Cork's green hills begin to break into the stony wildlands. Replacing cattle in the fields are horned blackface mountain sheep able to endure cold, wind and rain. Grass is standard fare for Quentin Gargan's flock, so when his whistle announces a feast of Irish oats, the sheep come running.

With sheep, chickens and a sod roof, Gargan and Watson's home—and its long six-foot-wide hedged lane—could be old Ireland. Except for the two 21st century-style windmills and the all-electric Citroen C-Zero Watson drives.

With one foot in the old world and the other in the future, the pair are long-time pioneers of the greening of Ireland. Nowadays Gargan is a wind entrepreneur, from his home supplying technology to wind farms around the world.

Household windmills like Gargan's are still something of an oddity in Ireland, but wind is an established part of the national energy mix, providing from four to 44 percent of total energy consumption. Contributing to the mix are hydropower, biomass, peat, gas, coal, oil, waste and imports, including nuclear power generated in Europe.

For Gargan, Ireland's Smart Grid is one more tool in a greener economy and lifestyle. Watson plugs in her car at the end of her day, but the way they've got their meter programmed, electricity doesn't flow to it—or their dryer and other big household power consumers—until the middle of the night. "By day, Ireland uses expensive nationally produced wind power," Gargan tells me. "At night, we buy cheap European nuclear power."

I'm feeling pretty green by the time I reach Dublin, so at Coppinger Row—one of the McKenna's Guides *100 Best Places to Eat*—I drink green. Not green beer; that's an Irish American specialty. Here I order a Flo & Basy, a concoction of Beefeater gin, St. Germain Elderflower liqueur, agave nectar, fresh lime juice and pureed Irish basil. It's so good I have another, along with pork belly and spring greens—both Irish and both local.

Of course.

The Story of My Hands

*Mother warned me that
what you fear comes upon you.*

"Yuck, Grandmother!" said 14-year-old Elsa. "What happened to your finger?"

Polish, copper for early autumn, flashed on nine oval nails, cut short to go with my short hands and fingers. The colored polish disguised the bruised, half-dead nail of my left thumb.

The tenth, on my right thumb, was unpolished and mostly bare down to the skin. It looked like something blind, like a mole. The old nail had fallen off again, pushed out by the stub of the new nail already the color of bruises at its ragged leading edge.

Would you believe torture?

"Really?"

No, not really. I don't want you to believe that, and I shouldn't say it. People are tortured, really, in countries all over the world, even here I'm sorry to say. It's not right to compare our little stuff to real pain.

"Yeah, like it's not right for me to say I'm starving to death when I just want a snack and people really are starving."

Smart girl. Plus, the truth about this is good enough, and there is some torture in the background.

How much you know about torture, I don't know. Before I was your age, in grade school (as we called elementary school in my day), I knew a lot about torture.

Martyrdom was big at Our Lady of the Pillar, where the nuns teaching us were pretty tortured themselves, though I didn't recognize it then, all by themselves in a classroom with maybe fifty kids. Lots of the boys were wild, with the savage close to the surface. Some of the girls were mean on the sneak.

To keep order, the nuns plied rulers on the boys and froze the girls with death stares. But their best weapon was God. Their God seemed about as bloodthirsty as the devil. Getting in good with their God would cost you so dearly that some of us kids thought we might be better off with the devil. I know I did.

We especially felt that way when Sister Alfonso, who taught third grade, would tell us about the martyrs and show us their pictures on holy cards. To prove their love of God, martyrs endured all kinds of terrible things. They were baked in metal ovens, roasted over spits, fed to hungry lions, pulled apart on racks, pierced in iron maidens, drawn and quartered, amputated and de-tongued.

Bad as all that was, and it all gave me nightmares, I was most bothered by the fate of the missionaries who came to the New World to save souls and, for their reward, endured painted pagan Natives (wilder even than the worst boys in our class) pulling out their fingernails.

I really didn't want that to happen to me. But I couldn't stop thinking about it. Even though my mother had warned me that what you fear comes upon you.

Even though the proof was right in my own hands.

Look at my little fingers.

"Oh Grandmother! What happened to your fingers?"

I marked you, my mother, Elsa's namesake, explained to me when I asked that very question.

In Catholic school, the deformity stood out. We brought our palms together in prayer many times a day, upright at heart center like a church steeple, each finger touching its opposite from base to tip. Everybody but me. I could, with isometric effort, keep my palms touching, and there was only a chink of a channel separating thumb from thumb and finger from finger.

But my little fingers stood out like sore thumbs. They touched at the tips, but the digits, rigid at the knuckles, bowed out in a long oval.

"What's wrong with your fingers? Straighten them out and fold your hands correctly," nuns in grade after grade had commanded me. Classmates tittered.

Mother! Why would you give me crooked fingers? I wailed.

What I feared came upon me, she replied.

What was she talking about, I wondered, and so may you.

Do you really want to hear this? I asked the second Elsa, my granddaughter.

"Is it gross?"

Yes, I said.

"I don't care! You've got to tell me," my granddaughter said, just as I had more than a half century earlier.

This is the story my mother told me—

"Your grandmother sent me to get a chicken," my mother began. "When I grew up, you didn't go to the store to buy a chicken already turned into meat and packaged in plastic. You went into the chicken yard, where I would go when we had our own flock. This fateful day, we were out of chickens. My mother gave me a few hoarded pennies and sent me to a woman down the lane.

"I was afraid of her because she looked like a witch. Whether she was or not I don't know, but even if she was a witch I had to go get our chicken. You didn't tell my mother no.

"When I told my business, she caught a chicken by the neck. I expected her to wring its neck. Instead, she tucked its complaining head under her arm. As she lifted her right hand, I saw that her little finger was crooked."

Mother didn't say *just like yours,* but I knew what she meant.

"What happened to your finger?" Mother asked the chicken lady.

"The words were out before I remembered I could be talking to a witch.

"At her reply I could have been knocked over by a feather.

"'When I kill a chicken, I don't want to waste an egg, so first I put my little finger up its rear just like this,'" the witch said, as she did just that. 'No egg,' she said, and flipped the chicken over by its feet with her right hand, grabbed its head with her left, and with one mighty swing ended that chicken's life.

"She handed the bird to me, then held up her right little finger. 'The first time I did that,' she said, 'my finger came out crooked.'

"Sandra," my mother said, "I was so horrified that I never forgot. Her little finger always worried me, and when I was pregnant with you, I marked you. What I feared came upon me, and you were born with two crooked little fingers."

"Grandmother! You never did that with a chicken, did you?" Elsa groaned, curling her lip and wrinkling her freckled nose.

Never!

Mother left the farm to go to work in the city when she was just your age, 14. I buy my chickens killed and plucked, though I did learn from Mother how to butcher my chicken for cooking.

"Did that really happen, what your mother said?"

I don't know, but Mother believed it, and I've never gotten a better explanation.

"Could something like that really happen?"

Your guess is as good as mine. Does what you fear come upon you? I never wanted to believe it. But I never forgot those martyrs' poor fingernails, and one clumsy summer I crushed the tips of both my thumbs. Ever since, the nails grow back only to fall off.

"Is it a curse? Was the woman really a witch?"

"You only know by a deathbed test," my mother told me. "If she's a witch, she'll beg for a broom as she lies dying. If you give her one, you become a witch, too."

I do not think my mother was a witch, though I was not at her deathbed as she died by surprise on an otherwise ordinary August afternoon. Still, I have hands that would do any witch proud.

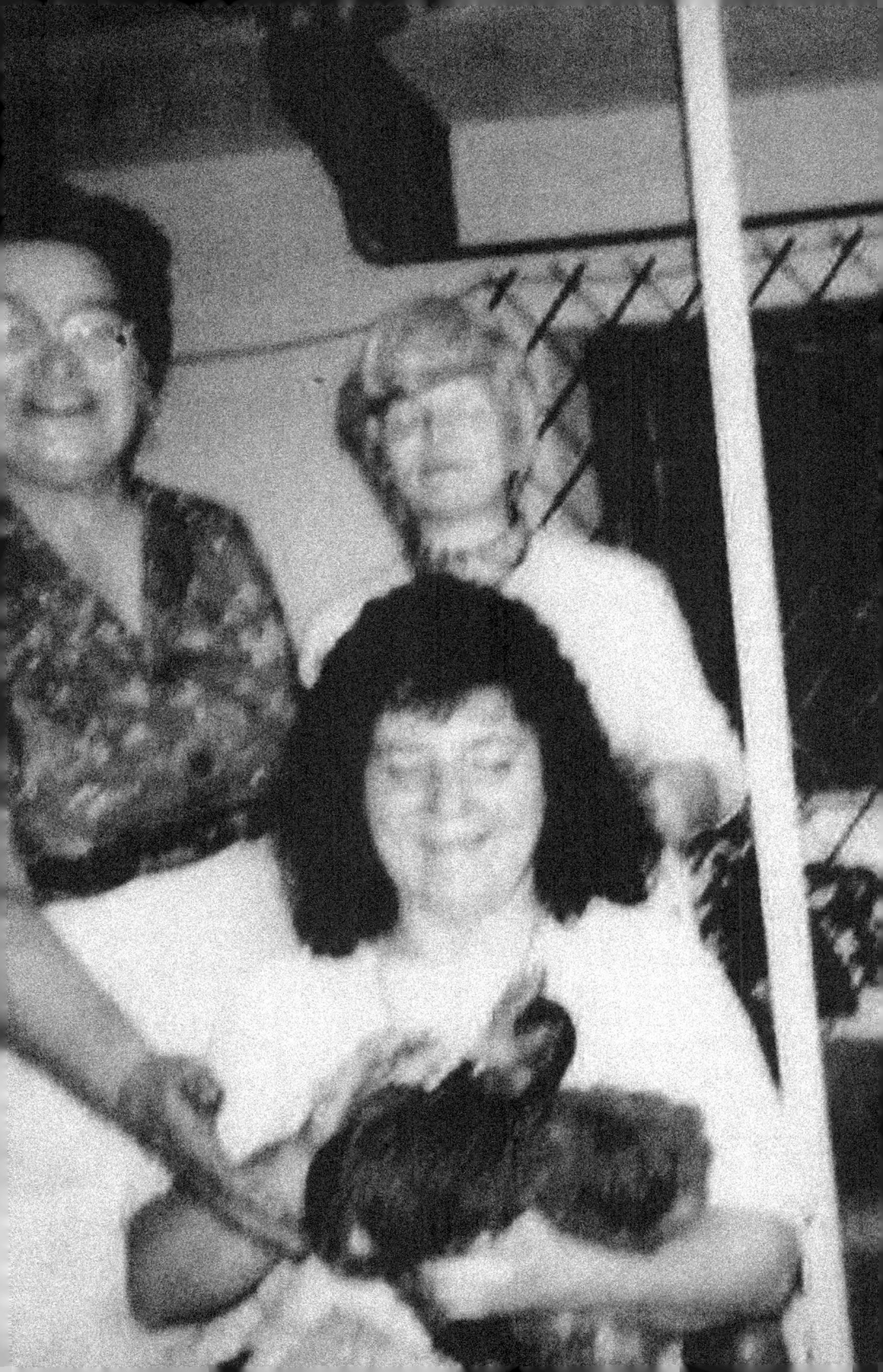

At the Mother Love Dinner Table

*When my son visited, it took six trips
to the grocery to prepare.*

When Nathaniel came home for comfort in the midlife crisis of living out his choices, I asked what he wanted to eat.

Food is my family's comfort zone. When my heart was broken, my mother fixed me chicken cacciatore with polenta, the way her mother had cooked it. By then Mother and I had been to Italy and she had rediscovered Italian cooking. I hadn't grown up with it—or with much of anything to do with her early life.

Her own broken heart shut that door, except when I begged her for stories. Most were about food. "Once we got the cow we never went hungry," she told me of her impoverished immigrant childhood.

No one who knew Elsa Olivetti Martin ever went hungry. To make it so, she and my father opened a restaurant.

Food was love in our family, and that was how we gave it best— me, like my mother.

Nathaniel had been a hungry child. He nursed voraciously for eighteen months. His first meal beyond breast milk, his 4-month-old Christmas, was a turkey leg. He gummed it lovingly.

Husbands and households changed, but meals stayed the center of our family life. We sat down together at the dining room table every night to eat on my Dansk Fluted Flamestone with grandmother's silver. By the time I got dinner fixed after work, it would be late, but when it came, everybody dug in. There'd be competition over who would get the last slice of liver with bacon and onions. After a stir-fry from the Joyce Chen cookbook, we'd have competitions, run by Bill—Nathaniel and his brother Alex's eventual stepfather—to see who could get the last grain of rice with his, or her, chopsticks.

Still, Nat always worried about where his next meal was coming from. He had been a starved child in another life, we imagined. Or he intuited hunger from his grandmother.

I shopped at a half dozen stores in the week before my 45-year-old son's first visit home alone in two and a half years. That was just for starters because after Nathaniel's arrival, Bill or I made a couple of trips each day for replenishment and specialties.

Nathaniel is an egg-eater, so I'd laid in two dozen. That purchase was serendipity. Our chicken-raising neighbor was having a 10 percent-off sale as her hens were laying more than people were buying. With the eggs, Bonnie sent me off with her homemade pickled beets.

Beet eggs followed, gorgeous globes floating behind glass. Cut one open, and you get sunrise: a ring of fuchsia, an inner circle of white, a golden center. Nathaniel loves beet eggs, but neither his wife nor daughter eats them.

We'd be eating a lot he didn't get with his family.

Fish would be his homecoming dinner.

Even if wife Liz or daughter Ada liked finfish—and they don't—St. Louis fish wouldn't be as fresh as Tidewater Maryland's. As this was February, fish meant a stop at the DC Fish Market on Maine Avenue, where Nathaniel had fond memories of the thousands of fish glittering on ice. From the back storage rather than the ice, Bill's favorite fishmonger, smiling, presented three massive flounder fillets newly arrived from just off Ocean City, Maryland.

That was their first stop after Bill retrieved Nathaniel from Reagan National Airport. The flight got in at noon, so after the fish market, the moment called for lunch, at Cafe Mozart, a long-standing DC German/Austrian restaurant.

❦

Awaiting family and fish at home after getting out the latest edition of our weekly newspaper, I turned the oven to high before switching to clogs.

After all those family dinners, I know how to do this, I reminded myself. I'm still doing it—though not so often nowadays, or so deliberately.

My half-risen bread dough for the ciabatta was in the fridge. I shaped the quick-setting loaf while still in heels and suit. It would be ready to go in the hot oven by the time I changed. The bread was Step 1 in an easy dinner that would warm my son's heart.

For years he had drooled silently over the picture opposite a much-made recipe in my Italian cookbook. "Why don't we ever get that?" he finally asked.

Tonight we would eat it. Just like in the picture, a platter of fish fillets flanked by a slightly tangy provolone from Eastern Market, on Capitol Hill, and a vinaigrette toss of garden arugula, roasted peppers and olives, lemon wedges as the garnish. Plus fresh bread and more olive oil.

It's beautiful, it's delicious and it's easy.

After a big hug when my tall son stepped in the door, I took two of those huge fillets of flounder, shook them in whole wheat flour and roasted them very hot, very fast, in olive oil and butter. The smell of baking bread heightened the anticipation.

As usual, we eat late. Bill serves good wine, so nobody cares.

Meals like that put us back in sync. They lubricate any talking we might need to do.

When Bill goes to bed early, Nathaniel and I talk about breakfast. He wants polenta with poached eggs under homemade pomodoro.

But come morning, those beet eggs are calling to him. He's thought out their pairing with the Amish bread-and-butter pickles and Maryland cider we've just brought home from our local-only market, along with just-caught Chesapeake Bay oysters muddy in their shells. Because Brussels sprouts were fresh this morning, we add irresistible bar-snack Brussels sprouts from a *New York Times* Magazine recipe.

All that is what we eat for brunch, along with the third flounder fillet. Add the last of the bread, a little more cheese and fresh radish sprouts, and brunch lasts a while.

As we eat, I recall long, slow breakfasts in St. Louis with my grandmother. After I got my driver's license, I'd pick her up on a Saturday morning. We'd stop at Pratzel's Bakery just off Delmar Boulevard on the way from her place to ours. Over toasted challah, pound cake and tea—very strong for her—we talked about all the things I wish I remembered.

"I remember breakfasts with Grandmother," Nathaniel says, meaning not my grandmother Florence but his grandmother Elsa, my mother. She still lived on the edge of the old neighborhood, and we could get real bagels, with lox and cream cheese.

"It seems like it was always summer, with us eating out on her patio," Nathaniel recalled.

Good memory, as my corollary memory has him running around in diapers—or less. Those were mothering's sweet times.

With cellphone, Instagram and sass, Nathaniel's nearly 12-year-old daughter has him as flummoxed as he did me in my turn. How to change a good kid's bad behavior? Gentle love, logic and knowing what you're in for stage-by-developmental stage: That's what the experts say.

I'm reading the experts now, too late to take back the reproaches, timeouts and punishments. On deadline to get him to daycare and me to work, I pried him out of toy chests and car seats, him clinging as tight as a starfish prizing open a clam. To escape timeouts, he'd climb out windows, wiggle through holes. Every bedtime, he'd pop out of his blankets like bread in a toaster.

To the want or need I couldn't read, he was irrevocably true. My efforts to make it otherwise worked no better with Nathaniel then his do now with Ada.

So here I am all these years later, begging pardon of my son as I stir sauce made from tomatoes ripened in the heat of last summer and homegrown winter garlic.

Maybe food is the best I can do, as it was the best my mother could do. We're a hard act to follow for Nathaniel, whose daughter is a picky eater.

Tonight we'll be trying to build bridges of food and drink with older son Alex and his family at dinner in the heated Biergarten of the Old Stein Inn, our traditional meeting place on the brothers' rare reunions.

As we eat and we drink, things done and undone many years ago keep their place at our long table.

On Saturday morning finally, its polenta and pomodoro, plus ancestral grapefruit surprise.

This is how my WASP grandmother ate it all those breakfasts ago. How extravagant, I thought, to eat a whole grapefruit—until this year's bushel put me in her Floridian shoes.

When you've got too much grapefruit, it's no sin to cut the top off a whole one. I use my sturdiest grapefruit knife to cut the inner circle of fruit from skin, then slicing the fruit, breaking fibers into a slush to be sweetened with a bit of sugar—Grandmother used heaping teaspoons—and eaten from the shell.

The polenta slips from its mold in a golden mound. The tomato sauce is red like August's setting sun. The poached eggs are perfect floating ovals. Nathaniel turns down a third, recalling that a fried duck egg had come his way at last night's German dinner.

Like his grandmother, Nathaniel doesn't like to end one meal before he imagines the next. "I never get oxtail soup at home," he says. If only we'd known.

"You used to make ossobuco, too," he suggests.

It's a miracle that I happen to have veal shank bones, frozen for a special occasion I hadn't known would be this.

Lightly breaded and browned, the cross-sections of meaty bone braise for hours in chicken stock and white wine. I'll finish the sauce with parsley and lemon, and serve the ossobuco Milanese with brown arborio rice risotto.

Between breakfast and dinner, there's more cooking to do. For Sunday's family dinner, there's new bread dough to stir up, and a cheesecake that wants to start early.

With all the family coming home, Sunday will be the night we satisfy Nathaniel's request for prime rib.

To decide how long to cook the huge beef, we must dangle it from Bill's vintage Zebco De-Liar fish scale. He'd been too staggered by the price to ask the butcher its weight, almost 10 pounds.

That means portions too big for Grandmother Florence's Haviland china. Bill resolves the issue of plates with seven of our big old Dansk ones, chipped full of memories. For tonight, renewed memories, prime rib and Bill's good wine make us a family.

"That was the roast I dreamed of," Nathaniel whispers as we clear the table.

Back with his family in St. Louis, Nathaniel texted that he was already missing us but feeling pretty good. I was glad, because I'd done about all the mother-loving I could manage. Since Nathaniel's visit, Bill has been cooking.

My Twin Son

A lifelong story

My Son at Three

My son can snatch a handful of sky in a stretch,
and hold the clouds and light and
raindrops in his hand.
He can wrap the cool night around
him for a cloak
and keep it through the day.
When morning wakes, butterflies covey
about him
Lighting on his face.
Birds go nesting in his hair—
They coo among the wavelets as early
spring they puff and pout
Among the tender grass.

My son phoned me last night. We chatted three-quarters of an hour about daily minutia: the peculiarities of our pets; the social indifference of my black cat, the news of his job. For the first time in three decades—twenty-seven years of that time devoted to creating and sustaining a family newspaper—Alex worked for somebody else. The new role wasn't second nature to this red-headed Aries male.

The Annapolis tour company where Alex works now changed hands after his first year there. The new boss, a specialist in running boats and keeping them running, was younger than Alex and brought in a new management style. Now Alex was suddenly earning praise—and liking it—for Sales and Marketing's smooth operation since he'd stepped in. And for his good disposition, which meant laughter in his office and people happy in their work.

127

This phone call was no longer an anomaly. Alex calls predictably nowadays. The routine is unusual for this family of mine, which is not one of those whose mother and children chat together every day. Ours can go days without phone calls, assuming a connection that doesn't need much refreshing.

Alex and I don't solve the world's problems on these calls, though we might talk politics or astronomy. Our topics can be trivial, and that's fine. For we're neither of us at a loss for how to engage the other. There's good reason for that. We are mother and son, he my life-changing first born, inexorably tangled in each others' hair and at it for half a century. Shared engagement was first nature to us, but not second nature.

I wonder why. Is it, as I suspect Alex believes, that I expected too much of him and too little of his younger brother? Perhaps he does think so, and perhaps he's right. Not yet have I achieved the self-awareness to judge all the terms of my imperfect mothering.

Or is it, as I believe, that Alex's lifelong independence is a barrier not to be breached?

If not one, then the other. Or maybe both. My unscientific approach to life is that most terms of cause and effect are more—or less—than you might imagine.

First or second nature be as they may, Alex and I spent nearly the last thirty years entwined as partners in a family business. That's not uncommon; 90 percent of American businesses are family owned. Short of the two succeeding pandemic years, we talked everyday, minus weekends and the occasional holiday, for more than a quarter century.

New Bay Times/Bay Weekly newspaper kept us both together and apart. We shared space and long hours in the same office, dedication to the same purpose, big decisions and hard choices, like how to keep going when it was uncertain we'd be able to make the next payroll. Alex felt the fate of the family fortune resting on his shoulders. With the pressure of the work and so many other potential reasons I barely understood, Alex and I sometimes smoldered in antagonism. We each thought the other was to blame.

None of that lingered in last night's call. Trust ran across barrier-free lines. Alex was proud of himself and eager to tell me so. At his new company, he was lauded for his skill in positive reinforcement. In himself he also saw the generosity others noted.

"I give praise rather than criticism," he said. "And everybody does the best they can."

I'd heard him describe himself this way before, I realized in musing on this turn of events. In his deep dive into youth soccer, he'd come to see himself as a team builder.

"I think of the girls and how they can enjoy the game rather than trying to be the team with the most wins," he said.

I watched a few games, and what he said seemed to be true. I saw no smoldering on the field. His daughter must have found working with her father comfortable because Elsa played a game for which she had no special talent from when she was a kid until high school. Perhaps he conscripted her, but I doubt it. She doesn't bully easily.

Alex surely liked the game. He stayed with it longer than Elsa did, coaching, taking over the reins of his league, finally refereeing.

Alex was reuniting with his good twin.

Back as an early teen, when he got caught up in Dungeons and Dragons, Lexey had announced he had an evil twin. Anything that went wrong, any fit of stubbornness, was the work of the evil twin. We didn't see much of that twin until puberty. Then we sometimes shared a home with him.

Up till then, we knew only the good twin. From infancy, Lexey was his own person. Along with soft red curls, he was blessed with curiosity and concentration. He got deeply into all he did, from fitting the thick wooden pieces of his baby puzzles into their same-shaped holes to polishing the silverware, a task that was part of the curriculum at his Montessori school, where he started at 18 months. For years my mother's hand-me-down silver, which we used for nightly meals, shone.

In disposition, Lexey shone, too. He was like a sunflower, turning to and blooming in the nourishing sunlight. For me he was a delightful relief from an academic day. For my mother, Elsa, he was an uncritical being into whom she could pour her unused helpings of love. His godmother, Linda, loved him for his own sake. His father was proud of his precocity.

Young parents who lived blocks from St. Louis University, his father and I filled our home with university friends, colleagues and students from the English as a Second Language immersion program where I taught. Lexey's babysitter was a nursing student happy to take him as a substitute for the children she longed to have. His best friends were grown-ups who thought him enchanting. Among them were Rolando Siman, an El Salvadoran perfecting his English for big things in his country's future. To Rolando, he was Alejandro.

Lexey kept his charm through my messy separation from his father. He was 6 years old when the mother of my to-be second husband came to stay with us during her husband's surgery. Lexey met her at the door, asking to carry her suitcase.

In the years that followed, Lexey, his brother Nat and I managed on our own. Bill, who would eventually be my husband, was the buddy and bringer of good times. But Lexey was the big brother and often parent in absentia as I worked a full-time job supplemented by part-time gigs, nourished a vast network of friendships and searched for my creative identity. Lexey seemed agreeable to that role. He was the kind of kid who said I can—so different from the brother who said I won't—always doing well in school, always up and at his 6 a.m. paper route.

Responsible as Lex was, his evil twin made fraternal acquaintance with Nat. Adept in mishaps and mischief, Nat could bug a bug. He matched the character of the dog Bill brought home,

Slip Mahoney, a beagle-German shepherd mix who never would do what anybody else wanted. When the brothers' stand-offs provoked Lexey into creative violence, there were, according to Nat, hammer chases and closet lock-ins. Plenty of violence, but no broken bones.

The evil twin was mostly a stranger to the rest of us. Even as Lexey made his own friends—many of them sons of my colleagues—he remained a kid able to win over adults. Our lives swirled with friends, then, for we were part of the awakened counter-culture emerging from the turbulent 1960s, the decade of Lexey's birth. He was part of the family for my girl friends, many who had watched him grow up while changing Nat's diaper at Cookie Monster, our cooperative daycare center. Bill's buddies took a generational interest in Lex. He was mentored by the constant stream of young craftsmen—post-hippies who'd given up the establishment for lives as artisans—who helped us restore the down-at-the-heels 1908 bungalow I'd bought us the week after I divorced the boys' father.

Lex's integration into a generation beyond his own wasn't all one sided. He cultivated all these grown-ups, showing them interest, spark and intelligence. He wasn't one of those kids who are like pulling teeth to draw out; he came out—and up to you—naturally, just as he had done to Bill's mother.

As Lexey outgrew his pre-teen plumpness, as hormones surged through him and he grew tall and buff and wore his now-auburn hair in a fro, we got to know his determination as well as his charm.

At 15, he got himself a bussing job at a restaurant in the suburbs and got himself there and back most nights—more easily after he talked us into helping him buy a car, though not the Jaguar XKE he noticed in the newspaper. In the same shopping center, he bought himself a pricey North Face gray down jacket that suited his sense of self better than the amorphous blue down coats I'd managed to afford at Southern States farm supply store.

At 18, Lexey talked his grandmother into buying him the family's first tuxedo for his high school senior prom. Part of his rationale was its adjustable waist. It would grow with him as he grew. For that same prom, he talked Rob Lantz, Bill's friend since childhood, into lending him his Audi so he could drive his date in style.

In between, in 1980 and '81, Lexey faced down first his father—with whom he was living in San Antonio as I attempted freelance life—then me, with his determination to live and learn at a democratic Sudbury School in Albuquerque. His belligerence as Bill and I begged, pleaded and commanded him home won the day. We concluded we'd live a more peaceful life without our little dictator, as he was known at home when his good twin had gone undercover.

The power of Lexey's will seemed superhuman to us ordinary mortals. The same will he showed against us—give in or be subdued—he pitted against the forces of nature. In Alaska for a wilderness adventure the four of us shared in August of 1982, we set out on an ill-timed crossing of a strait in Admiralty Island in two canoes: Bill and Nat, then 11, in one and Lexey, then 16, and I in another. Pulling us against the tide, Lexey paddled 1,200 nonstop strokes.

In 1984, our family split apart. Bill had been transferred from the *St. Louis Post-Dispatch* Illinois Capitol Bureau in Springfield to the Washington DC Bureau. Leaving our home, dog and cats in the care of house sitters, I followed him and took a job as editor of the *Hill Rag*. Lexey went off to the University of Illinois, and Nat spent that year—and a few others, off and on—in Richmond, California, with his father.

Lexey, the nearest to Springfield, arrived first back home for our Christmas reunion. We other three traveled from both coasts by way of St. Louis to Springfield to find Lex had bought a tree and strung the house with lights. We spent that nostalgic holiday in harmony, with the good twin.

Lexey had always wondered how I managed before he was born to set me straight. By his late teens, we entered a new partnership as he took on ever more responsibility for the family even as he created his own life. With Bill and me first in DC, then on the Chesapeake shore in Maryland, Lexey became our property manager in Springfield, a job that showed him how tough independence can be. Next, in a gap semester between school abroad in Nottingham and returning to the University of Illinois, he took refuge in our new home in Fairhaven Cliffs, Maryland, while undertaking its first adaptation.

He was barely back at the University of Illinois before the four of us were thrown together again, pulled out of our individual orbits by the death of my mother, their grandmother, Elsa Olivetti Martin (by then Allison). Over the weeks we spent in St. Louis that summer of 1988, mourning and managing her estate, Nat persuaded his brother to take on his guardianship at the chummery that Lexey was forging with college friends.

Nat grew up in a household of boys just a few years older than he, under their discipline yet enjoying freedom many a high schooler would envy. In various pairings, both sons stayed in Champaign-Urbana three or four more years. Then both boomeranged back home.

After finishing his master's degree in journalism, Lexey moved in on us with his girlfriend and each of their black cats—on top of our several cats, one black, and our 100-pound yellow Lab. His plan was to continue remodeling the house, making the whole lower level, where he had his room, livable space. He started by cutting a hole in the floor for a connecting stairway. Illinois friends joined to help him, and our shared household grew.

In our new extended family, whatever authority Bill and I had was foregone as we balanced life with two or three young, autonomous adults, each moved by forces beyond our understanding and probably theirs as well. Peace prevailed, mostly, so long as nobody's will challenged anybody else's. Acting out the internecine tension, brother and sister cats fought.

As the year of remodeling ended, in mid 1992, the girlfriend fled cross country, and Lexey returned to journalism. Over a semester's internship with *The Nation*, as an Alaska job slipped out of his reach, he was drawn in by a plan Bill hatched. We'd pool our talents—and invest our small family fortune—to create a regional, environmentally friendly newspaper. "Write good stories, and people will read them," Bill assured us, playing off a famous line in the wildly popular baseball movie, *Field of Dreams.*

The plan became a spider's web that entrapped us all, Lexey willingly, me kicking and screaming *No! New Bay Times*, as we christened our independent weekly "committed to the Chesapeake," would control all our lives for the next three decades.

From the beginning, Lexey, now Alex, willed his way into leading our shared enterprise. Bill, almost always diplomatic, stayed in the background, offering his journalistic skills as needed and, after we breezed through two or three family inheritances, plus infusions from his paycheck. My role was editor—and writer of all nobody else wrote. In the early years, we all spread ourselves like ice on water over the surface of whatever needed to be done. As the years passed—and there were many of them, passing so quickly that we seemed to be riding on a train with no brakes, the scenery racing from future to present to past—I stayed more and more in my own lane.

For all those years, Bill and I seemed changeless: the same house; always a boat (though we went through three); many cats; the same breed, size and temperament of dog when finally we replaced our beloved yellow Lab, Max; the same work: his the routine of daily and mine of weekly journalism. We even seemed ageless to ourselves and one another. The most notable change was our cars, and we had many, though even there stability came with my Audi TT, plated JRNLISM and driven daily—back and forth to *Bay Weekly*, as we renamed our paper at the millennium—for seventeen years.

Aside from *Bay Weekly*, Alex's life was as changeful as ours was stable. He bought a house, married a woman with a will as strong as his, bought another house, fathered and parented two children, lost his 20-year-old cat, bought another house, brought dogs into the family.

Alex changed in other ways, too. His will remained iron, controlling us all. But the good twin receded. He carried the weight of preserving the family enterprise and investment in an era when newspapers of all sizes across the country, including the independents that flourished from the '70s through the '90s, were folding like flowers past their span. The evil twin stepped forward to bear that stress. Out of the office, the good twin could come back, as he did when he threw himself into youth soccer with the same all-out determination as he'd powered our canoe against Alaskan currents.

So for many of the *Bay Weekly* years, Alex and I shared the same space and mission like those two earlier black cats, too close for comfort—but not always one another's good faith and trust.

Finally, twenty-seven years in, he had no more rabbits to pull from his magician's hat, no more to give. With the news that we should not continue and must seek a buyer, the good twin returned. Sad and humble, the good Alex saw *Bay Weekly* through to as easy a landing as we could manage.

My elder son and I stopped seeing each other daily at the beginning of 2020, a year in which our fate measured small against a virus that changed the world. In the years since, Alex's good twin has stepped into my life, phoning me every few days just for conversations with no edge to them. He does favors that he calls small but seem big to me, like bookkeeping for the independent publishing house, New Bay Books, that I made my next step.

When Alex was born, back when I was only 22, I told myself I'd be child free when he was my age, with years of my disrupted life ahead of me. Instead my life has been tangled with his, with good twin and bad, ever since. At 22, I was mistaken. Bringing a person into the world involves your life forever.

The Humbling

A tale from the ER

Slack, aged and aesthetically failing, my body is the patient here. My heart is failing, too. Diagnosed with atrial fibrillation, I relinquish my defenses.

First went the game face assumed this morning at my dressing table. Now three months retired and recreating myself, I continue to apply Bobbi Brown's age-appropriate makeup as if for work. Certainly for every visit to the doctor's office, where I'm the one "who doesn't look her age."

Today's two routine and one extraordinary doctor visits have beaten me at my age-defying game. My game face has fallen.

On the drive to my Maryland suburban county hospital, more defenses fell. I stripped off my heraldic badges of self-esteem: my mother's too-large diamond worn as a power ring. The heavy silver bracelet and onyx-studded earrings my husband brought back from tribal lands in the West. The thick, coiled choker from the Visionary Arts Museum, in Baltimore. They crowd into my designer sunglasses case. Where I'm going, I won't need sunglasses, either.

Entering these emergency room doors in the time of Covid-19, I abandon my hard-won identity. Newspaper editor...mother... teacher...writer...wife...poet...pot stirrer...friend and neighbor: None of that buys me much here.

As *Everyman* reminded morality-play goers and literary graduate students, there are places neither achievement nor wealth, face nor fame can accompany us. This is one of those places, and here I am supplicant, waiting for the surging tide of life-saving and pain-relieving to wash over me.

"You're lucky," says the age-mate volunteer who guides my wheelchair, her cotton-candy-colored hair bobbing with enviable energy. "We're not very busy this afternoon. They'll get to you quickly. No," she adds, revising her estimate. "Expeditiously."

As they do. In due time, the healing tide sweeps me along as relentlessly as a wave thrown at me by the Atlantic on an Assateague beach.

In Emergency Room 57, my last defenses drop. Shoes, stockings, trousers, jacket, linen sweater, silk chemise, bra, underpants: I remove the clothes chosen so deliberately this morning to seal me in style and comfort, stuffing a plastic bag labeled Patient Belongings. Under the fluorescent lights, I am dead fish-belly white. My legs are swollen, ringed by the elastic of the knee-high stockings, unlovely.

"Congestive heart failure," pronounces a nurse, one of four-dozen caregivers I'll meet between Tuesday evening and Thursday afternoon.

For the lifesaving hours my body is in their hands, I creep deeper through my brain folds to peek from the center of consciousness at what is being done to enable us to survive.

A blood-pressure band, my constant companion, grasps my left bicep. An oxygen reader cinches my left index finger with its thin Velcro strip. Hands invade my hospital gown to stick electrodes to my abdomen and chest; they lift my left breast back like a soft pear to surround my heart with sensors. Each gadget, like the devices on my arm, is attached jellyfish-like to long cords that tie me to monitors reporting my dire condition. Heart rate: 144 and variable. Whoa.

A port needled into my good right median basilic vein—the one that pulses in the crook of the elbow—yields a half-dozen vials of blood. Then it is reversed from giver to receiver and in two ports, nurses insert their assortment of mystery syringes. A port escapes the hands of technicians preparing a CT-scan with contrast, and dye shoots free like World Series champagne.

Before the night is out, my left basilic vein has its own two ports, and I am tethered to an IV. The phlebotomist must search my left hand for a stingy vein to take her blood.

When the diuretic shot into one of those ports goes to work, "You will pee like a racehorse," Terri, the nurse who happens to share my Zip Code, promises. She is wrong. Atop the bedpan to which I become attached—even the few feet to the toilet is too long a walk for my racing heart—I pee like the Missouri River flows, ceaselessly. My shame melts into relief.

The people flurrying about me are shameless. A bedpan swirling with warm yellow urine does not daunt them. When I fear it's full to the overflowing, I hoist myself into the dread reverse-table yoga pose, and it is whisked away as if it were any dirty dish.

Their ministrations are clinical, but there is such warmth in the ministering hand that my own wants to curl into it. In it I find my long-dead mother's touch when some illness of mine called forth the tenderness she held in bond, having received so little herself that she had less to give.

But these hands are surer than hers, hands that might strip off a bandage skin and all, before she fainted in horror at what she'd done. They peel off an IV patch so efficiently that not a hair goes with it— nor any skin—and with an apology to boot.

Deep in the night, in a quieter section of this life-saving station, a nurse named Angel joins in my care. My heart still races.

"Your heart can't work this hard for this long," she says, and, taking advice, she throws her book of drugs at me, bolus after bolus. Determined to take this heart thing in hand, she is giving me every-thing she's got. Her hair has curled in damp tendrils around her face.

"Did your name call you to your work?" I ask her as the drugs fight to do their work.

"No," she tells me, and in the dark hours there blooms between us the story of her father, fighting in Vietnam when she was a toddler, who called her his angel and came home safe. Thus Linda became Angel, and when she married, she changed her first name as well as her last.

"And me? Am I safe?" I ask her.

"It's in God's hands," she says.

While I do not believe the way she does, I feel I must be in the hands of angels, among these skillful women—and a few men—of so many colors of skin, countries of origin, races and religions.

Needy and naked as one can be in a hospital gown, I am humbled by so much charity. I wake in the morning with a more normal heart beat of 88—and variable.

Sandra Olivetti Martin

PART IV

The Character of Lincoln Land

Stories from Sandra's headlong dive into weekly journalism capture her Illinois' genetic connection with the sixteenth president. In **What It's Like to Look Like Abe Lincoln,** she corners Lincoln impersonators, who are many and whose presence can trigger near-mystical reaction in those who revere the great, gangling icon. In **Abraham Lincoln's Totem Poles,** she tracks carved statuary to Alaska, busting myths along the way.

To record her adopted state's essential sensibilities, she ranged from such traditional women's crafts as pie-baking and quilting to the delights of the Illinois State Fair to lives of the lesser-known and briefly famed—the masters in shoeshine arts, the homebirth prophet having a baby, a Middle East hostage arriving home to the land Lincoln bequeathed. She also began her deepest reporting, represented here by **Women Who Kill in Self-Defense,** the **Lawrenceville Peephole Incident** and **A Homebirth Teacher Has Her Baby.**—Editor's Note

What It's Like to Look Like Abe Lincoln

Lincoln lookalikes' phones are busy, their desks are piled with paperwork rivaling that of Abraham Lincoln.

They catch every eye and turn every head with the trick they play on time, these tall men made to seem even taller by six-inch stovepipe hats and the long cut of their black frock coats.

"Everybody does a double take," says Harry Hahn, the Abraham Lincoln of Mount Pulaski, Illinois.

"Grown-up people crush little kids to shake my hand," says Lester Davis, the ranking Lincoln in the Illinois town of Morrisonville.

There's a Lincoln in Lincoln, Illinois, of course. "That black uniform attracts people. I walk down the street and cars run into each other looking at me," says Charles Ott.

R. Frederick 'Fritz' Klein, the Abe Lincoln of Lincoln-obsessed Springfield, Illinois, says: "Old men's eyes fill with tears, little kids want to touch me. I don't know what I do to do it, but if I can stir that kind of positive effect in people, I want to do it."

Cities compete for their presence. Networks pay for their time. Photographers hunt them for pictures. Reporters hang on their words. Parks; plays; pageants and prayer meetings; fairs, films and festivals—all need their Lincolns. Lincoln lookalikes' phones are busy. Their desks are piled with paperwork rivaling Abraham Lincoln's old office in Springfield, perhaps even in the White House. They travel, expenses paid, to places they might never have seen, meet people who would never have noticed them.

In uniform, they stand shoulder to shoulder with presidents. They trade jokes with governors, senators, and mayors. They share headlines and airwaves with movie stars. Tributes of heroes greet them. Children tug at their beards and elders weep at their words.

In ordinary life, central Illinois' Lincoln lookalikes are ordinary men, family men, blue-collar working men. But dressing in black, donning top hat, frock coat and square-toed boots, they are transformed. Townspeople who don't know where Charles Ott or Harry Hahn live can direct callers to their houses if they say they wish to see Mr. Lincoln. What city would honor Lester Davis, who is a carney, handyman, and parts clerk? Lester 'Mr. Lincoln' Davis received just the fifth key to the city of East Moline. The fourth went to former President Jimmy Carter.

None of Abraham Lincoln lookalikes say they sought the role they fill. Tall, lean, and craggy, they saw in themselves only a not-uncommon prairie type. "I know Fritz Klein is as common as an old shoe," says Klein, of the man beneath the makeup. But in him others saw Lincoln.

For Harry Hahn, who will have been Lincoln for twenty-two years now, and for Lester Davis, who's been impersonating Lincoln for nearly twenty, Lincoln began with a beard. In the early 1960s, the Illinois towns of Mount Pulaski and Taylorville celebrated their 125th birthdays. Men were penalized if they didn't grow beards.

"Unless you grew a beard, you risked a dip into the horse tank," Davis remembers.

The $5 shaving permit Mount Pulaski required was too steep for Hahn, then a man with a young family to support. Both gave in and grew whiskers. But the lanky, over-six-footers towered above the mass of bearded men as something special. Hahn heard someone say, "I've seen a lot of Lincoln beards before, but I've never looked Lincoln in the face."

Before the celebratory summers were over, Harry Hahn had made his Lincoln debut in The Spirit of Mount Pulaski, a local theatrical production. Lester 'Mr. Lincoln' Davis had advertised Taylorville's festivities in every Christian County hamlet.

Hahn's Lincoln is a natural. "I was just born this way, " says Hahn, who at six-foot four-inches weighs 180 pounds and shares our 16th president's height, weight, shoe size, and family size.

"On April 14, 1865, Abraham Lincoln was shot," says Hahn, 59. "Sixty-five years later on April 14, 1934, I was born."

Winner of Lincoln look-alike contests at Springfield's LincolnFest in 1981 and at Hodgenville, Kentucky, in 1982, Hahn uses no makeup and prefers "visiting with the people" to "blurting out speeches." The man beneath his tailor-made modern-fabric Lincoln coat remains Harry Hahn, more likely to crack a cornland joke than stir the conscience with the president's words.

"I'm promoting Abraham Lincoln, and Abraham Lincoln was not just for the elite," he says. "People in Illinois love it. They tell me to keep going."

Something else also keeps him going. "Enjoyment too," adds Mrs. Hahn. " You're getting a little famous if not rich."

"I'm creative," says Lester Davis, who improvises on nature to make his impersonation accurate. Six-foot-two, 185-pound Davis adds an inch of lift to his square-toes boots, a stick-on mole to his weather-lined face, and a ballpoint pen cartridge to his hand-plucked goose quill pen. He wears only wool in the uniform he has assembled from second-hand stores, and regrets that his hat-brim is something over an inch and a half.

"When I'm doing this, I live Lincoln," he says. "If a man wears zippers and polyester, what kind of Lincoln is that? I've steeped myself in Lincoln and history. When somebody asked me when Lincoln was born, I told myself I better get with it or quit it," Davis says. He laboriously memorized excerpts from a dozen of Lincoln's speeches and offers them, together with answers to Lincoln questions, as the occasion demands.

"It took a lot of practice to get all his details," he says. But you can't sit there and do a program without taking a break, so I'm always throwing in jokes." Lincoln, of course, was a renowned storyteller and jokester.

"In a sense, I'm a nobody," Davis says. "But I go down red carpets lined with 350 people who paid $5 to see me, and there's the mayor standing there with the key to his city. I'm having the time of my life. In the twenty years I've been doing Lincoln, I never met a stranger. What happens the day I shave this off and go out there and stand all alone? This is my chance."

Charles Ott became Lincoln's Lincoln because he was the tallest man in town. "Once dressed, I'd always be above everybody," says the six-foot nine-inch Ott. Finding that he liked his appointed role, Ott grew a beard and added the touch that makes his Lincoln special—rail splitting—and has taken him all the way to Independence Hall. Ott's bigger-than-life Lincoln is a promoter: president of the Central Illinois Tourism Council; board member of Lincoln Heritage Trails; member of the Logan County Railsplitting Association and Arts and Crafts Guild. He serves as a goodwill ambassador for the state.

But promotion is not the only reason Ott has continued, after more than a dozen years, to don his home-designed and tailored black frock coat. "I've seen lots of places, received special honors, met many people. Playing Abe has opened a lot of doors for me," he says.

Playing Lincoln has whetted Ott's taste for history and given him a part in keeping it alive. It has also given him, he says, a special intimacy with the man he impersonates. "I'm told there are only a few people who have sensed Lincoln in his house, but it has happened to me, I have felt his presence," says Ott.

Felix Klein, central Illinois' newest and youngest look-alike, is a Lincoln with a mission.

"I'm more concerned with the message than with the medium," he says. The makeup he spends four hours applying is uncomfortable. He uses a toupee and ear props and has experimented with false noses. "Trapping around as Lincoln is not my style," he says. He endures because, he says, being Lincoln is "something to believe in much bigger than myself."

Klein's point is to "reach beyond the personality to the principles of the man, to challenge the American people with an aspect of history that few are aware of. When this nation was conceived it was a marvel of the world, not for its prosperity but for its concepts. The founding Americans knew what the answers were and how to implement them. Lincoln delved into the principles surrounding the writing of the Constitution. He understood the national tragedy that would undertake us should the American people ever be divorced from these principles.

"Following Lincoln's model of piecing together parts of speeches for new occasions, I combine what he has said in order to apply his principles to new contexts. That's not difficult for me because my principles are very much in line with his," Klein says.

When "approached by this thing," Klein was preparing to serve as a missionary in Asia. He agreed to portray Lincoln at a Hawaiian bicentennial celebration; although he had "no strong interest in Lincoln," he was the right height and weight.

"I had gone to Hawaii to find my life's work, but I certainly did not expect to find it reading Lincoln," he says.

The decision to accept the role as a way of life was a "slow, prayerful choice made over several years. Finally, it was kind of a revelation. I could see how Lincoln's words applied in my family, in church, in government, in national and international relations. I believed they were important."

He accepted his second destiny with professional deliberateness and dedication—researching, writing, planning and mastering foreign arts. Last March, he moved to Springfield, the appropriate launching pad for his new mission.

Now Fritz Klein, the reluctant Lincoln, is as caught in his role as any of central Illinois' other lookalikes.

"I love encouraging people," he says. "Their eyes fill with tears, They want to shake my hand. I don't know what I do to them, but if I can stir that kind of positive effect, I want to keep doing it."

Abraham Lincoln's Totem Poles

How it was that Abe in native art became one with bears, eagles, wolves, beavers, and whales. Frogs, too.

KETCHIKAN, Alaska—From island to island in southeastern Alaska, the Tlingit Tongass Raven clan fled their enemies, the implacable Eagles. The Raven's village had been burned, their weapons and generations of accumulated wealth destroyed, and their people enslaved. Stripped of everything but their canoes, the once-proud Northwest Coast Tlingits were now desperate refugees on the brink of extinction. Then—so the story goes—salvation sailed through the foamy waters of southeast Alaska's Inner Passage in the form of a United States ship named after Abraham Lincoln.

The Ravens took refuge under the shelter of Lincoln's guns. The ship's crew assured the shivering Indians that the great American chief Abraham Lincoln, who had abolished slavery, now protected them.

Thus "the Emancipation Proclamation came to the rescue, not only of the black serfs of the South, but in its shadow the Tongass tribe found asylum and escaped a terrible fate, the choice between slavery and extinction," wrote Judge James Wickersham in the 1920s. The Tlingit Tongass Ravens erected a mighty totem pole to show their gratitude, Wickersham's account continued. At the summit of the pole, in the place of honor, stood Abraham Lincoln.

For half a century, that story fanned sparks of patriotism. Because of it, in 1945, the Illinois State Museum mounted an expedition to southeast Alaska, the faraway home of the Tlingit and the totem poles. Because of that story, Springfield, Illinois boasts a Lincoln totem pole.

Judge Wickersham's explanation of how Lincoln was remembered on a totem pole makes a very good story—if perhaps not a true one.

There's no question that Lincoln totem poles exist. Visitors to the Illinois State Museum in Springfield, to Saxman Totem Park near Ketchikan, Alaska, and to the Alaska State Museum in Juneau can see them, as I have. Illinois' favorite son was carved atop a 51-foot red cedar trunk, probably in the 1880s, by the Tsimpsean artist Theida, commissioned by Raven Chief Yahi-Jeggi. Lincoln is as authentic an artifact of the totem pole as the ravens, bears, eagles, wolves, beavers, whales, frogs, and mythic humans who more commonly appear. He's up there all right. But why?

The answer may not be the one that Wickersham set forth so eloquently. But it is a tale that spans a continent and was centuries in the making.

Along its western edge, the North American continent rises in mountains, then tumbles in islands into the Pacific Ocean. This thin edge along Canadian British Columbia—no more than 150 miles at its greatest width—is southeast Alaska. Nature here is ruthless but not unyielding. She sustains grizzlies and eagles, salmon and seals, porpoises and whales, even humans.

Descendants of the hardy wanderers who crossed the Bering Land Bridge from Asia into North America settled this rough land some 30,000 years ago. Their villages faced the sea and backed into hills as densely wooded as tropical rain forests. The winters are long and dark and snowy, and the summer short and sweet. But the sea is rich. From it, the tribes of southeast Alaska took ample harvests. The long winters gave them leisure for art.

The forests gave them bark to beat into garments; roots to weave into hats and baskets; and wood to shape into canoes, hew into planks for homes, and carve into bows, utensils, masks and poles. As late as the 18th century, these tribes worked with tools of stone, shell and beaver tooth. Then the white men came, bringing iron and steel tools and the ability to fell giant red cedars, carve them into tall totem poles, and raise them as symbols of the heritage and pride of a family. Here, where the red cedars grow, totem poles flourished for a hundred years, from the early 19th to the early 20th centuries. Here and no place else on earth.

Spanish, French, English, Russian and American traders visited these lands, but Russia claimed them. Then, in 1867, Lincoln's shrewd secretary of state, William Seward, who had navigated tricky international affairs during the Civil War, purchased his "folly" from Russia while serving under Andrew Johnson. In short order, the United States established Alaskan forts and shipped in tax collectors.

One of the ships carrying the trappings of the American government to the Alaska frontier supposedly sailed in 1868 to the Ravens rescue, thus tying Illinois' favorite son to a culture just emerging from the Stone Age.

So said Judge James Wickersham. Wickersham was born in the southern Illinois hamlet of Patoka in 1857. In 1884, at age 27, the young lawyer moved to Washington state to become a judge. In the first year of the new century, he reached Alaska, where he helped establish the first federal court system and became a statesman and spokesman for the rugged territory. He served as Alaska's delegate in Congress from 1909 until 1933.

There, according to the Illinois State Museum's Cynthia Sietz, "he used his influence to correct the erroneous popular belief that his new home was nothing more than a vast expanse of ice and snow populated by scoundrels, Eskimos, and whales."

As the story goes, Wickersham was called on to speak at a Lincoln Day dinner in Washington, DC, in 1920 or 1921. There, in a flush of enthusiasm for his native and adopted states, he is said to have first told his version of how the Great Emancipator appeared on a totem pole.

In early 1922, Wickersham wrote a series of letters asking for confirmation of his story. Several native Alaskans agreed with his version. But one disagreed. That was William Paul, a prominent Alaskan lawyer, legislator and historian. Half Tlingit on both sides, he lived in the very Tongass village where the original Lincoln pole stood—disagreed. Wickersham's enthusiasm for his Great Emancipator legend was apparently undiminished. He published his story, romantically entitled The Oldest and Rarest Lincoln Statue, in *Sunset*, a promotional magazine for the Southern Pacific Railroad. The legend stuck, particularly in Illinois. A generation later, an expedition from Springfield would add a new chapter to the story.

Even before Wickersham's Lincoln dinner speech, the short-lived totem-pole era was failing. Whites had brought Alaska's natives not only the tools to create the tall totem poles, they had also introduced a culture of Christian ways and industrialized civilization. Missionaries condemned the totem poles as heathen idols and banned the lavish potlatch festivals that celebrated the wealth and status of a family who could afford a pole. Indians became workers, leaving their villages for towns built around fishing, canning and logging. Totem poles not destroyed were abandoned to rot in the villages where they had been revered as monuments. Uncared for, they decayed in a few decades in the harsh Alaska weather.

Again, the United States came to the rescue. The government recognized the cultural and artistic value of the totem poles and provided funding to save them. In 1916, virtually all of southeast Alaska was designated a national forest, named Tongass for the people who had ordered the Lincoln pole. Under the Forest Service's direction, several generations of preservation projects flourished.

In the late 1930s and early '40s, $175,000 was spent on a totem restoration project that employed 250 native Americans in rescuing, renovating, and recreating. Hundreds of poles were lowered and floated from thirteen villages to seven new totem-pole parks. Sometime in this period, a new generation of native carvers made at least two copies of the original Lincoln totem pole, which had been left to rot on Tongass Island. The original Lincoln was sawed off and sent to Juneau, Alaska's capital, where he remains, safe from the weather in the Alaska State Museum.

In 1945, recalling the legend of the Lincoln totem pole, the Illinois State Historical Library's Jay Monaghan (backed by W.C. Hurst, president of the Chicago & Illinois Midland Railway) traveled to Alaska in search of a Lincoln pole.

Monaghan's trip must have been an adventure. With few clues to where in southeast Alaska a Lincoln pole was to be found, he secured passage on a series of vessels until he found a pole he could buy. This was not the one in the Saxman Totem Park; it may have belonged to an individual carver. The price for the pole included some rare luxuries for Alaska: a case of Coca-Cola and a crate of oranges.

The 8-foot Lincoln with an 11-foot carved base was sawed off the undecorated, 31-foot connecting shaft and sent to Springfield. The shaft was left behind. In Springfield, a ceremonious welcome greeted the carvings. The Mid-Day Luncheon Club of Illinois, which likely had financed the purchase of the pole, presented Lincoln and Raven to the Illinois State Museum, The figures were put on display in the state's Centennial Building.

The State Museum proudly reported the legendary origin of its Lincoln Pole. Wickersham's story was a natural for thirty years, retold in magazines and newspapers, among them *Ford Times, The Apostle, Ambassador Times, Junior Natural History, The Living Museum, The Philadelphia Inquirer*, and the *Illinois State Journal*, in Springfield. In 1966, a fiberglass cast was made of the pole and the copy—now 50 feet tall with the shaft rebuilt—erected outside the State Museum.

But In Alaska, William Paul remained troubled that Wickersham's story had not faded away. Nearly fifty years after his first objections, Paul resumed research he had begun in 1922 to disprove the Wickersham legend and authenticate the true history of Lincoln's pole. He began with his memories of his own childhood in the Tongass village during the 1890s, and those of other villagers, some of whom had been boys when Thieda carved the pole in the 1880s. To this he added his knowledge of tribal customs and the oral history of his people. His lengthy and well-researched rebuttal appeared in 1971 in the *Alaska Journal*.

Paul noted that Wickersham's story contained a bit of fact but a good deal of fantasy. There had been a tribal war; the Ravens' village had been burned and Indians had indeed moved from island to island. But all this happened before the white men arrived. By the time American ships sailed into the Inner Passage, Tongass village had already been established. The people no longer needed to be rescued. There was a ship named the *Lincoln* that visited Alaska briefly, but it apparently had little to do with Tongass Island.

Paul added that the only Indians rich enough to put up totems were also those rich enough to own slaves and not likely to be eager supporters of the Emancipation Proclamation. In any case, slavery did not end in Alaska until around the turn of the century, many years after the appearance of the white men's ships.

Alaska totem experts agreed with Paul's demolition of Wickersham's story. But if Wickersham was wrong, how did Lincoln come to perch on that totem pole?

First, wrote Paul, we have the name wrong. The pole in question is more properly called the Proud Raven Totem. The date was off as well. It was erected in 1883, not 1868. As to what Lincoln was doing up there, he was carved to commemorate a Tongass Indian's discovery of the first white man some years earlier.

Important encounters had always given status to the people of the northwest coast. In earlier ages, an Indian who had met the mythic Raven would take Raven for a totem, his name for a clan name, and have the right to carve his emblem and escapades. But by the 19th century, the supernatural partners of long ago-encounters had become invariable identities. Thus the Proud Raven pole belonged to a clan of such size that half of the Tlingit nation that claimed hereditary rights to Raven identity.

More recent encounters could dignify living or newly deceased people. Sighting the first white man was a monumental event that could give the discoverer great prestige. So was discovering the first sailing ship or entertaining Secretary of State Seward, two other historic events commemorated on Tongass Island poles. Like the

Lincoln-Proud Raven totem, those poles were commissioned and erected by the families of the discoverers to claim their due respect. Poles' erections, typically accompanied by a potlatch festival, were costly: a once-in-a-lifetime event preceded by years of saving and planning. Hence the delay between sighting and pole.

The Proud Raven Discovery of the White Man pole was different from most because it required the artist to go beyond the conventional symbol-language of the totems to create a new figure. Thieda, the carver, needed a model for the mythic white man. He got a photograph of none other than Abraham Lincoln, national hero, whose picture was widely circulated in the years following his assassination. Lincoln's stovepipe hat may have impressed the carver, since tall hats were considered a mark of status.

Thus Lincoln entered the totem language of the Tongass Ravens not as himself but as the symbol for the white man. And that, concluded Paul, is the true story of the Lincoln totem pole.

Paul's revelations surely embarrassed the Illinois State Museum. The Wickersham legend lives on, on the backs of picture postcards, but no more was written about the Lincoln Pole. The fiberglass replica still stands, unharmed by the elements, outside the museum at Spring and Edwards streets in Springfield. But the real cedar sections of Lincoln and Proud Raven with a bear and a human figure are at the back of the first floor by a freight elevator. For all most of us know, our once-proud Abraham Lincoln Memorial Totem Pole might be just another improbable artifact of Springfield's Lincolnalia.

Take a second look at this odd result of the interweaving of Illinois lives with those of native Alaskans. In the carefully carved and painted figures, you can see the artistry of a faraway people, suggesting for us what modern Haida carver William Reid called "the completeness of their culture, the continuing lineages of the great families, their closeness to the magic world of myth and legend."

How far Abraham Lincoln traveled to return to us atop the Proud Raven pole.

After 444 Days, A Hostage Comes Home to Illinois

A town gathers on the day its citizens dreamed about

Paul Lewis, 23, came home in style last week . His reception was, he said, nothing at all like he'd known when he'd been home on leave. At Wiesbaden and Washington, at West Point and back home in Homer, thousands welcomed the freed hostage as a hero. For everyone who turned out, neighbor or stranger, being there meant something different.

Homer, Illinois, (pop.1,400) had lost one of its sons and now had found him. The faraway specter of an embassy stormed and Americans captured on that November day in 1979 had not been foreign news in Homer, situated 20 miles east of Urbana-Champaign, home to the University of Illinois. Among the Americans held hostage in Iran for 444 days was Paul, one of their own.

His father, mother, sister, and brothers lived in Homer, sharing its worship, its schools, its socials, and heavily of late, its news. "The Lewises are working people, the kind who pitch right in," as one of the town's residents told me.

Paul? "He was just your typical ornery boy," recalled his aunt, Shirley Buck.

Homer had cheered Paul on the football field. He had been Homecoming King in high school. Between high school and the Marine Corps he had gone on to Eureka College, Ronald Reagan's alma mater, staying until a dormitory fire put him out in the cold. Then, as a Marine sergeant he had volunteered to guard the American embassy in Iran, arriving in Tehran on the night of November 3, 1979. The next day history fell around him like an iron curtain, and the echo rattled loudly in central Illinois.

Over uncertain days and weeks stretching into months, Homer and its surrounds remained faithful. Yellow ribbons for remembrance appeared in Decatur, an hour west, before anywhere else in the nation. Before the symbol caught on around the country, every tree and post in Homer displayed a ribbon. The town set aside special days to honor Paul, and gave away flags tied with yellow ribbons. Even the tough guys of the American Legion Honor Guard wore yellow bows on their hats. In store windows, posters showed Paul as a long-haired high school graduate next to his photo as a brisk, alert young Marine. Daily the church bells in Homer tolled for Paul. Gloran Lewis, his mother, telephoned the captive embassy in the hope of speaking to her son. They wouldn't put him on the phone.

"Over uncertain days and weeks stretching into months, Homer and its surrounds remained faithful. Before the symbol caught on around the country, every tree and post in Homer displayed a yellow ribbon."

The crisis featured deadlock after deadlock, demand after demand. Watching it unfold, reading about persistent failure, became a national pastime. Throughout, the town shielded the Lewis family from the media. The Lewises and their town as a whole were branded as standoffish.

"We don't want you to think we're unfriendly," one man explained. "But the Lewises didn't know anything, couldn't say anything, for fear of making it worse."

Now, after more than a year, a period of captivity longer than people here could ever imagine, the town was ready to rejoice.

The day dawned sunny but cold. No snow in recent days but remaining drifts whitened the plowed fields in the rich surrounding farmlands. A January wind stiffened the freezing weather and pushed the flat winter clouds along. It was the kind of day you had to be serious to go out in. But for your efforts, you would get to see Paul Lewis as he rode down the town's five main blocks on Homer 290, the local American Legion's ceremonial vehicle. You would get to hear him accept tribute from his hometown, his neighbors, the entire state of Illinois. Gov. James Thompson showed up, as did members of the Illinois General Assembly and the U.S. congressman from hereabouts, Ed Madigan.

"A couple of years from now I'd hate to be telling people we stayed home washing dishes when only 20 miles away a hostage got his hero's welcome," said Hugh Gehrke, of Champaign.

Seventy-five-year-old Sarah Morris said she came from Allerton to "be part of the crowd. This event brings people close. I'm proud and excited to be here."

"If two old ladies come out you know it's important," said her companion Blanche Lyons, 79.

Along Main Street, there were nearly as many donuts as cameras, flags and yellow ribbons.

"We're here to celebrate, to make everyone feel more at home," said Salvation Army Lieutenant Steve Hedgren, 30, of Champaign. The Salvation Army units from Champaign, Danville and Decatur brought donuts, cookies and hot chocolate.

Danny Davis, 34, of Paris, Illinois, stood on Main Street with two flags crossed over his chest. One was Old Glory. The other, Confederate, had been purchased in Georgia. Davis had watched the hostage epic unfold on television, he said, calling it "so exciting, so emotional." So he came to Homer "to get in on the celebration."

"We've seen the death of Kennedy, Vietnam, Watergate, all those tragedies. It's about time America had something to make us look good. Now that we're back together," he said, "I hope we can have another victory. Over our energy problems. That will bring unity."

Church bells rang out a special meaning for Lowell Bergfield, of Arcola, who brought his 6-year-old grandson, Joshua Truex.

"Every time he'd hear the church bells ring, he'd say, 'grandma, pray for the hostages'. So we brought him to see the result of his prayers," Bergfield said.

Paul Lewis traversed Homer's five-block business district in a shining, 1939 International fire truck, ornamented in yellow bow. The parade traveled past the second-hand store and auction hall, past stores selling pets, pizza, and paint, past Buck's Cafe, the bowling alley and the bank. The parade was described as simply a motorcade after the Lewises had asked that the elaborate celebration originally planned be scaled down.

"Is that all there is?" one in a knot of Homer teenagers catcalled.

Brad Woolf and Chuck Hallett, both 15, and 17-year-old Lynda Butler traded political opinions.

Woolf: "Why didn't the government go in there and bring him home a year earlier?"

Hallett: "Seems like they sorta forgot, and let things slide."

Jim Rein, 16, said: "I never thought much about it before, but now I know I'd be proud to be like Paul in the Marines, or maybe the Air Force. Wow, I think I'll be joining."

As the motorcade turned, the seventy-member Horner Community School marching band played the Battle Hymn of The Republic.

Diane Propst, 41, a wind-chilled Urbana mother of four sons, said the music and celebration had left a lump in her throat. "I know it's impossible, but I tried to put myself in Mrs. Lewis' place," she said, as she snuggled her eight-year-old closer. "We couldn't not let Paul know we cared."

Jim and Diane McAlwee of nearby Sidney watched silently, their arms around each other's waists. "We're glad Paul got back. Peacefully," said Diane. Jim, a long-haired, fully bearded ex-Marine, nodded his silent agreement.

Paul Lewis, looking strong, resolute and almost at ease, was resplendent in his dress blue Bravos. His hair was newly cut into a crisp Princeton. He wore silver medals, scarlet embroidery and gold piping. In contrast with his finery was his becoming "aw shucks" manner. He looked the part of an American hero.

Capt. Vernon Peck of the Danville Marine Reserves cautioned the eager press before he submitted the young Marine to their inquiries: "Avoid long, drawn-out, double-phrased, windy, multifaceted questions. And as is the wishes of our new commander-in-chief, I'd appreciate it if you don't start assuming a half-crouch."

Finally, Lewis took the stage, relating a few details of his ordeal. He described the worst of his captivity as "physical abuse and some harassment," not torture. He said he agreed with the president that future acts of terrorism should be met with retribution. But he did not sound vengeful.

"I pity them," he commented. "I don't think we'll have to do anything. I think they'll probably destroy themselves over there. They are fools."

He felt overwhelmed, he said, to learn when he arrived back in the United States how people had invested emotionally in the hostages' fates. As far as heroes, he said that honorifics should be used for Vietnam War vets in the decade before.

"I think there are more heroes that came back from Vietnam than people realize," he said. "They made a great sacrifice and I don't think it was appreciated as much as it really should have been."

John Mohr, of Allerton, said afterward that one of his sons served in that unpopular war.

"It was hell on earth in Vietnam and we did not get our same boy back," interjected his wife, Evelyn.

"We did not get our same boy back," said Evelyn Mohr. "Because of that Agent Orange chemical defoliant used in Vietnam he's got a skin disease. "Now we're not begrudging the hostages their welcome, but I'd like to see the Vietnam veterans get something too."

For Eleanor Knickerbocker, 33, of Danville, Lewis' return was cause to praise the Lord.

"Sometimes I wonder if it wasn't all planned. I don't know, but there are ways of knowing. The John Birch Society could find out. Whatever it was, God overruled. This will show people how God answers their prayers."

A short time later, paper streamers littered the town's empty streets. Faded ribbons looked beyond ready to come down. Escaped balloons hung in the brown branches of an old oak tree. The lot where the Salvation Army hospitality wagon parked was vacant once more. In the Homer Community School, five cakes had been reduced to crumbs and eight punch bowls drained. Reporters from Chicago, St. Louis, and all over Illinois had filed their stories. Buck's Cafe was out of chili. The sign in the window was turned to CLOSED.

Like the whole town, Paul's aunt Shirley was worn out at the end of a day people had dreamed about. "I just hope we can get back to normal now," she said. "I just hope that Paul can settle down."

I think there are more heroes that came back from Vietnam than people realize," the freed hostage said. "They made a great sacrifice and I don't think it was appreciated as much as it really should have been."

Masters in the Arts of Shine

"Blasted means when you step out...your eyes must be struck with an explosion of bright."

I learned all about shoeshines from Mr. Burks, who was spending some time in the penitentiary. (I was there by choice, teaching.) Despite the rains of spring and the limits of style imposed by his temporary indisposition, Mr. Burks' sturdy black brogues were a marvel of sheen. The welts stitching uppers to the sole were brilliant white, as were the laces.

Mr. Burks taught me that while you can only buy distinctive shoes when you're flush, you can "blast" them whatever your condition. The shine, he believed, is father to the man.

"During childhood in the black neighborhoods of St. Louis, one of the most important things about dress was shoes," he said. "From laborers on up the social ladder, the final touch to an outfit was a shine. If your shoes were not shined, you were considered square. Your ensemble was incomplete without a shine. But more than shining, your shoes had to be blasted. They had to be distinctive.

"Blasted means when you step out of the shine parlor, pool room, or barber shop, your eyes must be struck with an explosion of bright. You are literally able to see your face in your shoes. In the faintest light, your shoes must gleam like patent leather," Mr. Burks instructed.

"Blasting shoes was an art. Through the windows I would watch shine boys work their magic. They could take the most ordinary-looking man that clomped through the door and with rag-popping, brush-slapping, foot-stomping rhythm, turn him into a strutting peacock. Shoes were a mark of pride. They gave the illusion of making it successfully in the world."

As this teacher learned, shoeshining is indeed an art, a wholly contained culture and a way of life. Even if it's not a booming business these days, there are signs it is heading for a revival.

In pre-Environmental Protection Agency days, when cities were sooty with the smoke pouring from belching stacks, you went downtown when your shoes got dirty. Shoes back then were not canvas, plastic, or vinyl; they were 100 percent leather, an investment you wanted to last. Shoeshine parlors flourished. There, business folk, gentlemen, hustlers, and hipsters—everyone on his way to making an impression—stopped, sat, got a shine, caught up on the latest news, got their money's worth of deference, all for the price of a dime.

"Salesmen, lawyers, doctors, politicians, even governors—you got them all," recalls James Haley, of Springfield, a master of shine arts whose history in valet services dates back over forty years. He observed that women, because their skirts caught on the bootjacks, were discouraged from taking a seat in the shine parlor; they left their shoes, with a smile and maybe a wink.

All the best hotels, and some that weren't so nice, had shoeshine parlors. In Springfield, Illinois, the St. Nicholas, Leland, and Abraham Lincoln hotels all had parlors.

"The bell boys and the shoeshine people worked closely together. The bell boy would bring shoes around to a familiar shop and we'd give him a little something. In that kind of network, both were making money," Haley said.

In the early 1950s, when a shine increased in price to 15 cents, Springfield boasted at least three successful parlors on top of a dozen or so smaller enterprises in barber and shoe repair establishments.

Some shine parlors were fancy, some plain, and some more than met the eye. More than one hole-in-the-wall looking like nothing but a stack of cigar boxes and a shoeshine fellow or two conducted "their real business behind closed doors," recalled a man who'd operated on both sides of those doors.

If women were discouraged as seated customers, during the war years they were briefly courted to become shiners. The fling did not last; the call was for women who looked good in low-cut dresses. The only ones who'd take those jobs were too tough, or unwilling, to offer a show.

The masters were older men. "There were nine guys at Nick's (507 E. Monroe) back in the early '50s, and I was the youngest," says Haley, who learned the art of distinctive shoe care more than two decades ago. "The old guys died and nobody took their place. The younger men thought being a shoeshine boy was a very degrading thing."

"Shoe shining is becoming a lost art. Younger men aren't getting in it. If you can't pass a trade on, it will pass out of existence."

The decline of the service trades, downtowns' decay and a cultural revolution in which black equality gained a toehold in the American conscience combined to put the majority of the nation's shoe shiners out of business.

But times are changing. In the old neighborhoods of St. Louis and Chicago, shine parlors are back. Meanwhile, shoeshine arts followed the flow of population from city centers to suburbs. Entrepreneurs have devised gimmicks to make the business catch on: shoeshine boys in tuxedos and shoeshine service subscriptions. Women have returned to the trade, less shy about showing flesh.

If the enterprise has not fully turned the corner, who is to say it won't? "Every minute somebody's born and there are thousands of pairs of new shoes, new leather coats, and hats, too. There's plenty of business out there just waiting," says James Haley the elder.

"I've been shining shoes twenty-three years. I did it to get through grade and high school. But I got kind of amazed at the way people could dye leather. It's an art," he says.

Along the way, he became a specialist in dye and refinishing leather. Whatever question one might have about keeping shoes distinctive, Haley has an answer. "There's spit shines and wax shines and super-special-deluxe shines. There's a lot of raps and gimmicks, but you get a guy who's been in the business twenty or thirty years and you're going to get your money's worth in advice along with your shine. For gossip and information and to preserve and beautify your shoes, people ought to use parlors as much as possible," he says.

Shining by itself is a dead end. "In shining alone, you just scratch out an existence," says the elder Haley, who's thinking about possibilities for a new business. "With a 'tip to top' valet service combining shoeshining and hat cleaning and while-you-wait pressing, then you'd have it made. You'd be offering a service people want, creating jobs, and bringing business back downtown," he says.

Haley is making plans. He's studied the changing times in service work and directions in the economy. And he's begun filling out the forms he'll need to secure space and legalities.

A couple doors north in Springfield, at the corner of Seventh and Washington, Nat Jett keeps history alive in a heated and air-cooled lean-to that's housed a shine parlor for ninety-four years. Jett has given up the dancing, rag-popping days of his youth.

"A lot of the old shoeshiners are dead. I'm going to retire myself in a few more years," he says. Meanwhile, he keeps his secrets, which include St. Louis-bought materials, to himself. "I get all the bankers here and the farmers, too. I been doing pretty good. I make a living off it," he tells me.

Gene Donaldson has shined shoes and blackened boots in Springfield for over thirty years, beginning at age 14 at the Seventh and Washington stand now owned by Jett. "The business has been very good to me in that it has given me all the necessities. Donaldson says. "Made me a living."

In the Abraham Lincoln Hotel, Donaldson is the sole shiner for mostly regular customers, the sort for whom shined shoes are as much a fact of life as neatly trimmed hair. The sparkling setting, with its revolving barber pole, gleaming plate glass window, and the lulling murmur of baseball and music on radios, seems part of something past—despite bullish sentiments about the future of shine. As Donaldson put it: "Shoe shining is becoming a lost art. Younger men aren't getting in it. If you can't pass a trade on, it will pass out of existence."

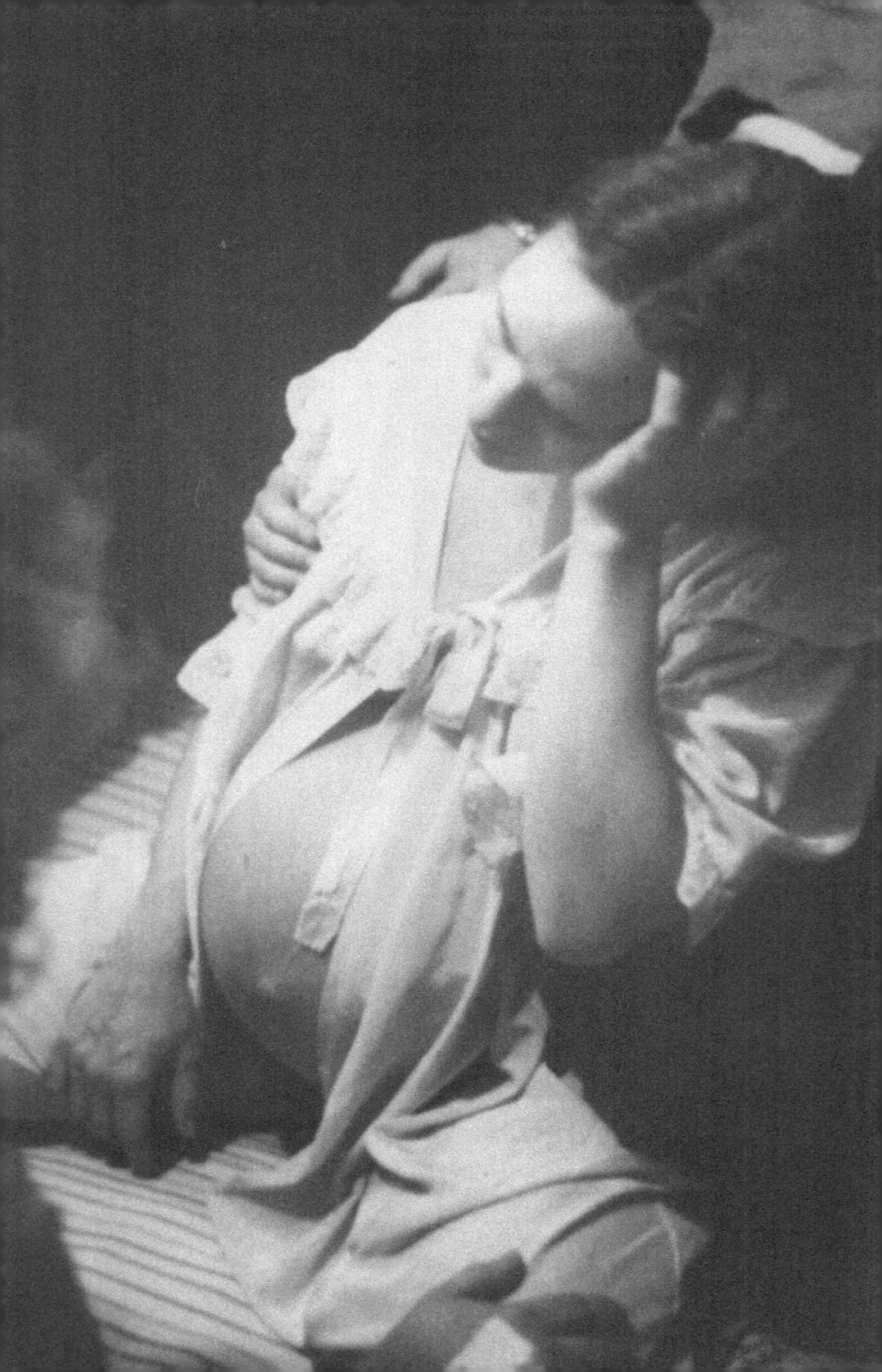

A Homebirth Teacher Has Her Baby

A priestess of childbirth at home puts her preaching into practice.

The room is freshly painted pale blue, a healing color. Through lace curtains comes the late afternoon sun, unexpectedly bright this early in March. In this country sitting room, which opens into a farm kitchen, the trappings of everyday life have been pushed against the walls. Here, on this day, a baby will be born.

Cat Feral is taking in her own hands the birth of her third child. At twenty-nine, she is Illinois' home birth missionary. Across the state, pregnant women are staying home when their time comes. Many have learned from her how to manage their births. Feral, Midwest coordinator for the California-based Association for Childbirth at Home International, is energetic, informed and something of a priestess among her earnest followers. Her work and life are inter-twined. She is so dedicated to her cause that for it, she says, she is "willing to put my body on the line."

Feral's choice to have this baby at home is beyond many people's understanding. In late 20th century America, scientific medicine nearly put an end to home births—until recently. Intuition was replaced by efficiency. Experienced female midwives gave way to schooled, objective male physicians. The antiseptic delivery room was perfected as the nation's birthplace.

In recent decades, technological medicine became accepted by an overwhelming majority of medical professionals and parents. But improvements on nature advanced so far that women who value mystery above efficiency rebelled at the dehumanization of birth.

Home birth reemerged as a reaction to the established, authoritarian system. And because the established birthing systems also were so uncompromising, independent women decided to back the right to bear children as they choose. But they found few traditionally trained doctors, nurses or midwives who would attend births on the parents' terms.

If having a baby at home these days is a choice of conviction, it also is an act of defiance.

In a recent year, just 1,895 of Illinois' 174,397 babies were recorded as being born out of hospitals, by choice or accident. Feral believes that figure includes only one-fourth to one-half of the babies born in planned home births. Because the state's old Midwifery Licensing Act was repealed as obsolete, Illinois has only a handful of licensed midwives, leftovers from an early age. In Chicago, doctors will attend home births. But for a nurse or nurse midwife to manage a delivery at home is to risk her license. A midwife who is uncertified can be sued for practicing without a license or, in the event of a catastrophe, malpractice.

There's been a debate in the Illinois General Assembly about what to do. Feral and her California-based Association for Childbirth at Home are under subpoena by the Illinois attorney general. Parents giving birth at home have been charged with child abuse.

Among the many issues at stake is the relationship of the paraprofessional to the mother and to the doctor. A second is the availability of medical information to non-medical people. A third is the issue of rights. Can people decide what they may or many not do, or must action await the state's permission? But the fundamental question underlying Feral and her parents' fights is whether the bureaucracies and technologies created to serve us have become our masters.

The growing number of women who stay home to have their babies are impatient with bureaucracy and lawmaking. What they want are specialists trained in the art and science of birthing, helpers at once resourceful in a critical hour and sensitive to the power of tenderness. Few such women are to be found. To get the ideal setting for birth, if not the ideal attendant, the radical vanguard is managing as best it can.

"Nobody at my birth will be functioning as midwife; collectively they'll all function as one," Feral told me. "I wish I had a midwife. I have faith in my birth team, but they're lacking experience, and therefore confidence."

Except for sterile cloths and fetoscopes (to measure the baby's heart tones before and during the birth), childbearing at home proceeds without modern medicine's bag of tools and drugs.

Critics contend that the homebirthers have thrown the baby out with the bath. They are horrified at what they see as disregard for proper order. Some even believe that entrusting an infant's survival to untrained hands in unauthorized settings is criminal. A Springfield, Illinois, obstetrician has said that if a baby dies in a home birth, the parents should be charged with murder.

The authorities have tangled with Feral. The Illinois attorney general's office sued after she and her organization refused to answer his subpoena for their records. The case was dismissed in circuit court. A state lawyer told me that for now, pursuing Feral is a matter "on the back burner."

If having a baby at home these days is a choice of conviction, it also is an act of defiance.

SUBMITTING TO LABOR

Cat Feral has gone into labor and she is submissive now rather than defiant. Her body is shaken with the awesome power of contractions. She has taught her birthing team the course of labor and birth, instructed them about what to expect and how to respond. But she is a woman in labor now, not a teacher. Her students have become her coaches.

As each new spasm ripples through her body, her coaches bear it with her, holding her shoulders, locking her eyes with theirs, soothing her with touches, chanting praise, controlling the rhythm of her breathing.

Between contractions, women minister to her like bees to their queen. Besides her husband, Steve McWhirter, Feral has many attendants; two for each role were summoned in the event of bad weather. Photographers are in the room; she wants slides from the day to use in teaching. Feral's two previous births did not meet her expectations; she was lonely, she said, and had no community of friends and helpers. This time, she is determined that it will be better. Not only is her child being born, her artistry is at stake. The birthing room is crowded with players—twenty-five of us, counting children.

It is 4 p.m. and since early afternoon, Feral has been in the first stage of labor. Her contractions last forty-five seconds and are easily managed through concentration, relaxation and breathing. In the four minutes between contractions, she is at ease.

Every fifteen minutes the baby's heart tones are measured and found correct. There is no fetal distress, which would be revealed by fast or irregular heartbeats. Contractions and the time in between are measured and recorded. Feral drinks juice or sucks on frozen fruit juice cubes to keep her strong and hydrated. Her attendants eat apples and lay bets on whether the baby will be a girl or boy. One, a new mother herself, is dressed in a flowing gingham skirt and apron overskirt that she has made for the occasion. Her daughter plays on the floor.

As another contraction fills the room, Feral's attendants rush to support her. She rises erect to her knees and hot compresses are placed beneath her stomach, as hard and symmetrically round as a taut balloon. Slowly, imperceptibly, the contractions increase in frequency and intensity.

"They're getting good and strong now, aren't they? That's what we want," an attendant says.

At 5:05, the contractions strengthen. "Let the tension go out through your palms," her coach says. And it does.

The kind of labor described in Feral's seminars on home birth, which we are gathered to witness, is hard for many of an earlier generation to understand. Echoes of screams, the clenching panic, desperation and pain seen in movies is a world apart. Feral and her disciples testify instead to relaxation, confidence and joy—though they acknowledge that home birthing is hard and potentially terrifying work, particularly in later stages.

"Do not let a mother close her eyes," Feral says in her seminars. "She'll be alone in the dark. Eye-to-eye contact is so important because you keep her with you."

Now Feral is listening rather than talking. "Feel your cervix open up...Stay relaxed...Let your body do the work," her coach says.

Feral is serene, heavy-eyed. Her robe is deep blue velour piped in satin ribbons in three more shades of blue. Her hair is long, her skin evenly pink, her lips red. After each tremor, her attendants wipe her brow with a cold cloth. For a contraction she stands, and she and her coach sway together. Her gown ties in the front with pink ribbons that fall over her swollen stomach. She flows with the contractions.

By 5:30, when the bright gold of sun reflected off the snow has slipped into silver, Feral has reached the transition between first-stage labor and birth. For the next half-hour to hour, she struggles with strong, erratic contractions less than a minute apart. Her cervix is dilating wide for the baby. As she has cautioned us to expect, she has grown restless and irritable. An unexpected touch or sound makes her recoil. The color has drained from her face. Between contractions, she falls forward on hands and knees to rest and keels over on her side.

"It's just feeling so intense. It's not that it hurts, it's just so intense," she says.

At six o'clock, it is time for the first pelvic exam. It is painful.

"How much cervix is there? I want to know that," Feral snaps.

"Less than the width of a finger," answers a coach.

"Keep it high, keep it light," the coach says. "Keep looking at me. Relax. Let your eyebrows relax, your forehead relax. Just let it happen. Slow...slow...deep breaths. You're doing a fine job."

Attendants listen to the baby's heart. "You're doing good; the baby's doing good," one of them says. "You're handling it real well. Remembering the loneliness of other labors, we weep for joy.

For the next hour, strong, hard contractions threaten to overwhelm the teacher-mother. For the first time she sighs—*aaugh, aaugh*—so deeply as she struggles to find a position. She is dissatisfied with the baby's descent.

"This baby," she says, "is going to have to work its way down." To help it, she rises and takes steps.

At 6:35, her water breaks, a nice clean gush. For a time she is calmer, alternating between expert and mother. Then she thrashes and moans.

"All you have to do is let it happen," she hears.

At 7 p.m., it happens. The birth, which has seemed so far away the past hour, is fast and almost frantic. A new set of sterile sheets and pads is thrown on the bed. Feral half-sits, half lies on a beanbag chair. Several of us have left the room to give her space. Then we hear a cry: "It's being born."

"Is the chin out?" Feral asks.

A baby is born, guided by Feral's hands into her husband's hands. It is minutes before we know whether this tiny, curly creature, white with protective vernix, is a girl or boy. The attendants rest the infant face down on the bed, cover it with warm blankets and check its breathing. We are back near the bed and we tremble, but the attendants assure us that the baby is fine and strong.

We reel with emotion. Minutes later Feral's stomach contracts again as the bright red placenta detaches from the uterine wall.

Attendants are busy—wrapping the baby, clamping the cord for Feral to cut, pouring fluid off the placenta to be measured, checking to see if it is intact and the mother safe.

The baby—a girl—and Feral are reunited. The pink little creature whimpers once and happily makes sucking sounds. After the ecstasy and exhaustion we learn the time of the birth—the seventh minute of the seventh hour on the third day of the third month.

JUNE 3, 1982
A DAY OF
REBELLION

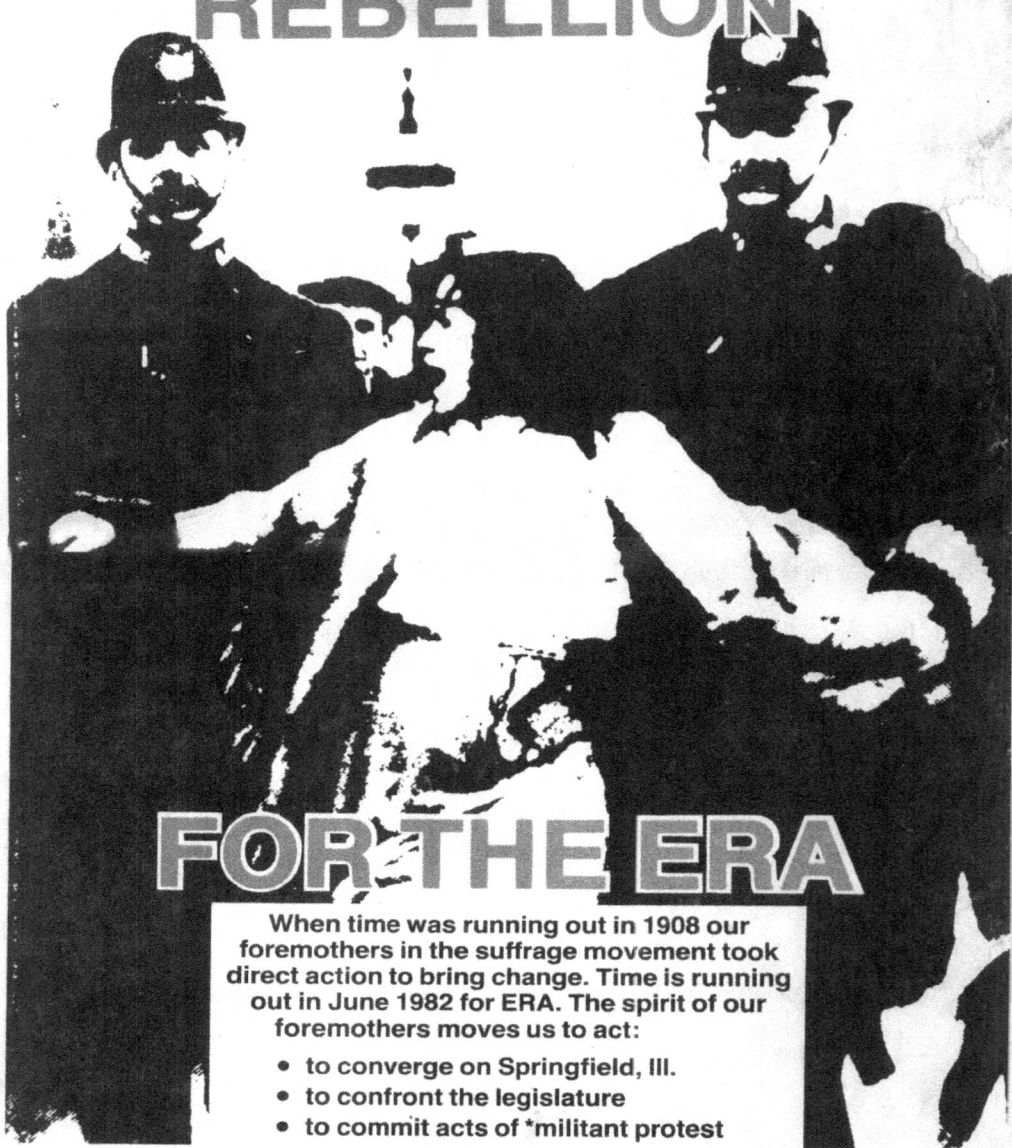

FOR THE ERA

When time was running out in 1908 our
foremothers in the suffrage movement took
direct action to bring change. Time is running
out in June 1982 for ERA. The spirit of our
foremothers moves us to act:

- to converge on Springfield, Ill.
- to confront the legislature
- to commit acts of *militant protest

*Define militant as you like: from wimpy to Amazonian

WOMEN JOIN US!

For information call Weaver — 217-398-3578

Fasting is Unladylike

*In the ERA wars, critics said committed protesters
went about their business in the wrong way.
Nonsense.*

They are accused of impracticality, imprudence, bad taste. They are
criticized because they did not prepare correctly, did not get medical
permission and did not spend enough money.

They are told they started at the wrong time. That they never
should have started at all. That they're hurting their cause.

Illinois Women's Fast for Justice and Grass Roots Group of
Second-Class Citizens hear that neither fasting nor frolicking in the
halls of the Capitol will change any minds.

Not so, say twenty-two women whose actions are adding a new
chapter to the long tradition of pitting conscience against injustice.
As they see it, nonviolent confrontation changed the past, and it can
change the future.

"Social change has never been won by persuasion alone," says
Mary Lee Sargent, the historian-organizer of Second Class Citizens.
"Success has always required much more dramatic confrontation—
militant, committed acts of civil disobedience,"

Two separate bands of women have come to Illinois' Capitol at
the eleventh hour of Equal Rights Amendment consideration to
put their bodies on the line because, they believe, absolute commit-
ment can provide the languishing proposed amendment the shove
of energy it needs.

In its early years, the second feminist movement this century was
as diverse and often as militant as the movement that won women
the right to vote in 1920. But with Eleanor Smeal's ascendancy to

the presidency of the National Organization for Women in 1977, and NOW's hold on the leadership of the movement to ratify the ERA, rational pragmatism became the prevailing strategy.

The "establishment"ratification campaign adopted the strategy of military men: All unratified territories were divided into theaters of operation, prioritized for their ratification potential, and the most likely targeted. From headquarters came orders and intelligence— newsletters, mass mailings, phone calls. Steady streams of money flowed to headquarters, and willing volunteers marched to a coordinated beat.

In NOW's organized, amply provisioned and rigidly disciplined system, every tactic has been subordinated to the larger goal of raising public opinion to such a crest that lawmakers would be swept along. The theory was that politicians count only what they can tally: voters; visits; letters; and, above all, campaign contributions.

Yet despite polls showing that a majority of Americans favor the ERA, despite the tactical victory in extending the original ratification deadline from 1979 to 1982, despite the best efforts of rational pragmatism, not a single additional state has ratified the amendment in five years. Indeed, the trend may be shifting in the other direction.

What to do now? "Redouble our efforts?" Smeal exhorted recently.

But this spring, rebellion cracked the solid front of rational pragmatism. A Springfield militant who identifies only as Katwoman put it this way: "We let the opposition set the rules for us. 'You can declare war on us but you can only use popguns from a distance', they said, and we agreed. When those rules didn't work for us, we thought we hadn't tried hard enough, and they smiled.

"We got screwed," she concluded.

On May 18,1982, seven women gathered in the Illinois Capitol and told the governor, the legislators and the world that they would eat no food and drink nothing but water until the ERA passed in Illinois—or failed nationally.

Not one of them resides in Illinois at present. That bothers some people, as does the unseemliness of their tactic. Gov. James Thompson and House Speaker George Ryan assert that fasting won't change any minds. GOP Sen. Forest Etheredge, who had been counted on for his vote both for the amendment and for changing the three-fifths majority required for passage, declared that he would vote yes on neither as long as the fast continues.

"They tell us the ERA will not pass because we have not been good girls."

Smeal, who gave the fasters money for lodging, says she doesn't "encourage" going without food. Their children beg them not to die. Their mothers plead with them to stop. Their fathers demand it.

Through it all they sit with serene dignity, unmoved in their determination, convinced they and their tactics are right for the moment and believing firmly that they have the duty to defy a political system that does not represent them. They hear their consciences no less clearly than did Jesus or Gandhi or Martin Luther King Jr.

"They tell us the ERA will not pass because we have not been good girls," said Sonia Johnson, who has spoken from a wheelchair since Day 8 of the fast.

Johnson says that she and the others have made themselves symbols of "the suffering of women that has remained invisible. As individuals, we have faces and bodies to make that suffering visible."

But this is more than symbolic. Gandhi believed that fasting opens doors to a moral force superior to any material force. He wrote that fasting "quickens the spirit of prayer…The effect of such action is that the sleeping conscience is awakened."

Johnson said that she and the others "believe that somewhere in these legislators are principles. We believe you can touch the good in everybody. We want them to begin to think about justice."

Dick Gregory, the comedian and civil rights activist who has joined the protest, described fasting as a force that releases "massive powers of love."

Mary Ann Beall, one of the fasters, observed that "the civil rights movement changed America. Black and white people now live side by side, if not in comfort, at least in peace. Gandhi changed the face of India in eighteen months, breaking through a caste system 5,000 years old and as deeply ingrained as our own system of domination of women by men."

On June 3, the Day of Rebellion, the Capitol Rotunda was alive with voices lifted in song. High-spirited demonstrators linked themselves in symbolic black paper chains and "relegated to the chamber pot" many of the arguments anti-ERA forces offer to explain their intransigence. Outside the Senate and House chambers, a dozen women chained themselves to brass railings.

The fasters proceeded spiritually, civilly, unlike their boisterously disobedient sisters in protest, who cheered and chortled and clanked and yelled and wore funny clothes.

"Whatever your fight, don't be ladylike," proclaimed the sign brandished by 57-year-old Doris Rutledge Busick, of Melvin, Ill.

For four and a half days, some legislators passing by treated the scene of women in chains as a joke. But beneath that comedy was a social protest as profound as the fast.

Being a lady means playing the game by somebody else's rules. Under those rules, too many women have lost too much for too long.

Rosa Parks ignored the rules.

Dr. King and his allies in the 1960s were told they were stepping out of line.

Gandhi was not afraid to heed the "still, small voice" that guided him in his campaign of nonviolent protest and mass non-cooperation against imperial rule.

Our suffragist grandmothers, whose gatherings and marching and civil disobedience won women in Britain and the United States the right to vote, were perfect scandals.

They broke rules. And they won.

PART V

Learning to Live
in Chesapeake Country

Sandra wasn't the first Midwesterner to fall into rapture upon landing in Chesapeake Bay Country. It's happened to senators (George McGovern among them), to congressmen, to Kennedys and various folks from the waystation of Washington, DC, who discover storied waters an hour's drive from the world's most powerful city. Sandra went beyond most of the smitten—starting a weekly newspaper, a heady financial and career move, one that enabled her and the many writers to whom she gave license to chronicle the glories and the goings-on in, along and beneath Chesapeake Bay waters.

Selections from those years chronicle her plunge into boating and fishing as well as the environmental decline of a waterway labeled "the immense protein factory" by Chesapeake Bay denizen H.L. Mencken. In these stories she writes of the afflicted (The Amputees' Picnic). She profiles certifiable Bay characters, writes about neighbors alive and dead (My Haunted Hood). The roots she sank in her newfound locale can be measured by the relationships she made, even solemnizing—after being ordained an Universal Life Church minister—a neighbor's daughter's wedding. Read the vows in Solemnization.—Editor's Note

Living on the Corner

Out my window,
the world takes its daily form.

Living on the corner washes you in the tide the way waves wash the beach. But people make the waves we feel on our corner.

On the first wave of morning come the crabbers. Waking in the 5 or 5:30 a.m. darkness, they fire up their truck engines. Subliminally, even in the deep of sleep, the departures register, and the sleeper knows who and how many have left the village.

Then, wave after wave, come the school buses, with a woosh of air brakes and folding doors breaking out of their rubber gaskets. Their arrival gathers kids, moms and dogs to chat and bark beneath my bedroom window. I've watched pregnancies advance, new babies appear on the scene, fashions and families come and go and kids transform into skittish adolescents.

Preteen girls preen and turn cartwheels or write their crushes' names in white rock on the asphalt road, while preteen boys are more likely to kick that rock. Smaller versions of many of these kids wrestled with my puppy, now a 100-pound dog. Their moms let them come alone now, or with their own dogs, who hang around after one bus leaves, waiting for the next.

Lately, a new crop has arrived of little ones with moms who push still littler kids in strollers, or ride them piggy-back up the long hill. Other moms, dressed for work, visit a bit until the buses pack up their kids, then rush away, too.

After the moms and the kids and the buses and even the dogs are gone, a sullen, late-sleeping teenage boy trudges up—too late. His mom will drive him again today.

Down the hill, the waves have washed the beach, tideline after tideline marking its advance and retreat in traces of pebbles, sticks and bubbles. Some days, the tide leaves behind swarms of ancient, barnacled, wriggling horseshoe crabs; others, a litter of flattened jellyfish, tentacles still rippling the ebb. Some days the tide throws up treasures; some days, trouble. Once, on Valentine's Day, the tide left a big red dog for us to bury.

Someday, it will leave me the biggest shark's tooth I've ever seen, lodged in an adjacent cliff since the Miocene epoch.

At the corner, the unexpected is routine, too. Twice this year, long after midnight, pounding at the door has started my dog barking and my heart pounding. Both times it was teenage boys, too old for school buses, who'd crashed their cars on the winding road. Dazed boys and parents and police crowded the early hours until it was nearly time for the crabbers to signal the next beginning. Once, after an imagined slight and egged on by girlfriends, the boys came back to the corner to fight our son with pickets they'd torn off a neighbor's fence.

Changeable tides drive the late-night teenage raiders, too. Some mornings, smashed car windows and mailboxes are left along the road, like tidelines.

Before the buses brought autumn, the human tide left another strange deposit on the corner: an orange Pennzoil box atop the fender of our *New Bay Times* truck. I saw it from my bedroom window, but I forgot it until a neighbor—whose running is one of the early morning tides—called me out to look inside. There, instead of a forgotten dozen quarts of oil, were five mewling kittens.

On the corner and on the beach, we only think we know the tides.

June Brings Ray Day to Chesapeake Bay

The cownose ray is a promise kept.

Baywatching is the sport in the Southern Maryland village where I live. In a county with no movie theaters, the Chesapeake is our silver screen.

Villagers name the day by what the Bay gives them. Any summer weekday, after weekenders have berthed their boats and returned to town, will likely be Heron Day, for the great blue giant birds that sweep down onto our depopulated piers like pterosauruses evolved to grace. Four times we've had *Queen Elizabeth II* Day; up and down the Bayfront, everybody turns out with binoculars to see her royal, ocean-going highness.

And now, in summer, we have Ray Days.

Swimming in from southern Atlantic waters, huge flotillas of these strange flapping kites with whiplike tails, radarlike sensors and voracious, gourmet appetites graze the Bay all summer long, mating and giving birth.

R. bonasus, otherwise known as the cownose ray, may be a nuisance fish with bad habits and an unbecoming, barnyard name. But hereabouts, the cownose ray is a promise kept.

Though not as celebrated as the return of the swallows to Capistrano, the cownoses' annual June arrival in the Chesapeake Bay is a sign of the same order. If such winged creatures keep their appointments, then surely the world isn't completely topsy-turvy. Our Chesapeake Bay, befouled as it is with toxics and supernutrients, still lures the marvels of the ocean to our doors. So dropping dish rag, garden hose or barbecue tongs, we villagers rush to the Bayfront to watch.

"If you get there on the right day, Little Cove Point is the place to watch rays. One day I saw what must have been a thousand of them there, banging into one another, leaping, flapping, cruising, chasing. The only way I can describe it is that they were playing," says Bob Lunsford of the Maryland Department of Natural Resources.

If a newcomer should sight a ray, they're sure to panic and cry, "Shark!" Then villagers explain to the greenhorn that Rhinoptera bonasus is only the shark's second cousin, though the devil fish's first. But despite our smugness, our hearts will be thumping.

After the huge gatherings of June have broken up, throughout the summer the lingering rays seem to fly in the shallow waters below us. Their undulating wings—actually broad, triangular pectoral fins fused with the body so that the ray resembles a pair of boomerangs set tip to tip—rise and fall. They stir the sediment of the shallows on the falling stroke and break the surface on the rise.

Knifing through the water, those dark wing tips do resemble a shark's dorsal fin. But instead of terror, it's pleasure that thrills watchers. For the rays we see are lovers, not hunters. In pairs and trios, the rays are dancing a mating ballet. Although the water boils with their ardor, these master dancers never fall from grace. True as herons to their horizontal axis, their wings beating the same slow and steady rhythm, the disk-like rays pirouette.

"Sharks with flattened bodies adapted to bottom dwelling." That's what Clarence Hylander calls rays and skates, the ray's first cousins, in his *Fishes and Their Ways*.

Seventy pounds of fish spread side to side in a disk propelled by a pair of horizontal pectoral fins nearly twice as wide as the fish is long.

Cownoses at their largest may grow to a width of seven feet, but more common are wingspreads of three to five feet.

As wicked as the whip-like tail looks, it is not the cownose's weapon. A finger-sized spike lurking at the base of tail and body is the real danger. Step on it, and the pain is excruciating and likely followed by infection. Exploring the Chesapeake, Captain John Smith encountered the business end of a ray and thought it would kill him.

What appear to be the topside eyes appropriate to a bottom dweller are actually spirades for expelling water. The ray's true eyes, round and bovine, are set close to the front of the head. Between the eyes, something of a channel divides the head into two lobes. Those lobes are copied by a second set of lobes on a soft fin just below. Together they make sense of this ray's name—at least if you know your noses. Cow nose and cow eyes give an unexpected familiarity— almost a gentleness—to the creature.

But the underside of the ray has a look to breed superstition.

The Biggest Teeth on the Bay

*The wonders of antiquity,
hawked on a country road*

Necks whiplash and brakes squeal on Rt. 2–4 near Solomons, in Calvert County, Maryland. It's no accident, just the show-stopping signs of local entrepreneurs Douggie Douglas and John Rue.

Whales! Great White Sharks! Fossil Teeth and Vertebrae! signs proclaim.

A vertebrae sale? Looking at the rolling green hills and farm fields beyond state comptroller Louis Goldstein's wide, undulant highway, you wonder what these guys can be talking about. Nary a wave, whale nor shark is in sight, and it's hard to believe, even when you know for a fact, that you're not too many miles from the Chesapeake to the east and the fat, swelling Patuxent River to the west.

So you swerve to the side of the road and you find out that there's more hereabouts than meets the eye.

"There's millions of years of history out there," says one of the fellows. "Waiting for you to find it," adds the other.

Sizing up John and Douggie's wares and listening to their sideshow spiel, words flowing and arms fluttering, you return to an age of giants.

Millions of years ago in the Miocene epoch, Chesapeake Bay was an ocean teeming with giants. Mastodon and rhinoceros visited these shores. Whales rolled and stingrays glided in the warm waters. Scallops grew the size of soup bowls. Crocodiles wallowed in the shallows. Sharks big as big as boxcars—big eaters fitted out with layered rows of razor teeth—preyed here.

195

The sharks that tyrannized those ancient waters seldom went hungry. Nature equipped each shark, then as now, with as many as 85,000 knife-sharp teeth. Whenever a tooth wore out—their useful life was as short as a week—a new one would come forward to take its place. The littlest might be as small as a thorn on a tea rose. But the biggest—the teeth of the extinct great white shark, Carcharodon megalodon—could be 7 inches long.

You doubt? Douggie and John will show you proof. John's big tooth is about 6⅜ inches; Douggie's, at about 6¼ inches, is not quite so long but wider. Both are between 12 and 18 million years old.

All that remains of other brutes and monsters is laid out for you to see and handle at Douggie's road stand at the entrance to Calvert Cliffs State Park. Ditto at John's stand, situated at the entrance to Calvert County's Flag Ponds Nature Park.

In addition to perhaps the biggest teeth on the Bay—teeth that weigh in at a pound and a half—you'll see small, medium and large sharks' teeth, as well as teeth made into jewelry. These teeth are for sale, of course.

There are full sets of sharks' teeth still situated in gaping, dangerous jaws; crocodile and stingray teeth; whale and porpoise ear bones and vertebrae; mastodon parts; and such ancient seashells as Maryland's own ecphora.

"It's just amazing. You never know what you're going to find. Once it gets in your blood, you never get enough," says John, laying stresses of enthusiasm on his words.

These guys are pros; they're hooked on fossils. Just about any time they're not here on the road showing and telling, they're in the water or on the beach, hunting.

"Both of us can get close to those old sharks," Douggie says, shivering. "I'll feel chills and think I've seen a dorsal fin when all I see is a tooth. But I know a shark must have been there."

There is the old ocean floor. All those teeth fell to the ocean bottom, as did the creatures whose mouths they once filled. In the sediment, flesh and cartilage decayed or were eaten, but parts and tissues hardened with calcium phosphate—bone and teeth— endured. Strengthened by enamel and petrified, the teeth of sharks and bones of whales outlasted the epochs.

Years passed by the millions as the ancient Miocene epoch yielded to the Pliocene epoch, and finally to the Pleistocene, our very own epoch. Twenty and more million years of history are deposited there.

Today the old ocean treasure trove is covered with sand and sediment on the Bay's bottom or thrown up by relentless geological shrinking and swelling as the 30-mile range of Calvert Cliffs. The Bay region isn't unique in hoarding Miocene fossils, but it's particularly rich. The cliffs, Calvert County's face on the Bay, are steep, rising as high as 100 feet, and often bare. As the cliffs crumble under the assault of winds and waves, beaches form at their feet. The beaches are larded with the cliffs' unburied treasure. And scoured by treasure seekers. Today the hunters of old have become the hunted.

Bayside children grow up hunting. Squatting on the strand, they sift the sand to discover fossils in their palms. Or a bored kid, following raccoon tracks for something to do, bumps into a big one protruding from a cliff.

Old timers may have collections of hundreds, if not thousands, of fossils. Some even have teeth as big as John's or Douggie's. Connie Smith, a 30-year beachcomber, stumbled over her six-incher on the marvelous beach at her old Girl Scout camp, Matoaka Beach Cabins. Jonathon Sheldon stopped by John Rue's stand to show off the gleaming white six-incher he found at Randle Cliff. A six-incher tonged up by an oysterman has been passed down for three generations.

As well as legions of pleasure hunters, the Bay supports several fossil clubs and inspires the Maryland Geological Society. Douggie, who has been at it for thirty years, has an extreme case of the lifelong fever that afflicts all the hunters.

"The hunt is fired by the thrill of discovery," says Smithsonian Institution paleontologist Dave Bohaska, a Calvert countian.

"Each find is something completely new, something no one has ever touched before."

Along the beach the hunters creep, alert as gulls aiming for dinner. Among all the grains of sand it takes to make a beach, fossils are secreted. The odds are against the hunters, but just as gulls eat, sharks' tooth hunters are rewarded—some more than others.

Douggie, who knows every beach and its likely rewards better than many of us know what's in our refrigerator, makes it seem like those old sharks are just keeping a date with him.

John Rue makes his dates on the Bay bottoms. "In between sand-bars are hard clay fossil beds. Furrows and ravines are natural catch traps," explains Rue, a scuba diver whose finds include "vertebrae as big as young tree trunks just sticking out of the bottom."

Diving's too easy, some land hunters complain, and compare it to shooting fish in a barrel. They worry that overharvesting, even greed, will strip their beaches. Rue, however, says that the sport teaches its own discipline: "Mostly I just admire and keep going. I can't carry home everything I find. If I did, my wife would get after me," he says.

On the beach or in the water, hunters pray for bad weather.

"Shifting, scoring sands, burrowing crabs, dissolving clay and storms push everything around," says Rue.

"We want erosion, storms and hurricanes—not to hurt anybody, just to stir things up," echoes Douggie.

Their eyes are gleaming.

You'd think a state would be proud of entrepreneurs who recover history and deliver it to roadside travelers. At least as proud as of its roadside markets featuring locally grown produce.

In regulation-crazed Maryland, think again.

A new state law to discourage roadside vendors of Carolina and Mexican furniture would ban Rue and Douggie from highways. They avoid the ban by selling on park land.

"They made me a criminal!" complains Rue, who's fighting for a variance on the grounds that Calvert fossils are a native product known throughout the world.

Says Douggie: "About half of what we're doing is entertaining people. While we explain things, they can pick 'em up and look at 'em, all for free."

Small Boat, Light Tackle, Big Fun

*It's like rediscovering an old friend,
that feeling of gliding.*

If you're like me, no matter how many times you've done it, launching is laced with doubt: Will this light craft and you merge like a Nereid or will you splash and spill? Then you've got your boat in the water and yourself in your boat and you push off and there, as paddle cuts water, is that old friend again.

These are new waters and new boats: on Maine's Lake Damariscotta, where *New Bay Times* contributing editor M.L. Faunce owns a cottage, I've barely said hello before being hooked by the lure of her little Manatee, a single kayak. When I ease out into the lake, the morning air matches the water, chilly and wet. It's a responsive little craft, short and agile and alive to both my stroke and the fast current of the channel that runs between a nice island and Osage Cottage's lawn and dock.

New, but not so different from the other waters I've canoed or kayaked—from Admiralty Island, Alaska, to Lake of the Woods, Ontario, to Lake Superior at Sault Ste. Marie to Lake Wappapello or even Mingo Swamp in Missouri, or the Mackinaw River and Lake Sangchris in Illinois, to the Pocomoke River on Chesapeake Bay's Eastern Shore to the Patuxent on the western to my home waters of Herring Bay. The glide is the same, the feeling that you are in another element yet one that is not entirely strange.

Rippling through water lilies, their white and yellow blossoms open in the early morning, over to the shore of that inviting island, I come upon another sight so familiar that my heart leaps: through the amber clear water shows the rocky bottom. I know in the tumble of memories why this sight so thrills me, something about being in the real world making you feel real yourself.

201

But you don't sit in one place—or stay with one thought—long while on the water, and a stroke later I see that M.L.'s Manatee, a gift on her June retirement after thirty-five years working for Congress and the government, can nose nicely into the shallows. It needs only a few inches of water; I'd already be stuck in my usual craft, a tandem sea kayak over 21½ feet long. In it I'd have put myself between a rock and a hard place.

But there are four more boats in Faunce's armada, more fish to fry this morning and the promise of another way of feeling realer on the water—though I must spell this one 'reeler.' So I leave this island—trusting that later I will feel the sponge-over-rock of its mossy banks—to cast my line upon the waters.

I renewed my taste for fishing in Western Ontario where, tangled for days in the chain of Lake of the Woods, I must catch my dinner or go without. By then the high balance of a canoe was second nature, sweetened by the pleasure of casting light little Mepps into the amber water over round rocks.

Rolling with the water, you hold your mouth like a fish, which I discovered in those meditative moments simply means figuring where a fish would like to rest: holding steady, perhaps, in the lee of a submerged log. You then cast into that sweet spot, feeling the arc of limb and line, high or low, watching the line float, hearing the plunk of lure landing. Now comes the thrill of current telegraphed along the line, the tug of the water, the wondering if there be fish.

Somehow there always are. So the time will come when your line suggests, then insists, and before you have time to say, *Oh my! A fish!* you'll be working it, giving line and taking it—all the time keeping your seat, which is as lively as if this boat on water were a horse beneath you—until you see the amber fish within the amber water. Then if you are sure and steady, you'll swing a big Northern or walleye pike into the net, and smelling its rank sharpness, you'll know you've landed a creature from another world.

For me, that's angling. Trolling Chesapeake Bay in a big, loud boat that does all the work seems to be many people's idea of fishing. Not mine.

But in the fall when the small rockfish make their way into the shallows as they do every year in Herring Bay, you can go out to meet them in a canoe.

This year, when I seek them, I'll have traded in my spinning rod for lighter tackle If—up here on this Maine lake—I can get the knack of fly fishing.

We've had our lesson. Out on the lawn, Maestro Lambrecht, our weekly newspaper's de facto publisher, has lined us up, practically a rogue's gallery of *New Bay Times*: myself, Faunce and classified ad manager (and sometime writer) Nathaniel Knoll. Kathleen Wilson, thank goodness, is a reader—or we would have to eat our own words. We'd rather eat fish with our Maine blueberries.

I'm here to tell you large-mouth bass live in that lake as surely as rockfish swim in the fall shallows of Chesapeake Bay.

We've felt with shock the length and lightness of the rod. Considered the taper of the line. Examined the leader. Compared the flies. Taken rod in one hand and the line in the other and attempted the art of wielding its length and lightness and all that line with no weight to give substance to its landing. At first, for most of us, line falls in a tangle, leaving us surrounded as if we were squirted with Silly String. It's limp, we're aimless.

Then, slowly, we get the swing, carry the tip of the rod just far enough back, teach the left hand what the right is doing, and the line whips in the lovely, limber arc beloved by the fly fisher. Not every time. Each success is bracketed by failure, when we're clumsily all thumbs and tangles. But surely we will find success.

Early the next morning my old fishing partner and I ease into no kayak but our old familiar craft, a canoe. Settling, we shimmy unsteadily, needing to learn this high perch all over again. How, we wonder, have we covered so many miles, so far from anywhere, in boats this slippery? Then we've got our seats and the paddles power us into the current and we move faster than it onto the far side of that island where, certainly, the fish live.

M.L. has seen hanging in the rocky shallows there a big fish with a wide, low-slung jaw.

So now, atop a lichen-covered boulder where the current idles, we dally, hardly paddling at all, twice a line's throw from the green shore. I have seen how Lambrecht swings and snaps the line, watched the wet fly swim back to the boat. He, too, has told of fishes: not quite as big as M.L.'s legendary lunker but big enough to feed two or three, big enough to talk about, big enough to grow bigger after you've set it free.

Now it's my turn, and here are those old friends again: the line, the lure, the loft and, eventually, the sweet sudden surprise when something live is on your line.

I'm here to tell you largemouth bass live in that lake as surely as rockfish swim in the fall shallows of Chesapeake Bay.

Editor's note: This piece won second-place in the category of Sports Column in the 1998 Maryland-Delaware-District of Columbia editorial awards competition.

Taking Three Hundred Horses For a Ride

Hoping to avoid the explosion with boat parts flying and bodies aflame

When you want to learn to sail, you find out quickly that Annapolis is indeed a sailing capital of the world. You can choose from a long list of sailing schools, including ones specially for women, children or handicapped sailors. Whether you choose Chesapeake Bay or follow a Chesapeake Country sailing school to an exotic destination, you can spend from a day to weeks on a boat learning wind, waves and weather, sails, sheets and spinnakers.

When you want to learn to take out a kayak and paddle and roll, you're also in luck on Chesapeake Bay, where kayaks are familiar sights.

But powerboaters? At least as many power as sailboats (and far more power boats than kayaks) ply the waters of Chesapeake Country. Propelled by the power of hundreds of horses and sitting on top of a reservoir of explosive fuel, power boaters are the last cowboys on the range. Many of us figured that if we can drive a car, we can drive a boat. You just turn on the key and go.

We were wrong.

"If you drive a car, you have to know what side of the road to stay on and what traffic lights mean," says Mickey Courtney, an even-tempered master mariner who teaches powerboaters the ways of their boats and the water. "People who buy boats with no training, it's like being on the highway without knowing what you're doing."

Maybe that's why you hear—heaven forbid your knowledge is any closer to hand than hearsay—far more frequently of how power-boaters have come to grief than have sailboaters.

CAUTIONARY TALES

From my first days in a powerboat partnership, I've stored away a cautionary collection of such tales and sights. Adding drama to my very first Coast Guard boating safety class were color slides—I remember them far better than how, say, to chart a course by compass—of catastrophic explosions set off by fuel fumes. Every time our tank is filled, my heart reminds me that it takes only a spark— even a loose bolt of static electricity—to ignite those seeping, invisible fumes. I recall human bodies flying through the air with smoke and debris, though I may be embellishing the scene.

Newly added to my catastrophic collection is the nearly averted demise of three generations of a single family. You've heard that story: how grandfather, father and daughter had taken a 20-some-foot boat out in wind and driving rain and, anchoring from the stern, had been swamped and sunk.

Only a couple of providential passings saved those lives. I think of that story as we're rocking at anchor—and I find myself thinking of it a lot, these prime summer boating days. I guess you can count on He who counts the sparrows counting you. Or you can learn the right way to set an anchor.

Just as cautionary are the catastrophes I've seen first hand. In the eight years we've slipped on Rockhold Creek in Deale, Maryland, I've seen two powerboats—one this year—piled atop the long rock jetty that protects the harbor. There they sat, their bottoms crushed like eggshells but otherwise undamaged, as if getting there had not been so hard—and at the same time so foolishly easy—as you knew it had to be. In strange waters, there but for the grace of my chart book go I.

What's a powerboater to do to be safe rather than sorry?

To avoid trouble once underway, Courtney says check your engine first.

"Oh gosh," he says,
"I've taught everybody,
the experienced to the
completely inexperienced.
Most recently a very smart
lady who bought a boat as if
she were experienced
but was very intimidated
by docking."

This is not me.

IN BETWEEN THE DEVIL AND THE DEEP BLUE SEA

I started my powerboating days righteously some years back with the US Coast Guard Auxiliary's course on safe boating skills and seamanship. For those regularly scheduled intensive classes, the Auxiliary actively recruits both sailors and powerboaters. The Powerboat Squadron does the same for power boaters. For boat operators born after July 1, 1972, a minimum of eight hours boater safety education is now required by law. But you're never too old to learn, advises the Natural Resources Police, who recommend boaters of any age take these classes.

Studying hard in my Coast Guard class, this old dog learned how many dangers awaited me in the deep blue sea and shallow brown Bay:

- Exploding from sparks igniting engine or cooking fuel;

- Capsizing from overcrowding;

- Swamping from anchoring astern;

- Getting stove in by a wild sea or even battered by a rogue wave (as in Sebastian Junger's *The Perfect Storm*);

- Losing my boat at the slip from an ill-tied knot;

- Losing my way due to navigational ignorance;

- Sinking after forgetting to tighten plugs (Are you reading this, Capt. Rick?);

- Crashing into pilings, wrecks or jetties;

- Losing power in the path of a big ship.

Large and small, catastrophes loomed. Proud as I was to pass the tough test concluding my 12-week class, I wondered how my headful of nautical knowledge would translate once in the water, where trial by error can carry a heavy price. When you learn to drive a car, you've got to get out of the classroom and behind the wheel. I hadn't done that. You don't, in even the best of these boating classes.

Some years later, a spell with WomanShip let me try my hands as well as fill my head. I wasn't switching to sail from power, simply tagging along with a friend who, with her husband, had bought a 26-foot Westerly Centaur in prelude to retiring to the water.

"Being able to handle your own boat and guide yourself through the water and wind is such an empowering experience," said Janice DiGirolamo, the wife of already empowered captain Philip Tinsley. Sounded convincing to me; five of us signed up for a three-day weekend with a woman captain who, as the school promises, never yelled.

With WomanShip, as well as sails and sheets, I learned how to take a look at an engine and set an anchor. But when I didn't do it everyday, I couldn't remember quite what to do—except in the galley. As I resumed my life as galley mate, DiGirolamo's other words rang in my ears: "It's so easy to give way to the one who knows the most."

On our boat, that's my husband. He captains it the way I captain my kitchen: with natural authority, expecting immediate obedience and not tolerating much clumsiness. It may be that we're prisoners of conventional gender roles, but that's the way it is.

Then a new boat entered our lives, a used but fine Sea Ray Sundancer. With it returned my empowering determination to handle my own boat. So when my husband went out of town one July day in 1998, I turned our boat into a Bay-going classroom.

PANIC DISCOURAGED

"Back down! Drop her into idle! Turn in! Now!"

Looming too few feet ahead is the extended prow of a long-nosed, very nice powerboat. But I am not panicking. The young pump jockey waiting to turn on the gas at Herrington Harbour South may be panicking. I can't be sure because I am not looking at him. If I were he, on top of all that fuel in the middle of all those expensive boats, I'd be at least concerned.

Concerned too is my sister at sea, contributing editor Carol Glover, another powerboating wife seeking the empowerment of guiding her own boat. I hear the scream she has stifled. But my teacher is not panicking. He thinks I can do this, so I do it, gliding on only my second pass with hardly a bump— and without clipping that overhanging pulpit—up to the fueling dock. Calmly, I am killing with one stone two of my most tenacious fears: fueling and docking.

Once we've tied up, I confess that I've never backed down (which is what he called going in reverse) before. Still, my teacher is unruffled.

This calmest of captains is Courtney, 57. I've chosen him for his cool as well as for his credentials. Editor of the venerable chart book *Maryland Cruising Guide*, Courtney has enough years on the water to have seen the worst and best of boating. He's spent over 25,000 hours navigating the world's waters.

Since his boyhood on the Magothy River and Cypress Creek, Courtney has nosed about the Bay, poking into just about every corner of the changeable Chesapeake. Any Bay place he's missed by boat, he's covered and re-covered in his day-by-day scrutiny of Chesapeake charts.

What's more, Courtney's an Atlantic veteran. "We left from Brighton, England, into Force 10 conditions," he recalls of a 1988 crossing in a 68-foot DeVries power yacht.

"Boaters on Chesapeake Bay would have been in a world of trouble," he says knowingly.

Courtney has rescued many a disabled boater on the Bay and off Ocean City, in his thirty years in the Coast Guard Reserve, and he has ticketed many a disastrous boater in fifteen years with Natural Resources Police. He's qualified to command 100-ton vessels up to 200 miles off the coast, and he's licensed to tow most anything. Courtney, who lives on the Shady Side peninsula, teaches the many skills of finding your way upon the waters, including celestial navigation.

"Oh gosh," he says, "I've taught everybody, the experienced to the completely inexperienced. Most recently a very smart lady who bought a boat as if she were experienced but was very intimidated by docking." This is not me.

All this is why I'm calm, cool and collected—despite the 300 horses beneath that throttle.

ALWAYS, EASY DOES IT

If I had backed down or turned away too ambitiously, we could have been in a world of trouble, as others have been before me. Courtney has seen it happen again and again.

"Somebody not used to doing that kind of thing would have panicked when they saw that pulpit and maybe grabbed the controls and threw it into reverse and with the wheel swung that way, maybe the bow would have swung into it. That's where experience comes into play. The more you do it, the more you realize, 'I don't have to do this in nanoseconds; I've got enough time to think about it before I react.'"

Doing it the easy way, after a quick reverse out of the way, I turn the wheel toward the dock, shift into neutral, and let momentum and the current carry us gently in.

Doing it the wrong way would have been easier. Following my gut reaction, I'd have wrenched the wheel away from the dock and the extending pulpit that was too fast approaching.

Courtney explains: "It seems like you're following common sense to turn away. But if you do, the stern will swing right into it. Instead, you've got to do something contrary to common sense: Turn the wheel toward it and go ahead. Then the stern moves out but the bow doesn't move significantly, and it pivots you in."

That's the point when everybody breathes again. Like the captains of WomanShip, Courtney doesn't yell. Even so, he can't forego an occasional exhalation of relief as we tie up, safe at the dock, bow line first.

A FUELING CHALLENGE

One fear is down, but another awaits me. We're not here just for practice. If we were just practicing, we'd be better off in open water. That's where to go, Courtney advises, to get used to the controls. To practice, I'd steer some figure eights. I'd float a cushion or a Clorox bottle held in place on sinkers and practice coming close to it, then backing up and down to it to watch what the wind does.

But we're here for fuel, and on the screen of my mind I see the explosion, the ball of fire, the bodies and boat parts flung flaming into the ruptured serenity of Herrington Harbour marina.

To avoid such a fate, we turn on the blower and keep it huffing throughout fueling. On our Sea Ray, the gas intake is low where the heavy fumes will drop into the water, so we don't close the cabin and hatches as you would on a larger boat with a higher tank intake. Otherwise, filling the 58-gallon tank is pretty much like pumping self-service gas: Watch what you're doing, don't top off and keep the nozzle in good contact with the tank rim and channel to avoid a chance spark of static electricity.

Like filling up your car except that in a boat—even one like this, with an automatic spark extinguisher—it's a good idea to sniff around in the engine compartment before starting the engine. That wasn't so bad, I say flipping off the blower switch. Except I'm the one who's got to get us out of here. But not alone.

Over the years, Courtney has developed a great exit move.

"Turn the wheel hard left, cutting toward the dock," he says.

Now that I know the ways of sterns, I know that the lower unit or rudder will kick the stern out. In the dawning light, I understand that I'm backing out.

"If you kick the stern out, you'll clear the dock," advises Courtney. "Then put it in reverse, straighten the wheel and back straight off." All you've got to do then is go forward onto your course.

"I showed that to a guy over at Tilghman Island at the oyster house. He thought I was showing off. No, I said, there's nothing to it," Courtney related. Once again, nice and easy does it.

UNDERWAY

Out of the channel—cruising at 1,000 rpms—well below the marked speed of 6 miles per hour—I'm reviving my faded knowledge of navigational aids with page vii of Courtney's Maryland Cruising Guide open on the dash. This channel is narrow, but it's hard to make a mistake.

"Red right returning" doesn't apply on the way out; that easy mnemonic guides you into port, not out. So I'm keeping the square green day markers on starboard, my right, motoring tight between red and green to keep to the dredged channel and heading for Rosehaven No. 1. It's just outside the one-fathom curve; inside is all tinted blue in the chart book to remind you that those waters are shallower than 6 feet. The numbers are feet at mean lower water. Use a tide table to find the day's highs and lows, so you can adjust with the water.

"You're always vulnerable when you're in the blue," says Courtney, pointing out on the chart the many wrecks at the bottom of Herring Bay. You see them as little footballs, their stitches the bones of the ship. One of them is the *Levin J Marvel*, whose sad fate I remember from a story I commissioned, and I'm drifting into a reverie about how many tragedies are buried in the mud of a well-traveled waterway.

Drifting, when Courtney reminds me this is no place to drift.

"One of a captain's responsibilities is to keep an effective look-out, which means looking around and not being distracted, which is one of the main causes of collisions," he says, and I see what he means. I'm on a near collision course with a sailboat. Whoops.

"You're on a collision course when you can see a vessel ahead or nearly ahead. When you're meeting head on, the rule is to turn to starboard and pass port to port," says Courtney, still cucumber cool.

"That's a one-whistle call, meaning you'd give him one short blast on the horn and he'd return the same signal in obscured conditions or at night."

But as I look starboard before pulling wide of the sailboat so we can safely pass port to port, I see a powerboat overtaking. Fast.

What do I do now? I want a simple answer, but we're in a give-a-woman-a-fish-or-teach-her-to-fish situation. Courtney is going to teach me to fish or, in this case, avoid collisions by knowing the rules of the water.

"If this were a situation at night," Courtney continues, "he'd have to pick up your sidelight, which is visible from dead ahead to 112.5 degrees, which is your arc of visibility. On the starboard side, where he's coming, your running light is green."

The sailboat's safe, but the other boat's bearing down on us from behind. My palms are sweating, but Courtney, somehow, is calm.

"Here's a good way to use that light to remember what to do. If a boat approaches on your starboard bow, he's going to see a green light, which means, to him, go ahead, as any green light does. So he's the stand-on vessel, obligated to hold course and speed, while you're the give-way vessel, obligated to change course or speed—and you've got to do that noticeably—and let him pass.

"On the other hand, if somebody's approaching on your port bow, he's going to see a red light, which means stop. Then you're the stand-on vessel and they're the give-way vessel and they have to give way to you. Your responsibility then is to hold course and not converge on his course, while he has to give away to you.

"You have to hold course and speed unless it's apparent to you that he's not going to take any action; then you're required to take an action."

This is what I'm thinking is about to happen while Courtney finishes this lesson.

"The arc of visibility from port and starboard lights combined is 225 degrees. Your masthead light is 225 degrees and your stern light is 135 degrees, so you've got 360 degrees of possible white light, and then you've got the side lights, the running lights, so you can see the aspect of the vessel."

As he speaks, the big, fast powerboat plows ahead of us and cuts across our bow. His wake comes rolling our way, and we're bobbing like a cork.

"Just hang on as we take the waves," says Courtney. "You don't need to be up on a plane. We can do a nice cruise at 1,500rpm."

ASEA, POINT A TO POINT B

By now, moving slowly, we've reached Herring Bay No. 1, a flashing green light from which we can take our bearings. From here, all of Chesapeake Bay—the wide world beyond too—is our oyster.

To cross the 10 miles or so to Tilghman Island, I'd follow an easterly course of 089 until I came to green No. 83, in 56 feet of water right at the edge of the shipping channel. On that trip, I take along my book from Cornell Maritime Press, *How to Avoid Huge Ships*.

If I'm out at night, Courtney reminds, I'd better know how to read navigational lights.

"When you know what to look for out there at night, you can pick up a ship's lights instantly. But get somebody with limited or no experience on water at night, they don't know what they're looking at or how to interpret it, and they can have mishaps, like people running under the hulls of barges. The barges can be doing 15 or 20 knots and it doesn't look like they're going anywhere. Or, perhaps, the ship's lights are so high, you don't know they're there. It can be highly dangerous."

Oh my goodness.

Do I really need to go all the way to the channel markers?

"No," says Courtney, "but you need to know the waters. I know a lot of people operate by local knowledge; they've found all the sandbars just by running aground on them. A Natural Resources Police captain remarked to me once you could plant corn in the rows his mate had plowed up by running aground. He's the same guy who ran up on Sandy Point jetty about six in the morning, then slithered down the jetty and jammed the lower unit of the outboard into the rocks. If it had been a little faster, it would have been like something out of a James Bond movie; he'd have flown right over it.

"People say, 'how can we be aground with all this water out here, and way far offshore.' Well, that happens. Along this whole shoreline, going north from Deale, be very careful. It's easy to run off shore. Especially in winter when you could have a Nor'easter going, you could be aground a mile or two from shore."

You could even encounter that treacherous Deale jetty.

NOT YET HOME FREE

We've had a safe trip, one for me as full of challenges as Odysseus' voyage. But the biggest of all is waiting for me back home: how do I get this boat back in the slip which, in the wind and current, is like backing into a moving driveway from a shifting street.

I know that I've got to put the boat back in the slip, which can be an adventure. Courtney has stories for every situation, but none of them top his docking stories.

"Backing in. I think it's some macho thing," says Courtney, illustrating his point with a story.

"A captain I know, a superb boater, one of the best, tied up at Sandy Point next to my patrol boat. 'I take these scientists out,' he told me. 'I work with Loran and precision positioning so they can set the current meters and maintain stations, and they don't say a word about that. But when I go back and back in the slip, they're all looking at each other, saying 'oh wow!'"

Couldn't I just slide the vessel in bow first?

"Some people prefer to have the bow in because of privacy," Courtney answers. "Some places, like up in Spa Creek, They dock bow first because they don't have enough water to put in stern first. But the best reason is that it's easier to back out than back in."

Now, I'm really impressed. But I know my husband won't be. I've got to get this boat in stern first, like he does and most people do on our dock. Courtney is going to teach me.

"I've seen people just throttle-jockey boats," he says. "That's not my style, 'cause I know what happens if your engines dies.

"One of the top-notch boat handlers I know used to back into the police boat next to me at City Dock. He'd round up way out in the harbor and start backing; he'd send this wave up on the transom he was backing so fast. Then at the last minute, he'd gun it ahead and stop short.

"I said to him, 'Jimmy, one of these days you're going to go ahead and the engine is going to die and you're going to be parked up there at an expired parking meter and get a ticket.' Well, it happened."

Thinking of Jimmy's fate, tearing his boat up and nearly sinking it in the slip with many people watching, I know throttle-jockeying is not for me. I'm really glad that, once more, we're going to take it easy.

"When you're approaching a close-quarters situation like slipping in a marina, one of the things I do myself is put the boat in neutral, maybe back down a little bit and kill all the wake in the water to watch what the wind and current is doing. Sometimes in the confines of a marina, you see something, maybe a current, entirely different, and you want to know which way the boat is going to move. Work with things like that rather than against it," says Courtney.

And somehow, nice and slowly, with considerable advancing and retreating, we slip right in.

Editor's Note: This piece won first place in the category of Sports Writing in the 1998 Maryland-Delaware-District of Columbia editorial awards competition.

For Bay Fever, The Cure Can Be Costly

There's another kind of pandemic out there that's hard to avoid.

I must down to the seas again, to the lonely sea and the sky,
And all I ask is a tall ship and a star to steer her by...
—Sea-Fever, John Masefield
English Poet Laureate
1930–1967

It begins with an itch. Soon the symptoms diversify: unfocused stare; distraction; restlessness. In Chesapeake Country, there's but one cure for Bay Fever. Get a boat.

When it comes to what kind of boat, cures diverge. Fishing, sailing, cruising, speeding, weekending, paddling, yachting, wind-surfing, styling, traveling, live-aboard, work-aboard. For every purpose on the water, for every season on the water, there is a craft.

This time of year, boats for all those purposes are splashing. Scan the Bay at winter's end, north and south and all the way to the horizon, you may see not a single boat. From January till the end of April, Bay traffic is light and specialized: Baybuilts for winter-working watermen, harvesting oysters; big freighters and container ships; work barges; frosty sailboats; and perhaps a kayak seizing the day.

Come the last week in April, the gap between sufferers of Bay Fever and their cure is as big as the distance between their boat and the water.

Wait: there goes one cure now, a big Grady White fishing boat on its trailer rushing back to the water. It's happening everywhere, this great annual return to Chesapeake Bay of the fleet that accounts for much of pleasure boating's $2.4 billion boost to Maryland's economy.

I must down to the seas again,
for the call of the running tide
is a wild call and a clear call
that may not be denied.

Maryland is home to some 210,000 boats, and many have spent their winter off the water. The exceptions are typically three: Wooden boats stay in the water because their planking might dry and separate out of the water. Daring fiberglass boat owners—often sailors or live-aboards—may challenge winter, often keeping ice away with a bubbler. Full-time watermen fish or oyster all winter long, then switch their catch to crabs or perhaps captaining charter fishing from spring through November.

"I just wash and polish it," says Maryland Watermen's Association president Larry Simns of the transformation of his *Dawn II* to a charter boat.

Many fair-weather boats live at home. Kayaks and canoes spend much of their time on boat racks, beaches or garages. Off water, lots of jet skis, wave runners, runabouts and fishing boats live on trailers.

Boats on trailers can get back in the water any day their owner is man or woman enough to bear weather and waves. Plenty of sailors and windsurfers rush out to catch a strong breeze on promising winter days, but typically anybody so driven is a fisherman or fisherwoman, commercial or pleasure. If you read Dennis Doyle's The Sporting Life in *Bay Weekly*, you know winter doesn't long divide from the water an obsessed fisherman with a boat on a trailer.

Tens of thousands of boats abandon the water to winter at marinas. They stand on the hard, in the picturesque parlance of boaters. A privileged few boats live under cover, in boat sheds or boatels. A boatel, one of the curiosities of the industry, is boat storage gone high-rise, where boats are lifted as far as four stories to berth in cubicles one above the other.

Last fall all those boats rose out of the water, by boat lift (a gantry on big tires that scoots belly bands under a boat), crane or marine railway. Before hibernation, boats were winterized and inspected. A boat on the hard rests on blocks or jacks. For protection from winter, many are shrink-wrapped in plastic, sealed with a blow dryer. Spring reverses the work of winter.

Now all that shrink-wrap is coming off, piling up in billows and challenging the marine trades industry with finding new ways of recycling. Shrink-wrapping is one of some 27,500 marine jobs in the state supported by boating. In April, all of them are in demand as boat yards buzz like beehives. Any day the weather is tolerable, do-it-yourself owners—like Capt. Paul O'Conner of the charter boat *Bay Hog*, who worked through March and early April on the hard at Gates Marina in Deale—park by their boats and go to work, scrubbing, scraping, polishing, repairing.

Visit a marina or yacht yard, and you'll see plenty of DC and Virginia license plates as absentee owners drive down to the water to scratch their case of Bay Fever with a few hours of work on boats small or large. Boats are notoriously fussy, and anyone visited by a mechanic will have a long list of repairs, along with dewinterizing.

Bottoms must be painted, but first comes the laborious job of scraping, power washing or sand-blasting (and, nowadays, baking soda-blasting.) It's a tougher job still now that we're thinking about how our messes spoil the environment, for it's got to be done under-cover—at least in Green Marinas, which are encouraged and certi-fied by the state.

Then comes the bottom paint, a toxic, anti-fouling coating that can cost more than $100 a gallon. With so much toxic work to do, careful workers dress up in suits and ventilating masks.

Finally, a boat needs washing and polishing. Now, the weeks of labor in the driveway or at the boatyard are paying off. The weather is finally warming.

Now only days—maybe even hours—stand between all those boats and the big splash.

And all I ask is a windy day
with the white clouds flying,
And the flung spray and the blown spume,
and the sea-gulls crying.

TROPHY TIME

Last week was the big launch of the first fleet of spring. Striped bass (aka rockfish) season opened April 21, and that regulated and highly anticipated event is the Easter of Bay fishers. It is their resurrection. Even Gov. Martin O'Malley hailed it.

"The weather forecast for opening day and the following week is nearly perfect," O'Malley trumpeted. "That, coupled with the robust numbers of large rockfish currently in the Chesapeake, should make conditions ideal for anglers and their families to enjoy a day on the Bay."

Through April, Maryland's 400-boat charter fishing fleet returned to the water in preparation for the big day.

"The last week, I've been putting in 18-hour days," said Glenn James on Opening Day Eve.

Past president of the Maryland Charterboat Association, James captains the 55-foot *Bounty Hunter*, the largest charter boat on the Bay, out of Rod 'n' Reel in Chesapeake Beach.

"On our boat," James continues, "we pick a project every year. This was the year to redo the interior—remodeling, paint, carpet, sinks, countertops—and like most boat projects, it grew."

With over 100 charter boats, Calvert ports more than any other county in Maryland, with the big marinas at Chesapeake Beach and Solomons and something smaller at Breezy Point. Anne Arundel County is home to more than 70 charters, with a handful in Annapolis, a few as far north as Pasadena, others in South County and a big fleet at Happy Harbor in Deale.

At all those marinas and piers, captains and mates have lately been scratching a near-intolerable itch by polishing and primping their boats. Sportsfishermen who fish on their own are just as avid. A few, like *Bay Weekly* columnist Dennis Doyle and his charter captain buddy Frank Tuma, of *Down Time* out of Breezy Point, practiced by hooking rockfish that must be released.

Then the Big Day was April 21, when the Trophy Rockfish season opened. "The whole charter fleet was out, along with the recreation fleet. It was boats as far as you could see; you could not turn around," said the Waterman's Association's Larry Simns of the season's opening.

That day let long-fasting Maryland anglers loose on mammoth fish that have returned from ocean life to spawn in the Bay. Rockfish responded to their own Bay Fever much earlier in the year; the late opening and ban on rockfishing in tributaries leaves most fish undisturbed until after they've spawned.

"It's going to be good," said James on the eve of the season's opening. "There are plenty of fish out there."

James and Simns agree that catching thus far has been hard work with April's cold, wet weather slowing the movement of big fish out of the tributaries into the Bay. Regardless of how well nature provides, this year's catch must be only half of last year's.

Over the past two years, the fishing was way too good. Protecting the precious species—on which Maryland's commercial and recreational fisheries depend—is a region-wide obligation, shouldered by the Atlantic States Marine Fisheries Commission. Maryland exceeded its quota in 2005 and 2006. This year's trophy season is limited to 30,000—half of last year's big fish quota of 60,000—and roughly the number of fish overcaught in Maryland in both '06 and '05.

This year from April 21 to May 15, the big-fish season, each angler is allowed to keep one legal fish per day. Legal fish measure 28 to 35 inches and 41 inches or more. Fish under 28 inches and between 35 and 41 inches must be released promptly.

Fifty-thousand of Maryland's 165,000 powerboats registered in 2007 are licensed for fishing. Even the National Marine Manufacturers Association can't say how many companies make fishing boats, but they range from john boats to, for example, a $440,000 36-foot Grady White Express, the boat Tri-State Marine salesman Robert Warren calls the "Mercedes Benz that floats in the water."

The fish are back, and all the owners of those boats have bad cases of Bay Fever.

I must down to the seas again,
to the vagrant gypsy life,
To the gull's way and the whale's way
where the wind's like a whetted knife.

A TUG RIGHT OUT OF A CHILDREN'S BOOK

The power fleet now returning to the water satisfies more kinds of fever than fish. Whether your fever burns for inflatables, personal watercraft, ski and wake-board inboards, cruisers, jet boats, pontoon boats, motor yachts or houseboats—you can likely find its cure at the Bay Bridge Boat Show, from April 26 to 28.

Five hundred boats from 132 manufacturers surround Stevensville's Bay Bridge Marina by land and water at this spring-cousin to October's famous US Sail and Power Boat Shows. About half the boats are new, and about half brokerage boats on second or third sale. Buy any of them, and you can get your boat in the water by May.

Boats range from the 20-foot Jet Dock to the 70-foot Marquis 65. Along with industry standards like Sea Ray and Silverton, Bayliner and Boston Whaler are custom crafts, among them boatwright Joe Reed's Thomas Point 40, built at Mast and Mallet in Edgewater. Few are sailboats.

Among them may be your dreamboat, the Chesapeake Classic Hooper Island Draketail; a Nordic tug that looks like it cruised out of a kids' book; a downeast Albin, Back Cove, Legacy or Sabre; a high-style European Apreamare; an elegantly pricey Hinckley; a rough and ready Boston Whaler.

Annapolis calls itself America's Sailing Capital, so the big surprise in boat registrations as reported to the U.S. Coast Guard by the Maryland Department of Natural Resources is the disparity between sail and power boats—at least statewide. Sailboats number only about 13,000 with powerboats more than 12 times more numerous—not counting about 19,000 personal watercraft.

You wouldn't think so looking at white sails speckling the Bay on a breezy day or counting the masts that tower over your marina. At two of Chesapeake Country's biggest marinas, Herrington Harbour North in Tracys Landing (where we keep our Albin 28, *Bay Weekly*), and Herrington Harbour South, in Rose Haven, sailboats dominate, about 60 to 40 percent, according to co-owner Hamilton Chaney.

Visit the yards of those marinas now, as boats return to the water—or cruise their docks in a month or so—and you'll see the diversity of the Bay's fleet under sail. Here and nationally, Beneteau, Hunter and Catalina are the popular leaders, but every second or third boat offers an exceptional eyeful.

To see the variety of boats under sail all in one place, however, you'll have to wait until the first week in October, when the US Sailboat Show returns to Annapolis, from the fourth thru the eighth, for the thirty-eighth year, bringing 250 sailboats to town.

"Any boat currently marketed by a foreign or domestic manufacturer in representation in the U.S. is in the Annapolis Boat Show. It has to be," says show general manager Jim Barthold. "The Annapolis show is the mecca for sailboat enthusiasts. It's the one show you have to go to if you're serious about looking for new boats and before you make a buying decision. You haven't finished the process until you see what else is there, and the only place is Annapolis."

If you haven't caught Bay Fever yet, boat shows are the place it's most contagious. If you're already infected, a boat show's where you're likely to cure it.

Sandra Olivetti Martin

*And all I ask is a merry yarn
from a laughing fellow-rover
And quiet sleep and a sweet dream
when the long trick's over.*

THE DRIVE TO GET WELL

Or you might find, as my captain and I have, that your fever takes a cure that's not on even these well-stocked shelves.

It's not that he and I are seeking two different boats. Our problem, as we search for our third powerboat, is that our combined tastes have diverged from production manufacturing.

Earlier boats were love at first sight. Back in 1985, when we bought our first, we'd just moved to the Bay. Like the guy who's fallen off the turnip truck, Capt. Bill bought the first boat he saw—a 28-foot cruiser of lesser reputation with a sharp design and roomy (and furry) cabin.

Looking back, it wasn't his fault; it was entrapment. First, he was a landlocked Midwesterner and a devout fisherman born under the water sign of Cancer. Second, the seller hailed from the town where we'd lived the last decade, Springfield, Illinois. And miraculously on his first trip out, Bill, known in part for his Flummoxed Fisherman columns, caught a trophy bluefish that topped 17 pounds. (He'd say: "The fish was so big that the picture of it weighed three pounds.") The boat lived long enough to disprove its name, *Reliable Source* (borrowed from a sassy, so-named *Washington Post* column), and to persuade us that the seller had help from lesser fish gods in hooking Bill up with that fish.

Our second, a neat little Sea Ray adorned in red, which berthed at Flag Harbor Marina in Calvert County, hooked us just about as easily. *New Bay Times* served us as well as any boat can for a decade. We'd been admiring its ilk for ages before we acted, which is easy. Not only are Sea Rays good looking, they're everywhere—forty models in sizes from 18 to 68 feet, last I looked.

228

This particular year and model, a Sundancer, is fishable, livable and big for its small size. In 23 feet, it's got V-berth and mid-berth, head and galley, two showers and nearly ample stowage. So when we contracted a new case of Boat Fever, we started looking at Sea Rays at boat shows and at Clark's Sea Ray dealerships nearby, one in Shady Side and one in Stevensville.

What we found was that Sea Rays—and others common in our midst, Cris Craft, Bayliner, Magnum—had changed starting in the 1990s.

Herrington Harbour's Chaney says boats are growing "longer, wider and more sophisticated, just like houses and cars. They're more technologically advanced, and owners require more: power, phone, all the services right at the slip."

They're slicker, as well. Sleek on the outside as high-end athletic shoes; sleek on the inside as floating plastic palaces. At under 30 feet, there's no place to put much of anything, and you sure wouldn't bring fishing poles stained with blood and guts into a cabin upholstered in puffy white satin. Even Sea Ray's Amberjack, a total fishing boat, couldn't seem to bridge the gap back to where we wanted to be.

So we've been haunting boat shows. By car and boat, we sightsee through boatyards and docks. We read *Soundings* avidly. We scour the Internet. We regularly find the right boat—Sabres, Back Coves, Legacys—at the wrong price.

> *And the wheel's kick and the wind's song*
> *and the white sail's shaking,*
> *And a grey mist on the sea's face,*
> *and a grey dawn breaking.*

SMITTEN

"When we listed it last fall, it sat," said boat broker Rob Begor. "Now it's spring, and people are calling. You're the second one this week to call about that boat."

I was falling in love, so the news of a rival fanned my ardor for the boat we were touring. Unexpectedly, this Albin 28 Tournament Express was looking more and more like my dreamboat. From obstruction, the raised engine box amidships had become an attraction, both a seat and a support for a custom-crafted picnic table. Until the picnic called the table forth, it folded cleverly up against the starboard hull, under cover. On port, three fishing rods would rack, horizontally. Aft were so many built-in fish boxes that some could be converted to storage.

But this was no single-minded fishing boat. It was one of a rare breed, customized right where I was seeing it, at Oxford Yacht Yard. This downeast boat, made in Rhode Island, had a local history, a quality I crave as much as stowage. New, this very boat was sea-trialed and reviewed by Jeff Holland for *Chesapeake Bay Magazine*.

It fills the bill, I see, when following the advice of *Soundings'* How to Buy a New or Used Boat, I've converted my boating requirements into a mission statement:

> *When I'm not at work in boating weather, I want to be on my boat. So it needs to be home and office as well as a fishing boat, cruiser, picnic and pleasure boat. It needs to look like a boat, not a bordello, and it needs to wash down well and clean up easily. All that plus diesel, GPS, a chart table, screens and well-railed sides I can walk around to the bow.*

Be still my beating heart. Yes, Bay Fever feels a lot like love.

MD 8242 BL

Never, Never, Never Give Up

Bernie's Big Day

You just wade out in the river,
give it all you got
Right up to your chest.
And then you pick your spot.

—Tom Wisner's "Bernie Fowler Day:
A Guide to Wading in the Southern Maryland Waters"

Back in 1988, a state senator donned coveralls, a broad-brimmed straw hat and a pair of white sneakers. Thus clothed, he walked into the Patuxent River. Now, Bernie Fowler has the most famous feet in Maryland.

They could have called him a madman. Instead, they called him a visionary. His wade-in has gained attention far and wide as the clearest measure of the health of Chesapeake Bay.

In 1990, The University of Maryland's Center for Environmental Studies honored him with its first Truitt Environmental Award. In 1993, Tom Horton introduced *National Geographic* readers to Bernie in his cover story on the Chesapeake. In 1994, the Maryland General Assembly designated the traditional wade-in day, the second Sunday in June, as Bernie Fowler Day.

"It's a wonderful way to bring people together and increase and hold attention on water quality," said Kent Mountford, senior scientist at U.S. EPAs Bay Office, an observer of the lower Bay and Patuxent River for over twenty-eight years.

This year, as its anniversary rolls around, Bernie's sneaker test is spreading across Maryland, from the wide, southern Patuxent River to the whitewater of the upper Potomac River, from shallow, central Herring Bay to northerly Otter Point Creek at the Bush River in Harford County.

It's Bernie's measure!
It's simple—yet profound.
We got a treasure!
You can't buy it by the pound.

It's not hard to understand why Bernie's sneaker test caught on. Chesapeake Bay casts a spell over most everybody, newcomer or old-timer, touched by its waters, and people throughout the watershed have pitched in to bring their beloved waters back to good health. But recovery is typically measured in the equations of scientists and expressed in the language of bureaucrats, leaving even the best-intentioned Bay friends scratching their heads.

What Bernie's doing, everybody can understand.

Despite his thirty years in politics, Fowler has never lost touch with what Shakespeare's rival Ben Jonson called "the language men do speak."

Speaking of his beloved boyhood river as chairman of the Patuxent River Commission a couple of years ago, Fowler said "the Patuxent River is still the canary bird of the Chesapeake Bay."

By canary bird, he doesn't, young readers, mean the Patuxent is a pretty river. Coal miners used to carry caged canaries into the deep shafts where they dug for black gold. Those same seams could be full of deadly odorless gasses. If the canary died, the miners went running.

"If you can't clean her up," said Fowler, "you're in trouble."

'Cause I ask you what's the profit
If we gain these worldly things
And foul the air and water
And all the life that brings?

So when another plain-speaking friend, Tom Wisner, suggested a little wade to Bernie a decade ago, the senator did not say no. Wisner recorded their walk in a poem called "Bernie Fowler Day: A Guide to Wading in the Southern Maryland Waters." Since then, well, the rest is history.

Well—we should do this yearly
On Bernie Fowler Day.
Dress up fit to kill
And wade out all the way.

BEHOLDEN TO THE BAY

To understand what Bernie's doing, it's well to understand where he's coming from.

Sixty years ago, the young Fowler left the comforts of Calvert County and the Bay's southern shores first to live in Washington, DC, then to fight in World War II.

After the war, he returned home with a $4,000 GI Bill loan to start Bernie's Boats, a rowboat business on Broomes Island, with a pier and a snack bar.

"Back then, I was my own bait boy, clerk, everything," he says, revisiting a story he loves to tell. "Soda bottles—Pepsi, Coke and Nehi, all flavors—were refillable. At the end of each day, I'd stack them outside. One day, when I was doing this, I saw these two customers drive by in their station wagon.

"I waved but didn't pay much attention. As I finished, they parked the car. It wasn't until they approached me that I noticed their daughter, Betty Lou—about my age and the most beautiful thing I had ever laid my eyes on. It was almost love at first sight."

Bernie and Betty Lou have been together forty-eight years—and never far from the Bay or its great southern tributary, even after he retired from the Maryland Senate in 1994.

From all those years in close touch with land and water, Fowler developed his grassroots environmental consciousness. "Earth was put together with such finesse. Everything we needed was here. All the beautiful resources of the world were here. To allow somebody for selfish reasons to destroy those assets is unconscionable," says the politician who speaks from his heart.

INCHING TO CLARITY

In the 1950s, Bernie—standing 6 feet—could walk chest deep into the Patuxent and see crabs swimming by. Visibility, he figured, was a good 63 inches. "It was crystal clear in the '50s," he said. "When I was a young adult, I could wade out there and chase the crabs."

In 1966, he looked down into the water for crabs and came up dry. That's how Fowler knew when the Bay and the Patuxent started taking a turn for the worse.

> *All the politicians gathered.*
> *They'd come from miles around*
> *To talk about the river*
> *That flows by Solomons town.*
> *Seems they had a problem*
> *Things were looking bad.*
> *They'd looked at all resources*
> *And used everything they had.*

By 1970, Fowler was campaigning for a seat as a Calvert County commissioner on a promise to clean up the Patuxent, which he then called one of the most polluted rivers on the East Coast. Upriver sewage treatment plants, discharging what later came to be referred to as "point-source pollution" were the heart of the problem. "Up until 1987 or '88, it was gross," Fowler recalled.

Fowler joined a lawsuit filed by Charles, Calvert and St. Mary's counties, eventually forcing the state of Maryland and the U.S. Environmental Protection Agency to live up to the Clean Water Act.

> *"If you can't see your cloppers*
> *There'll be trouble in this town*
> *We oughta sue those upper counties*
> *For the junk they're sending down."*

Then, in 1974, Fowler helped organize 400 community volunteers to write Calvert County's first plan to improve the environment. But the Patuxent wasn't getting much cleaner.

In 1988, Bernie and his friend Tom Wisner waded right into the heart of the problem.

> *It came 'round to Bernie Fowler*
> *And he stood among the best.*
> *He said, "folks, if you'll bear with me,*
> *I think I got a test.*

At that first wade-in, visibility was down to 10 inches. By 1989, the second year of Fowler's sneaker test, the water was so murky he could see only 8 inches down.

In 1992, all the attention focused on Chesapeake Bay seemed to be turning the tide. Visibility had crept up to 18 inches.

In 1993, when *New Bay Times'* first joined the wade-in, thirty people linked hands on the beach at Broomes Island and walked into the water. That year, Fowler—joined by Wisner, the diminutive U.S. Sen. Barbara Mikulski and, as usual, Betty Brady's fifth-grade class from Hollywood, Maryland—could spot a glimmer of his white tennis shoes while water lapped around his thighs.

In the cool, mushy sand, aquatic grass waved. A walker bent down to pluck a piece and give it to Fowler, who held it aloft triumphantly.

"The grass that the old red-headed ducks feed on is coming back," he said. "The year before last when we saw that, that's the first that we'd seen in over twenty-five years. We're beginning to see signs of it coming back. That's very encouraging. Aquatic species like that, you can use as a measure that is a little more effective than me looking at my feet."

The senator was pleased but cautious.

"We've still got a long way to go," he said. "Today is not a day to say we've won our battle."

In 1994, joining Bernie was Sen. 'American Joe' Miedusiewski. As well as wading, the two were running for the Democratic Party's nomination to lead Maryland, 'American Joe' as governor, Bernie as lieutenant governor.

"Sunday was a good day for a wade-in, bright and sunny. But not for good results," said Fowler. "A Southeaster Saturday night stirred the water up. We couldn't see below our knees." Official visibility was 28 inches.

> *"I think I have a measure*
> *That can't be beat*
> *You just wade out in the river*
> *And look down to see your feet."*

Peering down through the brown waters of the Patuxent River at his white sneakers in 1995, Bernie Fowler saw 12 more inches of long legs. In that watermark year, visibility rose to 40 inches.

Visibility was down a couple of inches in 1996, likely because of waves or water turbulence, but participation was up. Close to 100 joined hands and walked off the sandy beach into the water, keeping watch on their toes.

"Forty-four and a half inches." With those words, U.S. EPA Administrator Carol Browner announced the results of 1997's Bernie Fowler Day.

"That's a 20 percent improvement," said U.S. Rep. Steny Hoyer, a wade-in mainstay over the years, as he lifted the tape measurer up to Fowler's water-stained indigo overalls. In the crowd of nearly 200 people, about seventy-five waded into the lukewarm water.

In addition to Hoyer and Browner, Maryland Senate President Thomas V. 'Mike' Miller showed up—although he remained dry in suit and tie, begging out due to dress-up commitments. Wading in alongside Fowler were Maryland Comptroller Louis Goldstein and Maryland Secretary of the Environment Jane Nishida, as well as state representatives from both Calvert and St. Mary's counties.

Political heavy-hitters regularly join hands with Fowler to wade in, but 1997 may have marked a political watershed. "We had a power base here that is probably the largest we've ever had," Fowler said.

GETTING TO THE BOTTOM OF THE PROBLEM

What's beneath 44.5 inches of clear water?

Bernie Fowler doesn't pretend to be a scientist, but he can make the forces behind the turn-around pretty clear. Here's what the 74-four-year-old wader told me last week:

"In the last decade, visibility has increased from 10 inches to 44.5 inches. That represents a tremendous improvement, starting with sewage treatment plants. Most have now been retrofitted, taking nitrogen and phosphorus down to acceptable levels. That's the major reason."

Nitrogen and phosphorus—harmful nutrients in heavy concentrations—presently are the principal causes of Chesapeake Bay ills. They end up in the Bay from faulty septics, chemical fertilizers and the vast quantities of chicken manure from Eastern Shore poultry houses that farmers there spread far too heavily on croplands.

The nutrient pollution fertilizes huge alga crops that devour oxygen, curtain the sun and choke out other Bay life.

In keeping the Chesapeake Bay Agreement of 1984—the great compact to bring back the Bay signed by Maryland, Virginia, Pennsylvania, the District of Columbia and the federal government—Maryland pledged to reduce nutrients reaching the Bay by 30 percent between 1985 and 2000.

Fowler credits farmers for turning to so-called best management practices. Finally, Fowler said, environmental awareness has spread throughout Chesapeake Country.

"We've been able to bring into play school children throughout the state who can talk about water quality and environmental language and go home and tell their parents," he said.

"A more educated public knows it's an unpardonable sin to allow pollution to the Bay and its tributaries or contribute to its demise, and they're thinking of that when they fertilize their lawns or change the oil in their cars."

Fowler adds: "The Chesapeake is Maryland's heart. If we lose the Bay, the heart stops beating."

Next you take your peepers
And cast them slowly down
On the day we see our feet again
There'll be celebration in this town.

The Amputees' Picnic

Everybody cheers at shared good news,
but not everybody claps.
Not everyone has hands.

"The night of September 27–28 is my one-year anniversary," says the pretty girl, long brown hair swinging, who walks to the stage a little stiffly, with the help of a crutch. "I got in a car accident with one of my oldest friends." Of course, as every Marylander remembers with shivers, it wasn't the car accident that crippled 19-year-old Jordan Wells, of Waldorf. Wells could have walked away from that accident, achingly, but on two good legs—instead of one leg and one prosthesis.

It was the crash of Trooper 2 that crushed her body and, days later, took her right leg. The Maryland State Police medevac helicopter fell from the sky in rain and fog while flying Wells and her friend, Ashley Younger, to Prince George's Hospital Center. That crash killed four people: Younger, pilot Stephen Bunker, state police EMT Mickey Lippy and local EMT Tonya Mallard.

"I was the only one who survived," Wells says.

"I was thrown out the roof, but my legs were still pinned inside. I was found two hours later, hypothermic, with my back broken in six places, one side of my face crushed," she said, her fingers tracing her restructured eye socket.

"All the bones in my legs were broken below the knee—and my feet were just hanging on. I prayed to Jesus and cried out for help. Then, finally, I heard somebody in the woods."

This September picnic is not the first time Jordan Wells has told her story of that night just a year ago—and its aftermath. She's told it to family and friends, including the kids at her old high school;

to the Maryland General Assembly, in hopes of strengthening Maryland's Medevac procedures; and to the vast, anonymous audiences of ABC's Good Morning America and 20/20.

But she may never have had a more empathetic audience than here in the barn at Jefferson Patterson Park in southern Calvert County, where a group called Amputees Helping Amputees has just tamped down with slices of carrot and coconut cake a feast of barbecued ribs, pulled pork and hot dogs, all cooked on the spot by Randy's Ribs of Hughesville.

Here, when Jordan finishes, everybody cheers. But not everybody claps. Not everyone has hands. Eleven-year-old Dayton Webber, also of Charles County, lost his hands and lower arms, his feet and his legs to a terrible streptococcal infection that struck when he was 10 months old. But Dayton has running legs that put a bounce in his step. The Flex-Run legs are a match for his energy. "They're good for getting around, and they're fun," he says.

"Running legs are the way to go for an 11-year-old boy. There's not much walking," says his mother, Natalie Webber. "But he's just as able without his running legs."

"I play football and wrestle," he says.

On the blade-like extensions that attach by suction to Dayton's legs, he also runs track and rides skateboards.

Without any prosthesis, Dayton's done what any kid would at a picnic: tossed and caught a football with his father; moonbounced in an inflated chamber; eaten a hotdog and drunk a can of Pepsi for lunch; and then romped and rough-housed with friend James Culver, 10, of Lusby.

James, who lost two legs and an arm to a Strep Group A bacterial infection three years ago, came to the picnic with his new, 10-year-old-sized Segway. With it, says mother Cathy Culver, "he can keep up with kids on their bikes."

James isn't as talkative as Dayton, who's a natural at striking up conversations with strangers or speaking to a crowd. But James is generous, and soon Dayton, minus his running legs, is scooting through the park on James' Segway.

Ability is what the annual picnic of Amputees Helping Amputees is about. "You still move forward," says founder Scarlett Schall, an orthopedic nurse at Calvert Memorial Hospital who describes herself as "there when a lot of these folks got their lives back" through amputation.

"You can't say you can do whatever you want to do. But you try not to let that hinder you from doing anything."

Horrific as the stories are of these life-shattering bolts out of the blue, they are only prelude.

Last April, seven months after Jordan Wells's horror story began, she was able to bear her own weight and get her first prosthetic leg. A month later, she says, "I went to a gala and danced with three guys—the state policemen who rescued me."

To her great surprise, in two months, the sidetracked competitive swimmer "got in the water and won two gold medals and one silver" in the Paralympic Games in Arizona.

"And yesterday," she reports, "I started walking again after another surgery."

Triumphantly though Wells describes her "long—though not so long—recovery," no step is easy. "We share our stories to let you know that every day is not easy," says 47-year-old Wardell Swann of Hughesville, Md., a Paralympian and master of today's ceremonies.

At 38, Swann was a fitness fanatic. "I couldn't get enough," he says. A black belt martial artist with his own karate school, he was finishing five years of "physically and mentally strenuous" training to become a SMECO lineman. On the last day of class, February 24, 2000, Swann didn't feel well. The next day, he couldn't walk. Two months later, infection had stolen his legs and parts of nine fingers.

"We had no resources when he came home, " says Tammala Swann, Wardell's wife of seventeen years and mother of their two children, girls 14 and 10. "He had lost both legs. He had no use of his hands. I had to carry him."

Of his ordeal, Swann says, "When God takes so much, he gives you so much back."

Giving back is what Swann now does. He founded On Higher Ground to "share success through determination, education, motivation, support and hard work."

Thus Swann and his "sidekick" Dayton not only rushed to James' bedside in Children's Hospital. They got on the bed with the new amputee to "make him comfortable with who he was by making him comfortable with who he saw."

Who else could imagine the darkness surrounding a seven-year-old triple amputee whose twin sister has both her arms and legs?

Three years later, James' attitude is "so right," his mother says. He's learning Swann's message: "You can't say you can do whatever you want to do. But you try not to let that hinder you from doing anything."

A LITTLE HELP FROM THEIR FRIENDS

Technology helps. Prostheses and the people who invent, improve and fit them become, literally, the legs amputees stand on. Jordan Wells puts the prosthesis company Hanger next to God in helping her "every step of the way." Natalie Weber wants credit to go to

Annapolitan Dennis Haun, of Maryland Orthotics & Prosthetics, who fits her son Dayton with legs.

Today Dayton is giving thanks for another kind of technology, to another friend.

"One more thing," the 11-year-old says, taking the mike. "I just got a new bathroom installed by Greg Perez. It has a sink that's my size without my legs on, a shower with a head that goes up and down and a toilet that..." Dayton considers the right words "...does everything for you. It's also got a seat warmer. It's pretty cool."

My Haunted 'Hood

John's ghost lingers in the house where he died.

I live in a neighborhood of haunted houses. A couple are pretty scary: long uninhabited, running to run down, overrun by kudzu. Two or three more want to be mansions. Most are just ordinary houses, insofar as any house in this do-it-yourself village is ordinary.

Among our neighbors, ghouls, vampires and chainsaw murderers are poorly represented. We have recluses, and we have pirates. Over the years there's usually been a houseful of rowdy boys or young men. Two of them streaked through this year's annual hen-and-chick party, but they wore underwear (and masks).

Paths may be windy and dark, but most any house with its lights on will get trick-or-treaters on Halloween.

Lately, we have fewer. The ballerinas, witches and space travelers, as well as the streakers and other boys who seldom wore costumes, have grown up.

Mostly, we're just ordinary people, with the living spanning the political spectrum and the dead mostly beyond politics.

The dead? They seldom give up residence in our neighborhood. They continue among us as ghosts, haunting the houses where they once lived.

Where the rowdy boy-men live, grandparents Betty and Ed Becke haven't quite left. A couple houses up, Ed's mother Mrs. Beale hangs on amid the life of her granddaughter and husband. Another cousin moved with wife and toddler into grandparents' E.B. and Jean Smith's hauntings.

The Stewarts know Anne's mother is still around.

You don't have to be kin to see our ghosts. Even I, unrelated, still see shades of Sonia, Natalie, Myrtle and Henrietta. However the owner who followed Henrietta, who may have been a spook in real life, seems to have moved on.

Our latest ghost I don't think ever will. In life, John Lederer couldn't get enough of Fairhaven—nor enough done to finish his work here. In death, he seems to be carrying on.

I still see my next door neighbor's red Saab out of the corner of my eye. Still see his shadow passing through the house he couldn't bear to finish. Still hear his footfalls. Still wonder what project he's up to next.

John's next-to-last project was a tiny house.

I bring it up because the last one, went back with a curse to the drawing board. It never got restarted.

Death intervened, overcoming John by stealth like a colorless, odorless gas. Though his death was not by carbon monoxide, whatever killed John, in his undiminished prime at 69—heart attack, stroke or aneurysm—struck from within.

Struck and stole his breath away as he sat in his favorite chair, looking out his favorite window, down through the trees onto his beloved Chesapeake Bay.

What is John doing dead—when there was so much more in life for him to do?

The architect-builder and his occasional crew assembled the tiny house from construction remainders. They made it collapsible, able to be folded flat, strapped together and carried on a small trailer. Where John would carry it he said he didn't know. The last time I saw it, they'd given it a door as well as a doorway.

It was his playhouse, made from leftovers the way a pie maker makes a short cookie out of the trimmings of pie crust. It meant John was finished with the house remodeling projects that had occupied him since I moved in between the two small but not tiny houses he owned thirty-one years ago. Would have been finished had not wife Sheila—"the art director"—decreed that the understory must be completed.

Over thirty years ago the house, really a cottage, that occupied John was called Solace, so proclaimed by a now long-lost wood-burned sign on its shingle front.

Back then, John's house projects were mostly recreational. Skylights or refinished floors gave him a hobby and made the house more appealing for visits by wife Sheila Brady, daughter Michalea, and ancient black Lab, Reiver.

Their visits were sentimental journeys. Their cottage on our other side, then and for many years after rented, was the home to which they brought newborn Michalea. It was the house they'd bought and made fresh and livable, the house where all their dreams started.

By the time we became the Brady-Lederers' surrounded neighbor, the family had made their home in Arlington. Careers evolving, Michalea growing, they became who—and what—they are.

Husband, doting father, he became a development architect with Volunteers of America.

> *I'm a troubleshooter. I have to handle weird problems. It's always different. I work all across America, particularly troubled urban areas, Cincinnati, Chicago, Detroit, so we're part of that whole renaissance. Also rural areas: upstate New York, southern Louisiana and Puerto Rico. Our mission is to help those in most need. We acquire, build and maintain affordable housing.*

> *I travel all the time, but here are odd perks. I get met in the lobby of a senior development project by these 60-, 70-, 80-year-old people and get a big hug, and they say thank you. It's very rewarding.*

In the stories of friends, family and neighbors, John is a sailor, a thinker, a paddler, a reader. In him, one friend found a reincarnation of Tennyson's Ulysses:

I cannot rest from travel: I will drink
Life to the lees...
For always roaming with a hungry heart
Much have I seen and known; cities of men
And manners, climates, councils, governments,
Myself not least, but honour'd of them all.

In Fairhaven, on either side of me, John was the neighbor we couldn't set our clocks by, showing up now and again to sail an old catamaran in ripping wind. Or to start a visionary house remodeling project that might disintegrate before it was finished.

To one another, neighbors play a role simpler than real life; all those years side by side, we see only snippets.

Fifteen or so years ago, John's role in Fairhaven changed. Evicting his renters, he set more or less steadily to renovating both houses—at once. His first step was two copper roofs, the downpayment on his artistry to come. Then, importing his carpenter brother from Prescott, Arizona, he started on a third just up the hill.

This was building from scratch, requiring two wells, three septic systems and the best bio-digestive technology the flush tax had created—and permits, permits, permits.

Slowly and idiosyncratically and with some neighborhood consternation, John more or less finished—and rented—two of the houses, little gems that might happily have been cabins in a Scandinavian woods.

But the third house, the house of the family's earliest days, he could not, would not—no matter what the family or financial pressure—did not finish.

I called him our Penelope, after Ulysses' wife who wove all day, then ripped out her work at night so that the work in hand might never be finished.

That's the house where John died. That's the house he now haunts, on a schedule on which I can never set my clock.

Is John really there? Or is his haunting my imagination? Did Poe's murderer hear his victim's tell tale heart—or his own?

On that question humanity—if not science—is deeply ambivalent. We've made Halloween into an all-age costume party, celebrating it all the more fervently. We don't know what's in the darkness. But we know the darkness is there.

Solemnization

Of the Marriage of
Ariel Martinez Brumbaugh and Patrick Beale

Family, friends and neighbors...

Ariel and Patrick have chosen each other.

They have been magnetized by the inexplicable, inescapable force that draws two people out of their own history and sticks them together as one couple.

Magnetism is a wonderful energy: It binds two as one without changing either. Ariel with Pat is still Ariel: dauntless, daring, bubbling with effervescent spirits, quick spoken, sure she can do just about anything. Pat with Ariel is still Pat: succinct, watchful, celebratory, acting in his own time—though with an occasional fast-forward nudge from Ariel.

That's all in keeping with another truth of the physics of magnets: unlike poles attract each other and like poles repel each other.

These two unlike poles drew into one another's energy fields at bonfires where Ariel and Patrick found each other's energy warmer than the fire.

That was 2006, a summer Ariel decided "would be a really good summer to fall in love." They were 20.

Five months later, Ariel left Patrick half a world behind for her junior year in Australia. All the friends she went with were breaking up to be single in Australia. Pat and Ariel tried to, too but the magnetism was too strong.

Editor's note: In 2018 Sandra became an ordained minister in the Universal Life Church. She wrote this ceremony performed along the coast in Friendship, Maine at the wedding of Ariel Martinez Brumbaugh and Patrick Beale.

In five or six months, they figured out a way for him to visit.

"You're never going to let him go, are you?" a friend asked.

Ariel said, "No, I don't think I am."

In 2008, they moved in together. In 2015, they bought a house together and tested each other's resilience over years of remodeling. Through those years, they've lost and found jobs together. In 2016, they bought a dog together, Tavi the black Lab.

Finally, they decided they knew each other well enough, and liked each other well enough, to get married.

"Over twelve years, our relationship has deepened and changed, ebbed and flowed," says Ariel, the couple's wordy partner. I've always wanted that change, that adventure, that exploration to be with Pat."

"I knew that three years before he knew it and two years before he proposed," she says.

Finally, with a little nudging, he proposed. She is, after all, the person he wants most in all this world to spend his time with.

Two poles drawn together by magnetism create more than a union. They also create an energy field.

Today, as they take that next step into their future, Ariel and Patrick have drawn all of us into their energy field. We are their chosen people, their community.

We have followed them to Maine, Ariel's—and now Patrick's, lifelong sacred space—to surround them with love as they join in a new stage of their twelve-year love affair, wedding each other as husband and wife.

As well as love and nicely wrapped gifts, each of us brings heart-full of wishes for the future of their love.

We've each of us put some of what we hope into words, written them on pretty sheets of paper and tied them with ribbons to the tripod before which they stand.

That tripod is a metaphor suitable to the poet Ariel is: Patrick is one leg, she is the one leg, and they, united as a couple, are the third leg. Patrick built it for today, for Ariel, in the certain knowledge that its three legs make it unshakable.

Wafting around them as blessings are our hopes for their future.

Mine come from another poet. Once upon a time, the fast-burning Jim Morrison opened doors of consciousness with the lines

> *You know that it would be untrue*
> *You know that I would be a liar*
> *If I was to say to you*
> *Girl, we couldn't get much higher*

Fifty years of doubt and wonder later, I assure you, Ariel and Patrick, that high as you are today, you will get much higher.

As Ariel and Patrick join their futures to their pasts in wedlock today, we are well-wishers and witnesses. In the vows they now speak, they marry one another...

PRESS

The Hill Rag
12 Pennsylvania Ave., S.E.
Washington, D.C. 20003
543-6836

This certifies that
SANDRA O MARTIN
is a member of the editorial staff

ILLINOIS TIMES

Sandra OMartin
bearer

Fletcher Farrar
editor

BAY WEEKLY

The Chesapeake's Free Independent Newspaper · Since 1993

SANDRA MARTIN
Managing Editor

The bearer of this identification is an authorized
representative of Bay Weekly newspaper.

PRESS

Full Toll Free 800-579-0304

PART VI

My TT Tags Say JRNLISM (OU & A didn't fit)

Journalism became a ceaseless force in Sandra's life with ownership of a weekly newspaper for twenty-seven years, a weighty venture with deadline pressures forcing the rivers of writing to rise. During those years she continued training writers as she conceived and filled what would amount to 1,360 weekly papers while pursuing her craft with features and columns.

Her columns in the Her Car Tags Say JRNLISM (OU & A Didn't Fit) section of this anthology, reflect on the art and craft of journalism, from the weekly routine of her paper to its sale in 2020 to the 2018 attack on freedom of the press that took the lives of five colleagues, friends and competitors, at the Annapolis *Capital* newspaper.—Editor's Note

The Weekly Miracle

How each week we assemble a winning hand.

What will the cards deal us?

The drama of journalism is that you never know what hand the world will deal you.

Certainly, some stories are planned in advance; the ones that take lots of thought, digging and assembling are in process long before you see them in print.

Some stories are written so far in advance that the writer may be dead before the story appears in print. In that odd category may fall obituaries of famous long-lived people that were written by short-er-lived experts who knew them in their prime. That's more likely in big-staffed dailies than in *Bay Weekly*, where we hate to anticipate death or history, reckoning that the newsworthy moment brings its own truth.

Other stories have to hit just the right note at just the right time.

So it is that we trust, like card players around a table, that a new deal is always on the way. And we count on the chance—or luck—of the deal and our own ingenuity to make winning hands of whatever cards we are dealt.

That's a big assumption, and now and again in the friendless hours of 3 or 4am we journalists and editors alike wake in terror at not knowing where the next story is coming from.

But mostly, by morning, the cards start falling, often faster than we can manage them.

Obviously we're hoping for a royal flush, but everybody knows that kind of hand is a rarity. And when you're playing regularly— week after week for twenty-six years—you can make a winner of a straight or three of a kind.

CELEBRATING
26 YEARS
1993-2019

April 18 - April 24, 2019
Volume XXVII, Number 16

Bay Weekly

www.bayweekly.com

What's Your Recycling IQ?

*Recycling is complicated,
controlled by interacting
forces from the global
to the local level.*

Earth Day
Is Our Birthday

*It soon became clear that stories
lurked behind every bush.*

I don't burn my socks (yuck!). But I'd washed them (with much of
the rest of winter's heavy wear) and was walking out to meet warm
spring stocking-less in thin-soled shoes. When I opened the door,
April's wind twirled paper through the entry hall and drove me back
upstairs for a warm raincoat and pair of socks.

April's fickle ways always remind me of that April day in 1993,
when wind-driven rain tossed husband Bill Lambrecht and me in
our rented van like a boat on the Bay as we drove to Curtis Bay to
pick up the order of wire racks we'd use to position *New Bay Times*
Vol. 1 No. 1 throughout Anne Arundel and Calvert counties. It was
Earth Day, by design, and I had envisioned it as a descendant of the
sun-bombed, blue-skied, green-hued day I remembered from my
first Earth Day, *the* First Earth Day, back in 1970.

Now is farther from then than then was from Earth Day's first
day. Both landmarks are distant memories, but I know this about
them: In 1970, who (except the very wise) knew the mission we
tree-huggers accepted at the bidding of Sen. Gaylord Nelson would
be so long going?

In 1993, the future of *New Bay Times*, which would become *New
Bay Times—Weekly* which would become *Bay Weekly*, was beyond
imagining for its three founders, Bill, me, and son Alex Knoll. Back
then—and even now—we were citizens of the eternal present.
I think that's the time zone of people in the news business. Every
story, every edition, stretches from horizon to horizon. Past stories
exist as hazy memories, future stories as burdens you'll pick up as
soon as this issue goes to print.

So this morning I scratched my head and asked Bill, who I always blame for getting us in this business, what we were thinking.

I knew we wanted to tell some good stories, and that there were plenty out there to tell. It had taken barely dipping a toe into journalism to learn that stories were lurking behind every bush, and by *Bay Weekly*'s beginning, I'd been in the business going on fifteen years.

I knew we had the resources. Were the resources. Bill was a Washington correspondent and environmental investigative reporter winning some of journalism's biggest prizes. Alex had topped his Bachelor's in Rhetoric at the University of Illinois with a Master's in Journalism. He and I were both learning how to use those newfangled Macintosh computers to make pages as well as words. The miracle of electronic transmission had come unto us.

And Bill, our own Gaylord Nelson, had converted us to his own version of Earth Day optimism, styled after the recently popular movie *Field of Dreams*: If we build it, they will come.

We had the means and the desire. But what did we think we were up to?

"Did we think we'd make any difference?" I asked him.

Ten minutes later, I prodded him again.

Finally, he spoke. "Those were different times," he said. "Even after twenty-three Earth Days, people were just waking up to the shape we'd gotten our world in. Environmental awareness was at an earlier stage than the understanding of climate change is now.

"We thought we could show people what was happening, how the problems were taking shape on our own Chesapeake Bay. And how people were trying to turn the tide. How they were paying attention to what they had in a lot of ways, historic and cultural and recreational as well as environmental. How they were trying to save the best of it and make the best of it."

That was a lot of words from Bill, who treats words as currency and expects to be paid, ideally handsomely, for his.

They cut like a lighthouse beacon, magnified by a Fresnel lens, through the fog of memory.

That's what we meant by New Bay Times, I remembered. *Not only a new newspaper but also a new way of looking at our Bay and our world. A way that balanced taking out with putting back. I always liked that name.*

The going is slow. All these years later, that's still what we're doing.

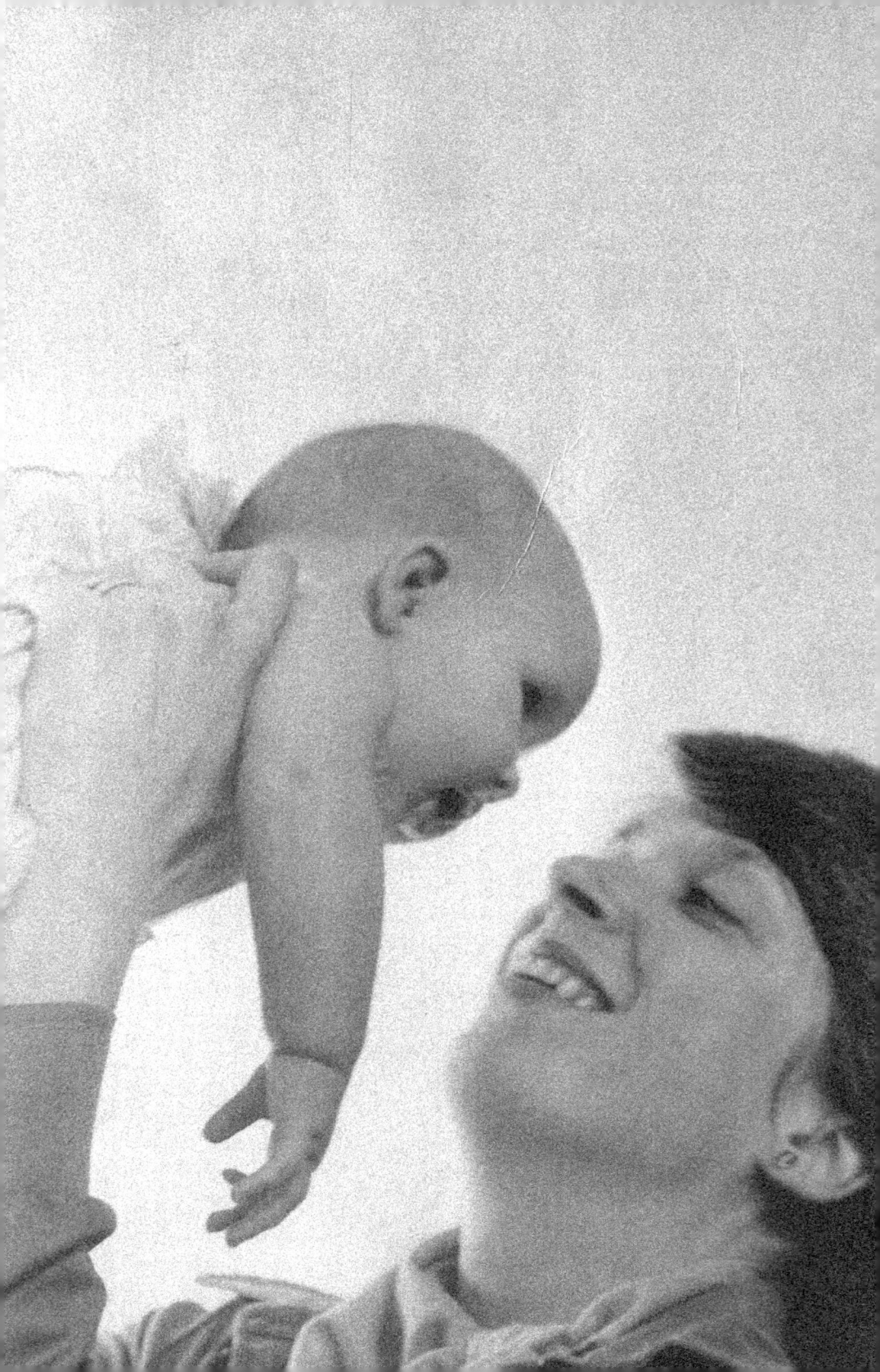

Death of a Proofreader

They rescue writers from
crawl-under-the-covers embarrassment.

Martha Lee Benz did not let you lay an egg. A woman of words, she made a career of policing the troublesome verbs lie and lay. She knew how to put vagrant apostrophes in their place. She vigilantly protected her writers from the error of their words—and her publications from having the egg they *lay/lie/laid* all over their pages and editors' faces.

For over a decade, *Bay Weekly* was the publication she protected.

In the early years of the paper, when I was editor, it occurred to me that we needed a dedicated proofreader. For our first decade or so, catching errors in our pages before they went to press depended on a shifting cast of writers. Now many of those standbys, like Darcey Dodd—who specialized in keeping verbs in the same tense throughout a story—had gone onto new things; in Darcey's case twins.

"I bet we can get a volunteer, some retired gem," I said, and placed a help-wanted ad in our pages of classified ads.

We struck gold when Martha Lee ("Thank you for calling me Martha Lee") Benz answered our ad.

"What makes you think you can do the job?" I asked.

"I worked as an editor for the National Planning Association in Washington DC, for more than thirty years," she said. "I'm retired, but I want to keep my hand in."

"You're hired," I said, swallowing my apprehension that this perfectly packaged professional woman knew my job better than I did.

Back then our office was in Deale, about 10 miles from her home, a traditional waterfront cottage in Holland Point at the end of Anne

Arundel County. When our office moved to Annapolis in 2007, she followed us, adding 32 miles to her round-trip commute. Year in and year out, as her arthritis grew crueler, she appeared every Tuesday for her afternoon shift. In later years, she carried her rubber-padded pens and seat pillow, as well as her trusty ruler, to help her with the job

Line after line she read, page after page as they flowed freshly laid out from Alex Knoll or Betsy Kehne's computer to the printer. Week after week she kept us clear, correct and consistent. No page was safe to print until Martha Lee scrutinized it. For no matter how carefully we worked, we'd always left things only she would find.

The only devotions she held dearer than her job at *Bay Weekly* were her daughter, Mollie Flounlacker, and grandchildren, Ian and Ella, whose births we celebrated with Martha Lee. Only their need for her kept her from her weekly place at her *Bay Weekly* desk and dictionary. (Well, also, her foundling feral cats, if she had the mobile vet calling.)

If she missed a week, we'd say, "Well, there'll be errors to find in this week's paper." Sure enough, readers would call to shame us with the mistakes they'd found.

So faithful was she that after she felt she could no longer make the drive, she hired a teenager as her chauffeur. Of course she didn't tell us. In she'd walk, impeccably, often beautifully dressed, as if for Washington, and we'd say, "Martha Lee is here. Bring on the pages."

In our paper and in our hearts, Martha Lee was one of us.

The Capital

FRIDAY, JUNE 29, 2018   A Capital-Gazette Newspaper ® — Annapolis, MD $1.50

| Gerald Fischman | Rob Hiaasen | John McNamara | Rebecca Smith | Wendi Winters |

5 shot dead at The Capital

Police respond Thursday afternoon to a mass shooting at *The Capital* that left five dead. A gunman shot through a glass door to the office and opened fire.

JOSHUA McKERROW/CAPITAL GAZETTE

Laurel man, the suspected gunman, in custody

BY CHASE COOK, PHIL DAVIS, SELENE SAN FELICE, E.B. FURGURSON III, RACHAEL PACELLA, DANIELLE OHL, JOSHUA McKERROW, PAUL W. GILLESPIE, DAVID BROUGHTON AND ROB HOUGH |
cook2-capgaznews.com

Five employees of The Capital Gazette — Gerald Fischman, Rob Hiaasen, John McNamara, Rebecca Smith and Wendi Winters — were killed Thursday when a gunman entered the newspaper's offices and opened fire.

"We are heartbroken, devastated. Our colleagues and friends are gone. No matter how deep our loss is nothing compared to the grief our friends' families are feeling," said Capital Editor Rick Hutzell.

Jarrod W. Ramos, 38, of Laurel, who had a long-standing grudge against the news-paper, is being held as a suspect in the deadly shooting, according to law enforce-ment sources.

The suspect targeted The Capital and used smoke grenades and a shotgun during the attack, according to law enforcement officials. Police arrived on the scene in about a minute after the incident began and did not exchange gunfire with the shooter, officials said.

The Capital's office is in a multi-story building on Bestgate Road with other businesses. Police said more than 100 people were evacuated.

Fischman, 61, wrote The Capital's editori-als, edited the editorial page and handled other editing duties.

Hiaasen, 59, was a native of Fort Lauderdale and a graduate of the University of Florida. He was hired as the assistant editor of The Capital in 2010.

Previously he was a staff reporter for The Baltimore Sun for 15 years. He was also a staff reporter for The Palm Beach Post in Florida and was a news anchor and reporter

at news-talk radio stations throughout the South.

His feature column appeared Sundays in the Life section of The Capital.

McNamara, 56, a sportswriter turned community news editor, was the editor of the Bowie Blade-News and the Crofton-West County Gazette. He has worked in various capacities for Capital Gazette for more than 20 years.

Smith, 34, a sales assistant, worked in the sales organization's office in Annapolis.

Winters, 65, covered various subjects as a community news reporter and the col-umnist for Home of the Week, Teen of the Week, and Around Broadneck columns — and more, but her background in public relations, having worked for two New York City agencies and had owned her own boutique agency in the Big Apple. Before her move to Annapolis, Winters began writing for AP Features, Copley News and a Manhattan weekly.

Inside
- More details on the shooting, Page A2
- The history of The Capital, Page A3
- Profiles of the victims. Pages A4-5

Online
- See more at capitalgazette.com

Journalists at The Capital found them-selves reporting on the gunman's attack Thursday as events unfolded. Phil Davis, one of The Capital's crime reporters, was inside the building when the gunman entered.

"Gunman shot through the glass door to the office and opened fire on multiple employees," Davis tweeted after he was safe. "Can't say much more and don't want to declare anyone dead, but it's bad."

WEATHER
TODAY
89 | 72
HIGH   LOW

Mostly sunny A7

INDEX

2 sections, 26 pages • Entertainment

Bridge	B6	Death Notices	A6	Puzzles	B6
Calendar	B7	Editorial	A8	Sports	B1
Classified	B4	Lottery	A2	Television	B7
Comics	B6	Obituaries	A6		

NATION & WORLD
Trump, Putin
The two leaders will meet in Finland in July A6

General 410-268-5000
Classified 410-268-7000
Circulation 410-268-4800

The Annapolis *Capital* Massacre

Antagonism to the news media played out tragically in Annapolis on June 28, 2018.

My newspaper is full of holes.

No, *Bay Weekly* hasn't forgotten a story here or an ad there. I'm using my in the larger sense that each of us newspaper readers invokes each day: *My* paper, as in the newspaper I depend on to tell me the daily story of our times, up to date and delivered to my door.

My newspaper each morning is the *Capital*. The holes—burned as if acid had dropped onto the paper—are the missing stories by Wendi Winters, John McNamara and Rob Hiassen, Gerald Fischman's signature unsigned editorials, the ads Rebecca Smith helped bring in to support the paper.

A week has gone by since the bloody, deadly massacre at the *Capital* newspaper, giving us time to encounter every hole.

Editor's note. Two of the columns that follow relate to the tragedy of June 28, 2018, when a lone gunman wielding a pump shotgun shot through the glass doors of the Capital Gazette newspapers in Parole, Maryland, a suburb of Annapolis, and murdered five staff members. There might have been more deaths had one of the victims, Wendi Winters, not rushed the intruder with a waste basket, giving others a moment to escape. The killer, Jerrod Ramos, disturbed about the paper's coverage of his criminal case seven years prior, in 2021 was sentenced to five life terms without parole.

Rob Hiassen's Sunday column would not have been comically breezy—had he lived to write the column of Sunday, July 1. Though we welcomed the tributes, the hole of his absence filled his space in the Life section of that morning's paper. For his readers, his space will remain forever empty.

Fischman's editorials, had he lived to define this week, would have put into words the feelings that grapple wordlessly in so many hearts. The paper's editors rose to the occasion of following his inimitable act. But his readers will always see the emptiness of his senseless death in his place at the top of the editorial page.

John McNamara. *Capital* sports page readers have been missing his insights since he moved to the *Capital* sister papers, the *Bowie Blade-News* and the *Crofton-West County Gazette*. Yet we readers projected the hole in our hearts onto the page and felt the depth of the void.

Wendi Winters, of course, made her posthumous deadline. We read her Saturday, June 30 Teen of the Week—profiling Anne Arundel Community College journalist Sarah Noble, moonlighting from what has been her day job as a student at Broadneck High School—with heartsore awareness of its irony. Death drained even Wendi's indomitable energy. A lacework of holes bled loss into the many spaces, especially Home of the Week, that would have been filled, in the course of a week, by the writer who so often—as the journalism saying goes—wrote the whole paper.

Those newspaper men and newspaper women died as they lived, with the righteous certainty that they held a place in history as its daily reporters.

Journalists like them thrive on the energy of the ever-goading deadline, and every newsroom buzzes like a beehive. Rebecca Smith must have fed on the high and felt that wonderful sense of shared purpose in hard work rewarded each day by the tangible, ink-and-paper—plus digital—proof of your achievement. Now her newspaper job has made her part of its death toll.

My newspaper is full of holes.

Yet in death, these journalists have written a story that will never be forgotten. It will lose its urgency in the news cycle. But it will never fade from the hearts and memories of its readers.

That's the Pulitzer Prize all of us journalists seek, for we know that the stories we've written today will be crab-wrap tomorrow. *Capital* journalists were well in on that joke. It's that read-today-gone-tomorrow syndrome that makes so many journalists avid to write their book. By their tragic, blood-soaked route, Wendi, Rob, John, Gerald and Rebecca have achieved permanence. Not even journalists would trade their lives for that, but having no alternative, they would appreciate it.

Which doesn't do a thing to assuage the pain—the outrage, the demand for justification—that radiates out from the center of each person's loss—from their family, to their friends, to their newspaper, to their community, and finally to the worldwide community of journalists and readers who depend on them to fill our newspapers, and our lives, with meaning.

Now we will have to find our way without them.

CONGRESS SHALL MAKE NO LAW
RESPECTING AN ESTABLISHMENT OF
RELIGION, OR PROHIBITING THE FREE
EXERCISE THEREOF; OR ABRIDGING
THE FREEDOM OF SPEECH, OR OF THE
PRESS; OR THE RIGHT OF THE PEOPLE
PEACEABLY TO ASSEMBLE, AND TO
PETITION THE GOVERNMENT FOR
A REDRESS OF GRIEVANCES.

THE FIRST AMENDMENT
RATIFIED DECEMBER 15, 1791

After the Tragedy

*Our city, and our profession,
have risen to the occasion.*

Would Annapolis become a Ferguson, Las Vegas or Sandy Hook? Places targeted by mass murderers can be tarnished by the mayhem and madness perpetrated there. At our safe distances, we may fear contagion, as if the climate that created one maniac might create others. Such places can become the destinations of sad pilgrimages or sociological studies of pathology, like concentration camps.

We will not.

With all the world watching, Annapolis has mounted a heroic response to the *Capital* massacre.

The *Capital* newspaper set the standard.

First, reporter Wendi Winters, armed herself with a wastebasket and recycling bin and ran at the man firing the smoking shotgun.

That action does not surprise me—or anybody who knew Wendi. She would have been outraged. And she would have been prepared. Wendi had, it has since been reported, trained to respond to an active shooter. Just as she had taken—and advised all her readers to take— Anne Arundel Medical Center's free heart-health assessments. She was, we all know, on the side of life.

Recognizing her heroism, the *Capital* has begun a campaign to award her the Presidential Medal of Freedom, an honor held by only 29 other journalists.

While blood still ran warm, we saw reporter E.B. 'Pat' Furgurson at work, taping Acting Anne Arundel County Police Chief William Krampf's press conference.

Then we heard reporter Chase Cook vow, "We are putting out a damn paper tomorrow." And they did, a perfect paper edited by mourners and written by reporters who had just missed their turn at death.

Those responses, single and collective, raised Annapolis to the standing of Shanksville, Pennsylvania, where forty passengers and crew crashed their plane rather than allow 9/11 terrorists to complete their mission.

Now our capital city is known as a place whence heroes rise. A place as resilient in our present as in our historic past.

Annapolis, Anne Arundel County and the state of Maryland amplified that message. Performing perfectly, police responded in one amazing minute, liberating the news office and hauling off the shooter, who'd cowered under a desk as if he were a victim rather than a killer.

Gov. Larry Hogan promptly ordered state flags flown at half mast, and Annapolis Mayor Gavin Buckley petitioned the president to lower the American flag, in national mourning. Now Buckley is planning a music festival honoring press freedom in Annapolis.

Within a day, tangible expressions of support appeared in Go Fund Me and The *Capital Gazette* Family Fund accounts. In twelve days, 3,748 people contributed $206,008 to the Go Fund Me account. The *Capital Gazette* Family Fund administered through the Community Foundation of Anne Arundel County raised over $400,000.

The Merrill Family Foundation, founded by the paper's former owner, donated $100,000.

Politicians and public figures through the state circled round Annapolis in such sympathy and support that we voters can now hold them accountable for action.

The *Capital's*—and its big sister paper, the *Baltimore Sun's*— whole community of readers expanded the circle even farther, locking hands and hearts physically and virtually in solidarity. We are joined in that circle of phone calls, emails, social posts, visits, memorial services.

Journalists made the circle huge. Papers across the country— from the *New York Times* to the *Missoulian* in Montana—covered the shootings as news and filled editorial pages and columns with empathy and recollections of the colleagues who died. As, with less poignancy, did all the other media, as well.

Reporters and editors retired or with other jobs volunteered their services to the *Capital* and the *Sun*.

One week after the massacre, at 2:33 p.m. on Thursday, July 5, the nation stood silent together in memory.

The nation—even much of the world—is joined in honoring the five dead *Capital* staffers.

As Annapolis has risen to this tragedy, with it has the profession of journalism.

As we well know, there is power in words. "Enemies of the American people" is a ferocious condemnation from president, Donald Trump. People looking for enemies believe that kind of labeling. From belief springs action.

Even we ourselves are affected. We journalists have bunkered down under shared siege. No, most of us didn't expect to be murdered. But we've felt threatened and responded to it with hunched shoulders, drawing in our pride in our work the way a turtle draws back into its shell in the face of danger.

In death, our colleagues have drawn us out of our shells. We are not enemies of the American people.

BAY WEEKLY

www.bayweekly.com • December 26, 2019 - January 1, 2020 • Volume XXVII, Number 52

CELEBRATING
26 YEARS
1993-2019

Good-Bye to My Newspaper

*After twenty-seven years, time to say farewell
to what we created*

We are, none of us, new to shutting doors behind us. As I write this letter, I am on the open side of the door. Once I finish it, I shut the door on a long chapter of my life. For I have saved this letter to you as the last thing I will write as editor of *Bay Weekly*. I'll not be able to open that door again except through memory. Fond as I am of memory, it is—another truth you and I both know—only a substitute for the real thing.

Nonetheless, memory and I have a lot to do with each other. It, and I, often revisit the pasts behind other closed doors.

If I ever get to climb in a time machine—which is an apparatus I've wanted to try since I was a kid reading comic books under the covers after bedtime—I'd go back in my life to the years when I was a youngish mother raising my own two kids.

I had divorced when they were little, Nathaniel 20 months and Alex seven years, and weeks after I had cried into the fountain of the Sangamon County Courthouse, in Springfield, Illinois, I had to take Nathaniel with me to the settlement on the little bungalow I'd bought for the three of us. A wild thing, Nat was sure to add drama to the transaction, and my heart was already racing with the enormity of it all. But what was I to do? The Illinois State Fair Opening Parade marched between me and his Cookie Monster Cooperative Daycare Center.

In our ten years in that house, the kids grew up. From a semi-sweet redheaded softie, Alex grew through a morning paper route and little-brother sitting (too often literally) and Dungeons and Dragons and an alternative hippie school to an immovable force

279

ready to go off to the University of Illinois. (This year, he's had that role reversed.)

Nat grew wilder until, pushing high school, he could brag that he knew every corner of the capital city from explorations on his oft-stolen Big Wheels and bicycles.

We had bad dogs and families of cats—including our best cat ever, BBK—and households full of friends that the incorrigible German-beagle Slip Mahoney sometimes bit, when he was home from chasing the train or getting arrested at the Kroger meat counter.

Bill and I were finding we couldn't do without each other, even as we flourished in separate lives. He was a rising star in Illinois statehouse journalism, and I had found my words in the Brainchild Women's Poetry Collective.

That's where I'd head my time machine: To not-very-exciting central Illinois to rejoin the real time of boys who smelled like dry dirt, when I was the woman who counted most in their lives (then their grandmothers) and I saw a dogwood tree through my kitchen window and hung all our wash on a line. Any day would do—after I set the wish-o-meter on an hour when the good times weighed in way heavier than the bad. I wouldn't, for example, want the dogcatcher visiting on the day I returned back home.

In the minutes I had there, I would be sure to suffice myself in every mundane image—the way light fell through that window and curls fell on Lexey's forehead when his hair, as usual, needed cutting.

When all that was mine every day, I was too busy with the everyday to pay close attention.

When the time comes when you close a door, already the weight of time has crushed each sacred day beneath the succession of days, compressing the features that once were oneness—the dinosaur as flat as the fern—into a mass of carbon. Finally from that mass, the diamonds of memory are made.

That time will begin for me, as the editor of *Bay Weekly* you may think of as your friend, after I finish writing this letter.

The process of transformation is twenty-seven years underway. Only in pale memory can I reexamine the moments that made up those years. I can't feel what I felt when that first issue rolled off the press. Yes, we were there, at Orville Davis' Newsprinters International printing plant in Waldorf. (Over my shoulder Bill remembers that he didn't mind taking the paper there to be printed because there was a good chance he'd buy another pool cue at a nearby billiard parlor.)

That printing press or another—we've had five in all, though that includes our second run with our friends at Delaware Printing Company—photo-lithographed good impressions on the giant cylinders of paper that fed through its webs and came out ready-folded as your paper.

For us, time was moving too fast for one day's impressions to stand out as different from another's.

So I'm not going to tell you about all "the times when"...though throngs of them are crowding my memory in photomontage, yelling, "look here!" Even if I could, how would I choose one over another?

But I can tell you that above and beyond the tensions that can curdle your stomach, I have lived my role as editor in deep satisfaction, as happy as when I was mother, if not always boss, of my little family homestead—though not often boss here either—of my destiny. Back then, thrive or fail they depended on me, and my work mattered deeply.

At *Bay Weekly*, the rules were the same. There'd be no paper to print if I couldn't fill it with stories, and my work mattered deeply. All the better that there was nothing in the world I could think of that I wanted to do more than find stories that needed to be told. There was always a place to put them, and always you to read them. Now and again you'd write to tell me one you liked particularly. What more could any writer want—except a paycheck to reward honest labor, and often I got that too.

Better still, as *Bay Weekly* has been a labor too big for one person, I got to do the work I loved best in the best of company. A college writing teacher in my earlier incarnation, I could—indeed I had to—inspire other writers and would-be writers to join our story-telling force. They inspired my favorite metaphor: Newspapering is a lot like baseball. I got to be team manager, and all those writers—hundreds over the years—were the talent, showing off what they could do, growing in skill, winning with the team.

Better still, because *Bay Weekly* is more than storytelling, I've gotten to work day in and day out with teams and players just as focused on their part of the game—ad sales, design, layout, business, delivery—as writers and I are on our storytelling. As in any good team, we've become one another's friends and extended family, over-looking one another's love stories, child- and dog-rearing, successes and traumas.

Best of all, I think, is the ride we've all shared on the electric surge of energy that pulses through a newsroom like a force of nature so that as you work—always chasing the deadline—you're high on the buzz.

I'm riding that buzz now, sharing the high with a newsroom of people, each playing her or his own position, each just this side of panic over whether we'll meet our deadline.

That's the door I'm about to close. I know my memory will repay me in diamonds. I just wish I could tell you about what I'll find on the other side of the door.

Next week, as we finish our era with 1,360 issues, I'll thank you for taking us this far and preview what lies ahead as *Bay Weekly* joins forces with Chesapeake Bay Media, on January 3, 2020.

Best of all, I think, is the
ride we've all shared on
the electric surge of energy
that pulses through a newsroom like a force of nature
so that as you work—always
chasing the deadline—you're
high on the buzz.

PART VII

Creature Features

Reporters, freelancers, salespersons and paper-deliverers were many at *Bay Weekly* in more than a quarter century, but office dogs were few. In a section devoted to animals, Sandra writes of two stalwart albeit furry employees, a not-very-dependable German beagle, a champion horse-next-door and the search for a companion for a lonely woman—her mother.—Editor's Note

Nancy Alberts' Horse Is Magic

The long-shot with his beautiful eyes on the Belmont Stakes greets visitors.

In the northwest corner of Anne Arundel County, Magic Weisner lives like the boy next door. When you come calling to the once-grand track, as we did last week, this 3-year-old is glad to see you. He cranes his long, warm-brown neck to look you over. He nuzzles you with a velvet nose. He displays oyster-shell teeth. He might even nip you, in a playful kind of way, if you take the liberty of patting the white star high on the bright bay's forehead.

That's when he's off duty. Take Magic to the race track, and you know where his name comes from. Like magic is how the horse next door runs.

The only person who saw the magic in Magic Weisner was his mother—his human mother, that is. Nancy Alberts owns and bred the 3-year-old thoroughbred, raising, riding and training him as well. In him, she saw "the horse of a lifetime," she says, a life for her that soon may change because of this horse.

From birth, he seemed to possess the great heart of his dam, Jazema. Jazema, is a horse that Alberts, of Jessup—and the Laurel Park race track—couldn't resist. She bought the daughter of Kentucky Derby winner Bold Forbes for $1 when crippled knees could have doomed the filly. But surgery, followed by Alberts' mothering, brought her to the track, where she started in sixty-eight races, winning fourteen times and taking home $86,000.

Some of those victories were in claiming races, meaning the winner goes to the highest bidder. Each time, Alberts tracked Jazema down and bought her back. When Jazema retired, Alberts bred her, though, she says, given her history, "I was a crazy fool." To Alberts' delight, none of Jazema's foals were "crooked."

With Ameri Valay, a horse that won $743,000 in his late 20th century career, she produced Deliver Hope, who has earned roughly as much as his mother. A second foal nearly died from an early infection. Saved by vet Alan Wisner, that foal became Magic Weisner, a slightly misspelled namesake.

MOTHERLY LOVE

Alberts, 56, all muscle and bone, a handsome horsewoman in midlife, runs a one-woman stable. Of the six horses she trains, she owns two, plus Jazema. Alberts knows her horses well. Like a mother, she feeds them thrice a day. A part-time groom helps her keep them sleek and brushed to a standard few human children attain. Every three weeks or so, she calls third-generation blacksmith Greg Wheeler to fit them with new shoes. She often exercises them herself, though a broken shoulder kept the wiry trainer out of the saddle much of this spring.

"A colt laid down on me," she relates. "I asked him why he did it and he didn't say a thing. I hate colts. They're a pain in the ass." Which explains why Magic Weisner must make his fortune on the track, not in the stud barn. He's been gelded, depriving him of parts essential for breeding.

Exercising Magic, as he's called at home, Alberts felt what he might do. When he got on the track—"after he broke his maiden and then his juvenile"—he proved to her he was "real special," as she puts it. In ten races, nine on his home track at Laurel Park, Magic won six times and placed twice. When the time arrived to enter horses in the big races of spring—the 2002 Kentucky Derby and the Preakness—Magic had earned more than $230,000. That's big money for an operation like Nancy Alberts'.

She skipped the Derby. But the Preakness, in Baltimore, was too close to home—and Magic too good a horse—to ignore. Alberts paid the $20,000 entrance fee, hoping to make money on her investment.

"I knew he had a good chance," she said. "Everything he won, he did it easy."

Odds-makers didn't agree. Magic Weisner arrived at the Preakness starting gate at odds of 45–1.

"I think the reason they didn't pay much attention to him was that I never took him out of Maryland," Alberts said.

THE SPORT OF PRINCES

Horse racing, it's said, is the sport of kings. In our day it's the sport of princes. This year's Kentucky Derby winner, War Emblem, aiming at thoroughbred racing's elusive Triple Crown, indeed commanded a king's ransom. The Thoroughbred Corp. paid nearly $1 million for War Emblem in April. The company is headed by a real prince, Ahmed bin Salman, the publishing magnate and nephew of Saudi Arabia's King Fahd. War Emblem's famous trainer, the white-haired Bob Baffert, has piled up enough high-stakes wins—four Preaknesses and three Kentucky Derbies—and heartbreak losses to hunger for a crown.

So what is Magic Weisner of racing's backwater doing gaining on royalty—and entering the drama of the Triple Crown, which is to horse racing what the World Series is to baseball? To win any of the three races over five weeks—the Kentucky Derby, the Preakness and the Belmont Stakes—a horse has to be very fast, very lucky, or both.

To win them all and claim the Triple Crown, a horse has to be legendary. That crown has been claimed only eleven times, and not in twenty-four years, since Affirmed won it in 1978.

The race for the crown began with the Kentucky Derby, on the first Saturday in May. The 125-year-old Derby is the most celebrated of the three Triple Crown races. The one-and-one-quarter mile race is run at Churchill Downs in the heart of Kentucky racing country, with miles of white-washed fences surrounding acres of bluegrass where herds of blueblood horses graze. Because of its fame, the Derby draws the best-qualified or most-hoped upon three-year-old thoroughbreds. Some two dozen vied to enter this year's race, which closes its gates at twenty.

Truth be told, any horse can win despite what the oddsmakers say. This year's winner qualified as a dark horse, the dark bay, War Emblem. Running at odds of 20–1, War Emblem leapt into the lead and kept it, astonishing fans and handicappers with a commanding, 6-length win.

Like Magic Weisner, War Emblem was playing out a Cinderella story. Until a month before the Derby, he'd raced in relative obscurity, in Illinois. But his victory in the Illinois Derby caught the sharp eye of Baffert, who needed a Derby horse. He turned War Emblem into a contender in weeks.

After the running of the Preakness, there's more at stake than the honor of the Triple Crown. First, the winner of each race takes hundreds of thousands of dollars from a million-dollar pot, divided among the top horses. Second, $5 million is promised by the recent corporate sponsor of the Triple Crown, Visa, to the horse who takes all three races. But that's a drop in the bucket to the third pot of gold.

If the winner is a stallion—as is War Emblem—he stands to earn tens of millions of dollars in stud fees, perhaps well over $100 million. The 1977 Triple Crown winner, Seattle Slew, who died this year at 28 in the days between the Derby and the Preakness, was still breeding mares a quarter-century after his success.

Expectation rises with the Triple Crown's second jewel. Maryland's Preakness Stakes is the shortest race of the three at a mile and three-sixteenths. Going into the Preakness, the Derby winner is on everybody's minds—though War Emblem is not necessarily everybody's favorite. Was he a flash in the pan? Will he prove sufficiently versatile to win another big race—another distance at another track? Assuaging doubters, experts remind that Baffert's horses won four of the last six Preaknesses.

Up in Baltimore on the third Saturday in May, the Preakness field narrows to serious contenders as well as a favorite son. In this year's field of thirteen, that son was Magic Weisner.

IN BALTIMORE, THEY'RE OFF

On April 20, in the Federico Tesio Stakes at Pimlico, Maryland's warm-season track, Magic Weisner finished second. Now, for the Preakness, Alberts hired the jockey who had bested her that day, Richard Migliore.

Migliore had never ridden Magic Weisner before the Preakness, the biggest race for both the horse and the jockey, a diminutive New Yorker at 5 feet-4 inches and 112 pounds. "It was a big step up," Migliore said of the opportunity.

Just before the race, Alberts told Migliore how to run. "Stay on the rail and run the last part," she said, recalling the instructions. Then Migliore donned Alberts' colors, red with a white band on the shirt, white with a red band on the sleeves. Alberts walked Magic Weisner into the paddock, saddled him and handed over her best hope for fame to Migliore.

Nancy Alberts is a small woman, a little shorter than Migliore, and in the owners' box, she couldn't see the track. When the race began, she sprinted to the nearest television.

"I saw as he was going round the first turn how he just sat there, which I planned to do, and got the rail. Then as soon as they went around the backside I never saw him again," said Alberts, reliving the seconds when her heart hardly beat.

As War Emblem overtook pace-setting Menacing Dennis, the cameras held a tight focus on the leaders. What was happening behind them, Alberts could only imagine. What her horse was doing when she couldn't see him was what she expected: finding a hole in a wall of horses. "You don't have to worry about this horse going through a tight hole," she'd advised her jockey. "You just have to steer, and he'll go wherever he sees any opening."

Indeed. Magic Weisner had dropped back to eleventh place after a quarter mile run just shy of twenty-three seconds. But the gelding, living up to his name, wove determinedly through the field to the flank of the princely, Baffert-trained War Emblem, who'd already vanquished Medaglia D'Oro, an oddsmakers' favorite, and Proud Citizen, trained by Hall of Famer D. Wayne Lukas.

Magic Weisner continued to accelerate, but he ran out of Pimlico track. War Emblem barely held off the unknown gelding to win by three-quarters of a length. Magic Weisner placed second.

"You want to win, but second is wonderful," Alberts said. "I'm very proud of him."

EVE OF HISTORY?

Nancy Alberts had nearly pulled off one of the biggest upsets in racing history. As runner up, Magic won $200,000, a pleasing dividend on a $20,000 entry fee. The renewed quest for the Triple Crown was the story of the racing world. But the tale of Nancy and Magic was a clear second. ESPN's Kenny Mayne called the upstart's run "the best part of the Preakness. One barn blessed with unlimited resources briefly shared the stage with mere common folk."

Now the Belmont Stakes beckons. It'll cost Alberts another twenty grand, but horse racing is a gamble she knows how to make. Horses are all Alberts has ever done. They're in her blood back to her grandparents, who owned the only livery stable between Philadelphia and Wilmington. Much of her life, she worked for trainer James P. Simpson while developing her own stable, one horse at a time. She tasted success a quarter century ago as groom to Simpson's Cormorant, who finished fourth in the Preakness Stakes, won by Seattle Slew, the tenth winner of the Triple Crown.

She has lived the life she wanted, Alberts told me. "I never dreamed of being in any big races. All I dreamed of was having the horses make money—earn their own keep—and be useful," she said. "I've had cheap horses, and no matter what I've had, I've made my living. I've got new cars and my own house."

Racing at Belmont seems the next logical step. "I want to go," she says, "because I want to win."

She'll be up against Big Money as well as Big Media, which will be rooting not for the underdog but for the first Triple Crown winner in a generation. But last week, she had the basics to tend to—new shoes for Magic and hooking her gooseneck horse trailer up to her truck and driving, with her brother following, to New York.

The make-up of the field of the third jewel in the Triple Crown will determine her strategy, how much of Magic's blazing speed to use and when.

There'll be more strategizing in Kentucky, where War Emblem is stabled. No longer is the Maryland horse obscure; Baffert and the prince know all about the Magic that nearly cost them the Preakness. Racing is a brutal business, and there are gameplans to thwart opponents and box them in.

But Alberts says she isn't letting Bob Baffert's big-money operation and quest for Triple Crown history trouble her. All that she's really got room to think about, she says, is her horse. "He just likes to be not in front, lay off the pace, then close," Alberts says. "He's got his mother's heart."

And if Magic has no magic in New York, well, Jazema and Ameri Valay got together again this spring.

Epilogue: *At Belmont, under jockey Richard Migliori again, Magic Weisner made Maryland proud, running fourth and winning Nancy Alberts another $60,000 in prize money. But War Emblem failed badly, stumbling out of the gate and nearly falling, en route to an eighth place finish, 19 lengths behind Sarava, a 70–1 longshot. Magic Weisner later won the Ohio Derby by a neck but was vexed anew by War Emblem in the Haskell International, running second again to the Kentucky Derby and Preakness winner. He won or placed in all but one of the stakes races he entered in a year's time and brought home nearly $800,000. But there would be no more success. He contracted West Nile Virus in the runup to the Ohio Derby and missed most of the next season. He returned for opening day at Laurel Park in Maryland—and finished last. He didn't race again. Albers, able to buy her farm after Magic's success, died, in 2012, of complications after a stroke. She was 65. The lifeline of another player in the '02 saga, Saudi Prince Ahmed bin Salman, was interrupted earlier. Bin Salman, the prince charming of global racing, died, at 43, in Riyadh, of a heart attack, two months after a version of the above article appeared.*

In Some Very Deep Woods

Love is better than leeches.

Camp Wood'N'Aqua sounded pretty awesome the afternoon its owners, the Alveys, pitched its wonders to the assembled third through eighth graders of Our Lady of the Pillar school. They illustrated the presentation with slides of Land of Lakes woods, paperbark birch trees, canoes and happy campers. I came home to tell my parents they had to send me. Persuasion took some doing. Wasn't the distance far and the stay long?

I was 9 years old and had never been away from home alone. I was also a pest, and I drilled them like mosquitoes around a campfire till they could take no more. Preparation was an adventure. Mother and I shopped for a shining black metal chest and filled it with neat stacks of required camp wear. She bought labels printed with my name and stitched them on every blouse, pair of shorts, jeans, underpants and socks, sheet and towel. She gave me lessons (that didn't take) on fixing my own hair. Along with soap and shampoo, we packed a hairbrush, hair bands and bobby pins. I added a stack of books and comics, and she tucked in tablets, envelopes and stamps.

In the grand dark caverns of St. Louis Union Station, Mother, Dad, my grandmother and most of the staff of the Stymie Club, our restaurant, waved. Some wept. I boarded alone. When the doors hissed shut, I was a stranger. The train trip north could have been my little ride on the Orient Express—had I not been in oxygen deprivation, holding my breath to keep terror at bay. Instead it felt like a first-timer's journey on a magical express train. Despite my stiff upper lip, I was already lonely.

On the very first day, of forty-two, I discovered that we girls weren't the only swimmers in Minnesota's thousand lakes. In the bathhouse, as we pulled off our wet one-piece swimming suits, we found shiny black blemishes on our legs and stomachs. Leeches lived in our lake. We poured on salt—boxes were on hand for that purpose—to remove the slimy, clinging parasites. I never went back in the water.

So why was I going back into the deep woods? I blame it on Bill.

"Let's go camping," Bill said as we bumped along a strip of country road in the middle of Illinois.

Driving to catch the night wind with the top and doors off the Jeep was how we cooled off in the prairie's liquid summer. The corn sucked up the humidity, and the humidity sucked us up.

"I'll turn north and we can just keep going."

"There are bugs," I countered as the swarm danced in the head-light beams. "I have to pee in the woods, which is no big deal for you, but it is for me. And that's not the worst of it."

"Bears shit in the woods," he said, as if that would win me over. "It'll be fun. Nobody will be able to get hold of us. We'll be all on our own."

Back then, a person could get out of touch. Telephones were teth-ered to wires. Get past the wires, and you'd be off the grid. To find you, they'd have to send out the Royal Canadian Mounted Police. Because Bill's plan took us to Canada.

Florida was too hot. Colorado too rocky. California too far away. And all had their own bugs, I knew. I couldn't think of any place better. Wherever we went, we'd be fishing. That was part of the deal with Bill. I wasn't my mother, a fishing fanatic, but she wasn't Bill's girlfriend. I was. And what a thrill that was. Finally, it was my turn to sit in the front seat with the dashing guy, blond hair blowing in the wind. With Bill, I'd go fishing.

Sticking as close to the Mississippi River as we could, we traveled up the spine of America.

"What do you think?" he asked as the Jeep ate up the roads.

In Illinois, he told me stories. Of course, one of them was about the time he was parking in the woods (with another girl) and heard scratching and banging on the truck. He tore out of there, he said. The next day he found a bloody hook hanging on his bumper. I reached over and slapped off his cap.

The backseat was out so all our baggage could go in. We'd even brought the iron skillet, along with our camping pans and coffee pot. On top of the pile, Bill made me a nest, padded with the sleeping bags we'd snatched from the kids' beds. I could climb up and look truckers in the eye before I fell asleep.

We ate eggs, biscuits and gravy or chicken-fried steak at truck stops, and we stopped for ice cream when I said so. Only at Duluth did we bear north for International Falls—which records some of its lowest temperatures in the civilized world—rather than northeast, for Ely, the jump-off to Camp Wood'N'Aqua. About that far north, I first put on my new birthday sweatsuit, my very first such attire.

This was nothing I couldn't handle. We were having an adventure. Living it was better than reading about it.

"I think it's pretty cool," I said. "If we see a Dairy Queen, let's stop."

I remembered the peppery, clean smell. Ozone. Ozone came out before a storm. I'd smelled it at Camp Wood'N'Aqua, canoeing over lakes thick with water lilies. Now it wafted over the Minaki Trading Company along the Winnipeg River system, at the village of Minaki—little other than a general store, Holst Point Lodge and the Canadian National Railway station.

I searched the sky low above for the speck of the tiny Piper Cub floatplane that was our mode of conveyance to deeper into Northwest Ontario. But I couldn't see it or hear the mosquito buzz of its engines, either. An hour earlier, when the little plane finally lifted off the lake, the sun had been shining, bringing, unexpectedly, one of those short-summer moments when you can bake in the 50th parallel north. But clouds rolled through, bringing lightning and thunder with rain that sizzled as drops fell on hot rocks deposited by glaciers. Now I was sticky under a plastic poncho.

Bill? Well, that was the question. With both Bill and me aboard, plus all our luggage, bush pilot Dave Schneider had been unable to pull the floatplane off the water. We'd taxied the lake twice before he gave up, waterskiing the plane back to its little dock.

He'd fly Bill and all our bags to the drop-off point where the canoes waited, it was decided. Then he'd come back for me. I was still waiting for my ride somewhere in the sprawling Winnipeg River system, while Bill had flown off with an outfitter he'd found in *Outside* magazine.

Had the plane gone down in the storm?

"They're just fine, eh?" said the woman who found me, forlorn, trying to pull the plane into view with the magnet of my stare.

"Dave knows what he's doing. Come in out of the rain and we'll have a cup of tea."

Change had glaciated my life over the past five years. I ricocheted from wife to independent woman—if I could stand on my own two feet, holding tight to two kids. On a new landscape, I was training myself out of worrying about what might come next. If he was lost, that was news I'd deal with when I had to.

Though I started to compose a news story. Bill would merit that, not just a regular obit, since he was in the news business. And plane crashes are always news. Writing us out of this life is a game we play, when our circumstances turn dire or embarrassing.

Illinois Statehouse Reporter and Bush Pilot
Missing in Canadian Backcountry

I had the headline. But rather than write the story, I said yes to a cup of tea.

"I'll brew a pot," said Mary, whose compound at the Minaki Trading Company had made room for Minaki Outpost, her son's wilderness outfitting partnership with Dave Schneider. "It'll cool us down."

"Hot tea? Not iced tea? To cool down?" I asked, sticky wet from the greenhouse effect of my poncho, now hanging in the mudroom.

"We're part of the British empire," she said. "Iced tea is one of your American inventions."

I dropped a cube of sugar into my china cup and sipped warily. The cooling effect was not immediate, but it was pleasant to drink tea and chat in such a civilized outpost of the great Canadian wilderness. Like all the buildings on the compound, including the big house, this one, the shop, was a modern-built log cabin. Skeins of heavy yarn—off-white, brown, gray and tweed—were shelved in cubbies filling two of the walls. The style was rustic, and furniture built from peeled-bark logs. Cold-winter Fair Isle-style sweaters, sox, caps and gloves hung on display.

Mary knitted as we talked, thick needles flying through hand-spun heavy yarn that tapered from almost-pencil thick to toothpick thin.

I was a knitter, too, and before Dave walked in, which I barely noticed, I had bought one of her sweater kits. With fifteen skeins of yarn, new oversized needles and a checkerboard pattern, I had all I needed to knit up this nice, local wool in a Canadian Native design. Naturally, I chose the fish design.

"Nothing to worry about, eh?" said Dave. He'd dropped off Bill before the storm rolled in. When it came, it was so quick that he'd landed in a cove to wait it out.

"There isn't much shelter at the canoe landing," he said, "so Bill likely waited it out under a canoe."

Bill was out, waving at us with a bit of Robinson Crusoe desperation, when the Piper Cub banked over a pebbly spit of land along the lake an hour or so later. We were packed up and moving almost before the plane was out of sight. Heavy loaded as it was, our aluminum canoe slithered across water the color of brown bottle glass, and you could see through to the stones and grasses in the shallows, rocked in sunlight. Farther out, the lake was very, very deep, dark and cold. Here it was friendly. We flowed through it as easily as a fish.

Bill, too, told me had written a story, A-copy for our obits, he described it, words he expected would be found someday. He hadn't begun until a couple hours after his abandonment, when it had become certain to him that our plane had gone down in the storm.

Of course it was tough writing beneath that metal canoe amid the lightning strikes and the banging of hail. But he reminded me that once he'd written on deadline in an airplane hangar, on a five-gallon bucket of joint compound. Below zero, planes revving, their exhaust making him dizzy. So scribbling in his notebook wasn't all that hard as long as he could keep it mostly dry.

"And we never even got to eat a walleye," was the kicker.

Which reminded me, after losing hours of daylight, that we would have to camp somewhere, and eat. We were trying to think like a fish, too, for that was our hope for dinner. Line streamed behind us as we paddled, with light rod-and-reel outfits across our legs, the grip of the cork rod tucked under a knee. I was the first to feel the tug on my line.

"Whoo!" I said and dropped the paddle with a clatter.

The fish had succumbed utterly to the tiny treble hook dangling from my zero Mepps, and the noise spooked him so that he fled toward the deep, stealing line from my reel. I am not a fisherwoman but I channeled my mother, equally skilled with such a tussle, whether out of Key West or on a Missouri lake. Holding fast against the plunging force, I resisted his escape. The momentum shifted, and cranking the spinning reel, I pulled him surely to the boat. I maneuvered the fish-heavy line back Bill's way, and he netted it, without losing his paddle. A toothy, dark-speckled walleye.

For this specimen, we'd brought that heavy iron skillet. Fileted, it filled it nicely, and the skillet sizzled over the campfire Bill built from downed pine. Potatoes rolled in boiling water in the tin pot wedged on a rock among the embers.

It was an ideal campsite we lucked into shortly before the sun disappeared, on a promontory above the shore where we beached the canoe and Bill cleaned the fish. Earlier campers had made it homey, with a fire ring of stones and a rickety bench.

We made coffee, pouring the potato water into the tin pot to drip through the ground beans, and sweetened it with B&B.

We drank the coffee as we ate the potatoes and my fish and thought life was pretty swell.

In the night, outside the tent, a hare was as noisy as a bear, which we were certain was about to attack. The storms would return the next day and the day after, and we'd be cold, our clothes sodden, as we struggled with a fire. That would be the worst of it. There was more of the better of it, two paddlers in sync in this great big world.

How Did the Turtle Cross the Road?

With your help, hopefully.

Has the world ever looked more beautiful? Probably, in some pristine past, but in the eye of this beholder these late days of spring sparkle with perfection—and when the sun doesn't come out give us moody skies reflected in shady green.

Who doesn't want to be out in times like this?

Somebody who does is the eastern box turtle. That beloved little fellow with the high domed shell crawls out of the leafy cover of the forest floor this time of year to see the world. There's a lot to see and do after months of hibernation. Like all of us, turtles have their ranges, within 250 yards of the nests where they were born, according to the Maryland Zoo in Baltimore. That's home, where they forage, mate and lay their eggs. If a road cuts through it, turtles take it in stride.

Unless we have the luck of a turtle visitor, that's where we're most likely to see them, carrying their camouflaged shell on fast little clawed feet. Stop to check this harmless fellow out, and you'll see how it got its name, for it snaps its shell closed like a box. Inside is a safe place to be, so box turtles have little to fear from predators—except us.

Taking a box turtle home for a pet is a bad idea. You cannot manage for them as well as they can for themselves. Unless you do careful research into what to feed them and how to keep them, they're likely to starve. Certainly they won't be making any more baby turtles.

The loss of just one adult box turtle from a local population each year could wipe out that population, for box turtle reproduction is a lengthy, tenuous and oftentimes inefficient process. Females typically produce small clutches of only three or four eggs a year, and temperature extremes, heavy rainfall, fungus and predators frequently destroy the eggs.

Even when an egg does survive, the hatchling—again having to struggle against weather, predators and other hazards—has a slim chance of reaching adulthood. It takes years to fully develop the stronger, protective adult shell and years of habitat familiarity to attain some degree of relative safety.

A female who is able to survive her first several years, reaching reproductive maturity, can produce a few hundred eggs during her lifetime, which can reach seventy-five to 100 years. From this entire lifetime of egg production, only two or three hatchlings may reach adulthood to sustain the population.

When you see a turtle crossing the road, the right thing to do is help her or him succeed. (You'll know it's a him if you get a glimpse of his eye before head, tail and four legs snap into the shell's safety. Males have red eyes.) If, of course, you can do so safely. It's not only our scenic byways turtles cross. You'll see them, and cringe, on main thoroughfares, even highways.

The other day, a woman driving in front of me stopped her SUV, hazards flashing, on Rt. 2 approaching Aris Allen Parkway and ran, arms flapping, to save a box turtle. Normally, you'd carry a rescued turtle to the side of the road it was seeking. Impossible in this case, so I imagine she took it back to the patch of wild from which it was heading.

If the turtle you hope to rescue does not snap into a box shell but remains exposed, pointy bill snarling at you, it's likely an aptly named snapping turtle. Cautiously, very cautiously, pick it up by the shell, not the tail, but well back so it can't turn its long flexible neck to bite the hand that rescues it. Save a turtle, and there will be more to see in years to come.

The
John F. Kennedy
of Dogs

*All muscle and poetry,
he swam in Chesapeake Bay 4,000 times.*

November 13, 1987-August 13, 2001

All we could see when Max was a pup were big feet and butt-up crouches that exploded in legendary romps.

"I don't know why kings and queens bothered with jesters, for nothing's funnier than puppies and kittens," said our son Nathaniel, then 16, who missed the start of his school term to start off the butter-fat yellow Lab puppy who joined our family on January 1, 1988.

Max came to us from St. Leonard. In his litter were eleven, six black and five yellow. At eight weeks old, he was the one with the tennis ball in his mouth. He was so cute that our other son, Alex, dropped out of school in England to bring up the pup.

In the fleeting, rollicking moments of puppyhood, we couldn't foresee the big-hearted old bag of bones who would, 5,000 wakings later, drag himself up rocks and hills to stay close to the people who were the king and queen of his universe.

All we could see for many more years was a hero of a dog. Strong and tireless in his long prime, he laughed at hills, calling encouragement over his shoulder to humans whose poor two feet couldn't carry them so ably as his four enormous leather-podded paws. After a long, cool drink of water—lapped fresh from the garden hose or, even better, salty from the Bay or muddy from a favorable puddle—he'd sleep long and hard until you'd say, *Max, are you ready...?*

Max was born ready. You want to walk in the woods in the fresh snow? Sure! He'd lead us in the track of his huge footprints, marking the white way with yellow blazes. Hey, fellows, he'd say, dig this! And he'd dive nose first and snort his way into this wonderful element.

He knew the Chesapeake even better than the woods, visiting it over 4,000 times. Into the cool liquid of its element, he'd surge after his ball, returning to us as a streaming white seal. Then as a wet dog, he'd trot up to shower us with spray before shoving a sandy glob of a ball into our hands—or dropping it on our laps.

In the water, Max was muscle and poetry. Want to go for a paddle? Sure! he'd say, and lead us in our kayak as if we were water gods and he was a Naiad pulling our chariot. When his favorite season returned to freeze the Bay, pursuit of that inevitable ball would send him careening over ice.

How, in those long days, could we foresee a time when our playful companion's steps were so numbered that his big feet could carry him no farther than the corner...the mailbox...the front stoop...no more?

How could we have imagined feeble this able creature proclaimed by his neighbor, lawyer J. Richard Ronay "the John F. Kennedy of dogs"? His fighting weight ranged from 95 to 105 pounds, but Max tried fighting only once or twice before setting his feet on the path of peace. Among our cats, he became sheriff. For our friends, he invited a return to harmony. Grown men with emotions encased in armor rolled on the floor with him, running their fingers through his stiff, yellow hair and stroking his buff velvet ears. Strong men were vanquished in many a game of tug with Max.

No matter what their age, women couldn't resist Max. His first girlfriend, Stephanie Linebaugh, courted him young and courted him old, calling him her best boyfriend. Many more followed—

Ariel, Betsy, Christi and Christy, Emelia, Farley, Georgia, Jennifer, Linda, Liz, Sonia, and Vicki—asking if Max couldn't come out to go for a walk in the sand or a romp in the fallen leaves. Would he like a cheeseburger? A massage?

Max didn't care much about other dogs, but he never met a person he didn't like. In him, in turn, many people met a dog they couldn't help but like. He waited with kids for the school bus, cheering the gray of the early morning. At *New Bay Times*, where he worked for seven years as receptionist, fear and indifference to his species gave way to Max's persistent advances.

How dared you resist a 100-pound dog who'd dropped his heavy head in your lap? Or who looked so adorable? He looked good in pictures, too, as you've seen on many a *New Bay Times* cover; he was sketched and painted in oil. Even strangers Max could reduce to tears, for in him they saw the image of their own best dog. That's how we saw him, too.

For when the time we could never imagine came upon us, all the days of Max's long life returned to us in a tumble of images too vivid to be mere memories. Old and feeble, he was all the dog we'd loved so long.

On the August morning when his frail body finally released his fearless spirit, it was hot as we held him, and we dreamed of lying together by the fire. Having achieved the wisdom of age, Max understood that dogs were mortal. In those last moments, he asked us to tell you that his only regret was the grief of those who loved him. Then he was young again, and romped into the universe.

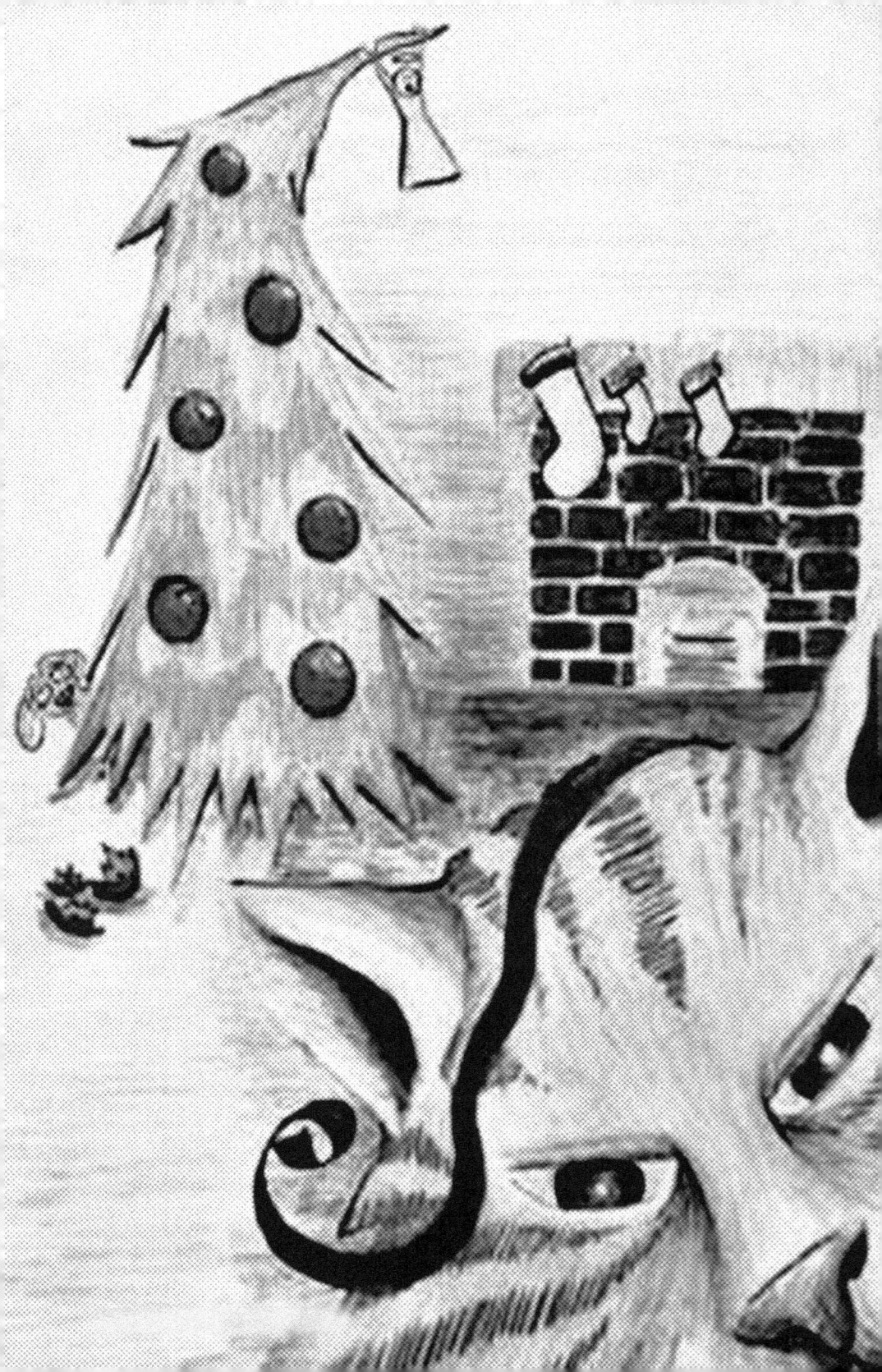

The Christmas Kitty

Prescriptions for loneliness can be hard to fill.

Christmas is a hard time to find a kitty, but Bill was dogged. He should have known that this quest wouldn't be easy. Except at dinner time, there is never a cat when you need one. When it is time to go to the vet or come in for the night, where is the cat? Your *here kitty, kitty, kitties* fall on deaf ears. Even a white cat disappears into the background—be it the green of spring or the butterscotch of leafy autumn—when you want him.

This was a lesson Bill could have learned from experience. But he was an investigative reporter, doggedly persistent in digging up the buried bones of chicanery. Finding a kitten ought to be a walk in the park. So when his wife said, "While you're back home for Christmas, why don't you get my mother a kitten?" he'd said, "I can do that."

The diagnosis was loneliness, seasoned with boredom. With too much time on her hands, Bill's mother-in-law was sure to get into trouble. After a lifetime of giving orders and moving walls, if walls needed to be moved in the pursuit of her goal, Elsa lived alone. She had not a thing in the world more she needed to do than clean and re-clean her empty three-bedroom house. Not a person whose comings and goings she could direct. Even her dogs, yappy little things that might have needed a lot of management, were listless.

Elsa's daughter, Sandra, who lived far away, had inherited her mother's conviction that she knew best. Now what she knew best was that Elsa needed a kitten. Her conviction had been growing since Elsa tamed Little Black Kitty.

"I know what you need," Elsa had said when the tiny refugee puffed up to twice his size and sidled away like some midnight genetic cross between a crab and a cotton ball.

It had been summer on Chesapeake Bay, and the crab pots were full. Elsa fed the foundling on backfin crab and cream. Eating, he had won her heart. As this feline climbed trees, hopped in the canoe or stalked a crab that escaped from the bushel, Elsa rediscovered the forgotten truth that nothing's more fun than a kitten.

But when the time came for Elsa to go back home, she left her kitty on Chesapeake Bay. "I don't see how I can take him on the plane," she said. "And what would the dogs think?"

Now with her every phone call she wondered how her Maryland kitty was doing. Christmas loomed blue for Elsa that year. One grandson was in England, the other on the West Coast. She couldn't visit, and Sandra couldn't come home. Except for Bill's brief Christmas Eve visit, Elsa would be alone.

"What Mother needs," said Sandra, "is a kitty under the tree."

Bill became a man with a plan.

THE QUEST

"Leave me a key so I can come back this afternoon," Bill told Elsa, after she'd fixed him one of her famous breakfasts.

"Don't you have to get home to your family?" she asked. It was Christmas Eve.

"Not right away," he said, setting out for the Humane Society of Missouri shelter.

Kittens always came easily to us, and frequently. They jumped into our arms from doorsteps, followed us home, were wheedled into our lives by friends whose mama cat had had a litter or by neighbors who had spied a kitty family living in a cinder block behind a church.

Now he'd come looking for a kitty at a place that certainly smelled like a cat, reeked like the big-cat house used to at the famed St. Louis

Zoo. But the only cats in residence on Christmas Eve were huddled and suspicious in their confinement, hard cases around enough to know when a fellow was looking for a kitten. They didn't bother with cute come-ons.

Neither did the human intake worker. "A kitten at Christmas? You've got to be kidding. Kittens aren't born this time of year, and if we had an odd litter, they'd be long gone."

"That's my problem," Bill told his father-in-law over a hot cup of coffee.

"Are you sure you wouldn't rather have an eggnog with a shot of bourbon?" asked Gene Martin, who lived right down the road from the shelter.

After their divorce, Gene and Elsa had settled into a spat-filled brother-and-sisterly-ness. A plan that would certainly take Elsa by surprise and might inconvenience her suited Gene just fine.

"A kitten," he said, rubbing his hands together. "I bet those damn dogs of hers won't like that."

Armed with a thick phone book, the two men settled into conspiracy. Among Gene's standards for competence was the ability to manage the phone book. At that skilled task, Elsa was only so-so, and for too long a time his only daughter threatened to be no whiz, either.

So Gene approved when Bill skipped the letters K and C and turned instead to Animals. He found welfare leagues and societies for the protection of living things. But there was nary a live voice at any number.

"It's Christmas Eve," said Gene.

"They're probably all volunteers," Bill sighed.

Among the messages shrilled one busy signal.

"That's way out in the county, anyway," said Gene, who knew places the way GPS does today. Outside, heavy skies pushed the temperature down in a hurry. It looked like snow, and Bill's parents' home in Bloomington, Illinois, was many hours away.

Bill turned to Pets. There, after pet cemeteries and pet salons, he found pet shops.

"Here, give me the book," said Gene. "We'll start with the nearest one."

The phone rang a long time—six, seven, eight, nine rings—before it connected. "Hello," Bill shouted, hearing the connection just as he was about to break it. Then the line died with a terrible thump. When he called back, it was busy.

Three more numbers were busy, too. The fourth rang and kept ringing. The fifth picked up, eventually, and after six or seven interruptions, Bill got his question out.

"Kittens?" the voice at the other end demanded. "You want kittens? You and four dozen others. The only cat around here is dead in the back alley, got run over by a UPS truck. If you want a cat this Christmas, you'll have to steal it."

For Christmas cheer, Gene and Bill had eggnog after all. Then they put on their thinking caps. Under Bill's, a hunch hatched. He trusted his hunches.

"I think I'll try that one in the county again," he said. "The first busy one. Read it again to me, Gene."

On the third ring, the number answered.

"I'm looking for kittens," Bill blurted, before the voice on the other end could speak.

"He wants to know if I have a reservation," Bill whispered to Gene.

"Tell him you do," said Gene.

And Bill's answer must have been the right one, for the low, slow voice said they'd be open until 12 noon, locked up at 12:01.

A KITTEN WAS STIRRING

Bill set out for the county. Before he could make it to the car, wind snatched his directions. But he might remember them, so away he went, over roads clogging with last-minute shoppers.

He thought he knew the way, and he might have, but one wrong turn led to another.

Far away from anywhere he'd ever hoped to be, at three minutes after noon, he pulled into a convenience store about as forlorn as the cats he'd seen that morning. Maybe those cats weren't so bad. Would the shelter still be open?

The Yellow Pages had been torn out or blown to Kansas in the outdoor phone kiosk, which seemed to be situated in a wind tunnel.

Maybe the shop hadn't closed all the way, he told himself. He called Gene. After all, he'd come this far, and the store wasn't as far away as he thought, Gene guessed. He might as well push on—and put off the sighs he'd hear calling home to Maryland to confess failure.

Bill pulled up at only 12:10, maybe later with the clock in his rental slow. The lights were off, but one truck was still in the back lot, its engine running and windows defrosting. A good sign.

The store's back door opened and a sweet-faced girl emerged, carrying a cage that swayed and thumped in blue canvas. Bill shoved the shifter into park and ran to the newly locked door.

"He's a tuxedo and he's not exactly a kitten," she said, lifting up the canvas.

"More like a teenager," she said, pointing to a hunched fellow. "He's mine. His sisters—one's black with white spots and one's white with black spots—have gone back to their foster homes for the holidays. They'll be back the day after Christmas. Can you come back then?"

Bill decided to go back to Elsa's, leave her presents under the tree and get on the road. There'd be plenty of time for kitties—and plenty of kitties—in the months ahead, maybe for spring. Eventually, Elsa would move to Maryland; maybe that's when they'd get her a kitty.

He took the turn onto Olive Street Road with the grim realization that for Elsa, too many Christmases have come and gone without kittens under the tree, or wishes come true. He wouldn't have turned into the strip mall if it hadn't occurred to him to bring some decent bagels home to Maryland, which has none, from the neighborhood deli. So what if they weren't quite right for Christmas; they were good. He wouldn't have seen the pet store if his parking space hadn't been snatched by a grinch who probably had more troubles than he did.

If he hadn't, what the heck, gone in, he wouldn't now be turning into Elsa's driveway with what may well have been the last kitty in all the city, in a cardboard box. He'd had to out-maneuver a whining kid for whom the right pet would have thick skin and cold blood. He'd virtually (actually?) snatched the kitty from the little spud. The fellow on the phone had said he might have to steal a cat, hadn't he? Bill never had paid money for a cat before, and this one went for $35. But he had Elsa's kitty, and the kitty was orange.

SAM THE CHRISTMAS KITTY

"I suppose you know what that husband of yours has done?" Elsa demanded when Sandra picked up the phone. It wasn't a question.

"He thinks he put one over on me. But I knew he was up to something. The dogs told me something was wrong in the boys' bedroom, and when I opened the door, there *this* was, curled up on the bed staring at the dogs and me.

"It's hardly a kitten, all ears and elbows. And Bill's note says he's a boy, so he'll probably pee all over. It says his name is Max, but that was my brother's name. I'm going to call him Sam. Kitty-Cat Sam," she announced.

"He's bad," she went on. "He's taken the ornaments off the tree. Where is he now? In my lap." Over the long-distance line, Elsa chided and Sam purred.

Sam was trouble. He never got over his fondness for Christmas ornaments. After Christmas was done and Elsa hauled the artificial tree down to a basement corner, Sam plucked off its red, silk-thread ornaments and, in his mouth, carried them one by one upstairs.

Her yappy dog duo went in and out as they liked into Elsa's fenced backyard. But Sam, who had proved his skill as a climber, had to stay inside. Spring had come and all was green before Sam got to go out. He stayed in sight, chasing sunbeams as Elsa raked and weeded. But when it was time to go in, there was no Sam. Elsa called and called and set out little dishes of chicken cooked just for him, but darkness fell and still no Sam.

She sat up late, but still no Sam. In bed, she tossed and worried. After one in the morning, her ears pricked. She sat up. She listened. And listened. Yes, faintly she could hear Sam's voice.

The night was warm and her nightgown flimsy as she searched for him in the yard. Her flashlight beam found him, high up in the budding apple tree. So Elsa, well after midnight, clanged out her late husband's extension ladder from the shed and braced it against the tree, as Sam cried piteously. Up she climbed. Sam jumped onto her shoulder. That's the image her next-door neighbor recalled when, awakened by the racket, turned his flashlight upward. There was a ladder, Elsa and Sam.

"He's always playing jokes on me," Elsa reported to her daughter. "That Sam's a lot like Gene Martin."

EPILOGUE

My mother died that August, when the apples on her tree were nearly ripe, and Sam had taken to batting around windfalls instead of Christmas tree balls. For the last seven months of her life, Elsa was never bored and seldom lonely. With Sam on their case, even the dogs seemed to have taken out a new lease on life. After Elsa was gone and the dogs were adopted by friends, the Yorkshire terrier named Nathania for her grandson surprised her new owner with a litter of puppies. Sam became a college cat. But that's another story. Now, a granddaughter has been born to carry on Elsa's name. And that is another life.

The Dog Days of August

Recalling four-legged friends who love us unconditionally with more understanding than we realize

"A dog," Mark Twain wrote, "can't be depended on to carry out a special providence." His case in point was "Prov'dence's" failure to depend on Uncle Lem's dog—appointing Uncle Lem instead—to soften the three-story fall of an Irish hod carrier. The Irishman lived, but Uncle Lem's back was broken in two places. "Why didn't the Irishman fall on the dog?" Twain's storyteller asked. "Becuz the dog would a seen him a coming and stood from under. That's the reason the dog warn't appinted."

Clearly neither Twain nor his circuitous storyteller, the legendary Jim Blaine, had ever met a Canine Companion for Independence. Prov'dence had those two born a couple of centuries too early to meet this lineage of dogs appointed to stand in for humans in the most remarkable ways.

The way we humans tell the story, Prov'dence has put us in the driver's seat, giving us "dominion over" the animals. The dogs who train as Canine Companions for Independence, mostly Labrador and golden retrievers, lead the field in responding to benevolent human domination, for they dedicate their lives to doing for their humans what they can't. Acquiescence has, I think, a lot to do with the breed. Though sorely lacking the training to train dogs, I did pretty well at bossing my two Labrador retrievers, but not so well with my beagle-German shepherd mix Slip Mahoney. Cats seem to have misread the domination clause of the Bible.

All together, my lifetime experience with these and many more dogs and even more cats suggests that mutual adaptation

319

was the key to the flourishing of our mixed-species relationships. Neither dog nor cat could I ever convince to be other than what its nature dictated.

Some of the ways Slip Mahoney remained true to his nature are too embarrassing for me to mention, and even the best of my dogs and cats had the occasional flea and flaw. Some, like my best black cat BBK's fondness for bread and baked goods of any sort, were often charming. Others, not so, as when our pandemic pussycat Innocente brings in birds for a game of Who's Got It.

Within the parameters of their nature and mine, I've had the best relationship with the creatures in whom I've invested the most time and attention—Innocente excepted. So now that I have no dog, I wish I'd spent more time working with my two oh-so-willing Labs, Max and Moe, to develop their latent talents. Every day, I miss the mutually adapted companionship of a creature, cat or dog, who gives me his best (for the last forty years my best animal friends have been males) in return for me giving mine.

The air this time of year is fragrant with the caramelized sugar of sunbaked vegetation and bittersweet with remembrance as well. Amid celebrations of so many birthdays of friends and neighbors are so many days of loss that paging through my anniversary book feels like walking through a cemetery.

Personal losses are magnified many times over. The widely beloved outdoorsman Bill Burton, whose columns you read in my newspaper from 1993 to 2009, died on August 10, 2009. My mother, Elsa Olivetti Martin, shares her 1998 death day, August 6, with the tens of thousands killed in Hiroshima in 1945 at the birth of the atomic age. Max took his last breath on a steamy August 13.

So I rejoice that this time of year marks nice life-saving anniversaries as well. July 30: fifty years since Medicare and Medicaid created lifelines to health care for senior and poor Americans. August 14: eighty years of Social Security turning wages into lifelong income. You probably don't remember the battles preceding that entitlement, signed into law by Franklin D. Roosevelt in long-ago 1935. But 1965 and the battle led by Lyndon B. Johnson remain in many memories. Together, those two landmarks put the Affordable Care Act—the turmoil surrounding it and the eventual good it may achieve—in perspective.

Perspective is a good thing now that our nation's law-making factory seems to have turned to sausage-making.

That, reader, is where you're heading, as *Bay Weekly* co-creator and editorial consultant Bill Lambrecht—who has reported in Washington on national political doings for a noteworthy thirty years—turns our Dog Days storytelling in that direction.

"Bill," I said. "I've had my say on the dogs you and I have shared; now—at the fourteenth anniversary of our dear dog Max's death—it's your turn."

Here's what he wrote, under the headline Capital Leaks:

> I suspected growing up that your dog reads your mind. Now that more dogs have entered (and, alas, exited) my life, I know it's true.
>
> Back in Illinois, there was Slip Mahoney, the roving German beagle, apprehended and jailed seven times (once at a Kroger meat counter). Mornings, Sandra would head off in her silver Gremlin to her newspaper job in downtown Springfield. My consuming thought: How to secure the house to prevent canine escape.
>
> Slip, of course, would have caught that brain wave, exited through an unlatched door (or right through the screen), and begun weaving his way through traffic on a Gremlin-sniffing mission.
>
> In Maryland, there was Max the yellow Lab, formerly employed in the salaried position as *Bay Weekly* Office Greeter. On his days off, we'd go fishing in the old Sundancer, in Borg-perfect sync. He'd get excited as me spotting a bluefish feeding frenzy. One day, after a tip about "acres and acres of huge breaking rockfish," he seemed to share my nagging sense that something was wrong.

He whined as we raced to the slip. Then oddly, he stayed in the car, watching forlornly, while I discovered upon boarding the vessel that I'd left the rods back on the patio. Of course when we'd finally got our gear together and motored out on Chesapeake Bay, there was nary a fin in sight. (I'm hangdog myself at this moment recalling that today is the anniversary of Max's death.)

Then came Moe the yellow Lab, who held down at least three jobs. At *Bay Weekly,* he was sidekick to Nipper the Notorious (a Jack Russell who owns the Maryland state record for biting humans).

On Capitol Hill, Moe was my security detail. (I'm speaking here about protection from members of Congress, patrolling the 'hood with glazed eyes and the look of someone eager to take a bite out of your neck.)

There too, on the Senate side of the Hill, Moe was ambassador at large. Around our condo, he'd buddy up to senators' poodles and wrestle in Stanton Park with young female aides who'd kick off their heels and roll in the grass. All the while, he'd stay plugged into my thinking, like that morning during the October 2013 government shutdown when we walked along the south side of the Capitol building.

I'm wondering, as we walked, why the zealots therein, in malicious and ham-handed fashion, had shut down a sizable portion of the federal government.

Moe, leash-less but usually well behaved, big-nosed his way through azaleas and lifted his leg on the limestone foundation of the Congress of the United States.

He plowed back through the bushes, looked up at me smiling and communicated a question: Whaddya think of that? I petted him.

Empathy. That's the emotional partnership shared by the man who needed a friend in Washington and, following the advice of Harry S Truman, got a dog. Our thirty-third president obviously understood that our four-legged friends love us unconditionally—and with more understanding than we realize.

—with Bill Lambrecht

Farewell, Moe

NOVEMBER 12, 2005 – NOVEMBER 29, 2014

"He's just a dog," we would say.
Many saw more in him.

Angel of God my guardian dear,
to whom God's love commits me here,
ever this day be at my side
to light, to guard, to rule and guide.

I never expected the guardian angel of grade school prayer to be corporeal. Certainly not a dog.

The stiff fur of a yellow Labrador retriever covered 105 pounds of vibrant muscle. His chest, where the fur whirled in vortex, was broad and deep. Foot pods were thick and black, indifferent to the ice and stone. Lower legs were strong with long bones, springy with tendons. Lips black as pods fluttered in elastic opposition to podal density. Quivering whiskers rose from black pores. Ears were soft as silk purses, eyes big, brown and soulful—an angelic giveaway.

Moe was pure creature, the far end of the spectrum from pure spirit. Yet he was a guardian angel to a T.

By my side? Twenty-four/seven.

Moe was my dictionary for the words *dogged and hounded*.

I have been dogged. I have been hounded. You do not need to hear the trumpet bay of beagles, bassets and blue ticks to experience hounding. A dog you belong to has no need to track you like a fugitive. He has you. Moe hounded with big brown eyes, deep breath and proximity.

I came to morning not at the alarm clock's siren summons but at Moe's silent hounding, head on the side of my bed.

Dog presence softly told the hours of my day: time to eat...time for a walk...time to play in creaturely abandon...time to be companions.

Waking time, breakfast time, waiting time. Moe was a study in patience. He waited through all the diversions that stood between one place and the next.

Come on, I'd say, *we're going now.* Still he'd lie, giant head between shapely paws, until key in hand I opened the door. Only then would he rise, joint by joint until the whole dog stood, stretched nose to tail and trotted into whatever came next.

Next, for roughly 1,700 days, was getting into the car, which for Moe was the lifelong effort of a 100-year-old dog. My car is small, a coupe, so he squeezed into the back seat like yarn threading a small-eye needle.

I calculate that he and I drove 100,000 miles together in my little Audi TT. You might have seen us together. He made, I'm told, a memorable sight, with his big head out the window. Parked, I'd often open the hatch to give him air. Resting his head on the seat back, he'd put on the look of the world's saddest dog as he awaited my return.

Moe was my assistant at four *Bay Weekly* offices, one in Deale and three in Annapolis. (He also had a Washington, DC office, where he assisted husband Bill, but that is their story.) At work, his job was not demanding. Mostly, he'd lie on his cushion under my desk, waiting for lunch, for a biscuit, for a walk, for the ride home, for whatever tedium and pleasure those hours would bring.

The best of the pleasures were wild romps through the woods with Nipper the Holy Terrier, a Jack Russell of considerable notoriety, also dead this dog-bereft year.

*Ever this day be at my side...*Yes, Moe was.

Moe's presence was mostly insinuative. But it could be intrusive. He could sound a clarion bark that shook pictures off the walls, deer out of brush and souls out of hiding.

As my guard, he was potentially formidable. I never locked my car when Moe was in it, and seldom closed the windows. Who would enter a confined space occupied by a 105-pound likely growling creature with inch-long canine teeth?

I stepped out of offices urban and rural into secluded lots at all hours knowing that Moe stood between me and whatever might lurk in the shadows. I slept through the midnight creaks of an empty house fearless of all intruders but ghosts. Moe guarded our house—and all inside—with authority.

But Moe was more than a guard dog. He gave us the light and guidance I was taught to expect from my guardian angel, even one appearing in such unexpected form.

To whom God's love commits us here...

If those words mean what they say, do they not promise the constancy of God's love in day-in, day-out presence that is, if not intrusive, perhaps dogged?

If God's love dwells in all creation, it may not be so far a leap of faith to find a divine outreach in a dog.

Some force for which I can find no better explanation emanated from Moe. The very sight of that big dog broke down the barrier of conventions that separate us from one another. Beautiful women kissed this dog as if they were princesses and he their frog. DC suits fell to their tailored knees to embrace him. Old men buried their fingers in his fur and wept for their lost dogs. Friends or strangers, loners and gregarians, people fell for Moe.

He's just a dog, Bill, or I, would say.

Many saw more in him.

"He's a magnificent creature," a last-days friend pronounced. For even as brain cancer advanced, Moe kept his magic.

For the nine years that were Moe's eternal present, I felt that magic every day, so it needed no words.

On Moe's death, it found words.

All the days he was at our side, our lives were lighted, guarded, ruled (dog walk is the unbreakable rule) and guided.

Just a dog opened our hearts.

Sandra Olivetti Martin

PART VIII

Misbehavior

In Illinois, Sandra was drawn to the stories of women in deep straits or preyed upon. The most invasive of these assaults is depicted in the Lawrenceville Peephole Incident, recounting the fate of two women who discovered they had been spied upon while using their factory's toilet. Acquittal for a woman who kills her husband is the disturbing focus of another story.

Writing for *Illinois Times*, Sandra was on hand for a spectacular skyjacking, with a teen girl reprising another, earlier skyjacking drama in which her mother was shot dead—for the love of a magnetic prison inmate.

Sandra sheds her cloak of objectivity in a story from the Equal Rights Amendment wars about a woman in deep legal trouble playing the game of political campaign cash. The title is true to its tone: Wanda Was Wronged.—Editor's Note

The Lawrenceville Peephole Incident

*Gawked at in private moments, sisters
Ruth and Etta demanded justice.*

Runoff of a record 42-inch snowfall, followed by March rains, have swelled the raging Embarras River until no longer are its marshlands visible anywhere in Lawrence County, Illinois. Life has been as tumultuous for sisters Etta Briggs and Ruth Harrington since they learned that male workers had opened a gaping peephole above the women's toilets in the Lawrenceville computer-parts factory where they worked as inspectors.

"I was proud of my job," says Ruth, 41. "I never thought they'd do us like this."

After a determined confrontation with managers of the electronics factory and its parent company, the sisters were fired. Now, resolute and out of work as the seasons change, they have sued both Lawrenceville Industries Inc. and its parent company, Central Enterprises Inc., of Evansville, Ind. With attorney Mary Lee Leahy, a veteran of Illinois Gov. Dan Walker's cabinet and high-stakes legal fights, the sisters threaten to rock the boat in factories wherever women are oppressed and demeaned.

In their first interview since the Lawrenceville Peephole Incident changed their lives, the women told me of the odyssey that led them to Leahy and the Seventh Judicial Circuit Court, in Springfield, where they are seeking in excess of $120,000 in lost wages and damages.

"Late on a Friday night in January, 1978, just about an hour and a half before our shift ended, we were having our coffee break," Ruth begins.

"Etta was in the restroom and I was in the cafeteria, sitting across the table from one of the young fellows at work. 'You know', he says, 'there's a way to see into the women's toilets'. I don't know how my face looked, but he must have seen something because right away he added: 'What are you looking at me for? I haven't used it yet.'"

A world they had known, and trusted, for seven years collapsed during that coffee break. How had a peephole over a restroom used by as many as eighty-six women gone undetected? Whoever did it has not confessed. Until they testify under oath, all Ruth and Etta will say publicly is that what they saw when they looked through the peephole from the other side showed that it has been a male perversion for quite some time.

From the toilet side, the peephole appeared to be an innocent ventilating fan that never worked in all her years on the job, Ruth says. A staircase led to a landing above the restroom, and from up there the ventilating fan served a different purpose. Its cover swiveled aside on one nail. Through the grillwork covering the blades, "you could see everything in the two center stalls," Etta says.

Who were these men? How many had lurked in the shadows of that storage balcony, peeping at women, their friends and coworkers, using the toilets.

"Nobody knows," says Ruth, who ranks twenty-third in company seniority, shaking her head at possibilities that pain her to ponder. "But turnover has always been high at Lawrenceville Industries. Surely it wasn't everybody. Some men wouldn't stoop to that. But that's what's so terrible. Any one of them might have. We haven't been mixing much since we found out."

Shaken, the sisters didn't know what to do. Perhaps it hadn't happened to them personally. Hadn't they always preferred the end stalls, the ones out of range? No, they likely had been victims, gawked at in their most private moments.

Reluctantly, they acknowledged what they already knew: They had been watched. Slowly, they sorted through options. Etta, the bolder of the two, immediately told her husband. Quiet and conscientious Ruth couldn't tell her husband alone. She brought him to Etta's carefully appointed mobile home where the two families faced the scandal together.

"Shamed, spied on, betrayed, hurt, disgusted—you can't know how we felt," Ruth says.

What kind of factory was this, where women toiling could become a circus attraction? Ruth says she knew of no behavior like this prior to the discovery.

"Nobody went out of their way to harass the women," says Ruth. "Sure, there were differences in the way men and women were treated. If a woman's machine went down, she was given another job, even one out of her section, while the men under the same conditions could loaf or read. Once the plant was slowing down because we were about to go out on strike. They brought cleaner and had the women scrub scrape marks off the floor, while the men watched. But never anything really low down."

Why did these men do it? Why bother when *Playboy* and its dozen imitators show more? Marilyn Moquin, a development counselor in Springfield, offers this explanation: "Just as rape is more a crime of violence than a crime of sex, this may be a desperate power play. It's as if the intruders were saying, 'we have it over you, without you even knowing we can look down and see you in a vulnerable position. You're demeaned and that makes us better and stronger.'"

Gary Morgan, co-director of the Sangamon State University Learning Center, offered an explanation that wouldn't pass muster with victims. "You don't understand how sex works in men if this surprises you. Peeping is the oldest sport in the world. In toilets or not, here was the real thing. I don't want to justify what they did, but I don't think you have to go very far to explain it."

However many the toms, whatever their motives, for Etta Briggs and Ruth Harrington the incident was a sick joke better suited to the pages of *Hustler* unregenerate than to real life.

333

Bad turned to worse for the sisters. They complained about the peephole to their supervisor, who in turn reported it to plant manager Tom Osmond. The sisters fully expected that things would be set right with sealing of the peephole. It would have been an easy matter in a factory where people used tools to fix things.

"We didn't want revenge," Etta says, "but it just wasn't right."

Adds Ruth: "We went there to work, not to be spied on."

"It's only right," Etta continues, her Illiana accent intense and her jaw set, "that the men should be questioned and the guilty ones made to answer for what they did. Otherwise things like this can keep happening. It's not only for us. Women shouldn't have to be treated this way.

"They wouldn't even have to question all the men. It's not hard to find out who's supposed to be where. People are pretty well watched here."

Less than a week after the discovery, in January, before their 3:30 p.m. shift was to begin, Ruth and Etta spoke with Osmond, the plant manager, and a representative of Central Enterprises to find out what action had been taken. Neither man responded with information.

When I reached Osmond by phone, he described himself as "just working for Central Enterprises...I'd rather you spoke to them."

Robert Mounts, the company's vice president, also had little to say. "I know what happened and I know why," he told me. "But we're a business; I don't want to get involved."

Ruth and Etta came away with the sense that neither of the men understood what the fuss was about. The plywood cover had been nailed back in place over the fan, and they were told that they should return to work.

"But," says Etta, "if it's been moved once, it can be moved again. There is no way for a person in the restroom to tell whether the cover's on or off. We want it fixed right."

When the women pressed their case, they were told that they shouldn't "feel that way," as Ruth recalls. Worse still, they were told, "and unless you report to work today you can consider yourself terminated."

They didn't go to work, and on that day, January 11, they were fired.

Relating the conversation, the sisters grow pensive and struggle for words to represent what is so natural to them as to transcend words. It is a fundamental right of privacy, they write in their lawsuit, which was "violated and destroyed."

Ruth, often the summarizer of the pair, elaborates: "We stayed out not only to force them to fix it but because we naturally thought they would fix it so we could go back. We couldn't work under those conditions."

Losing their jobs has meant the loss of their inspector salaries and the seniority they accrued over the years. That's hard in an area where layoffs of junior workers are common. It's harder still on the Harringtons given that Ronald was laid off from his job at another factory shortly before Ruth was fired.

It's hard, too, on pride. "I used to imagine how awful it would feel to be fired," Ruth says. "Nowadays, people ask me why I'm not at work. I sure don't want to tell them about all this, but if I don't say anything they can imagine even worse."

They also lost their health insurance and a year's vacation pay, which was due to be handed over soon in a lump sum.

Determined to fight, Ruth and Etta have come out swinging. "Even now, I can hardly believe it's me doing this," says Ruth. "But I look again and here I am."

Their husbands and families are behind them and they have each other; neither sister can imagine waging this fight without the other.

Above all else and beyond a doubt, they believe they have right on their side. They don't need lawyers, or bargaining units, or precedents to tell them what they know as familiarly as if they'd given birth to it. Down in their eastern Illinois farming community spattered with oil-related industries, justice is alive and well—at least in the minds of the two sisters.

"It's only right," one or the other says time and time again.

But in the crazy-quilt justice system, knowing what to do and how to do it is separate from knowing right from wrong.

The Constitution doesn't spell out rights of workers. Its writers were concerned with creating and regulating a government. So the courts have traditionally shied away from scrutinizing the relationship between a business and its workers.

"Business nowadays is as powerful as states were back then," says Larry Golden, president of the central Illinois American Civil Liberties Union and a political studies professor at Sangamon State University. "The Illinois Constitution goes further in protecting citizens from these new super powers. But the legal territory of what rights individuals have when they go to work remains pretty much uncharted."

After the labor turmoil of the late 1800s and early 1900s, Congress passed the Wagner Act to bridge the power gap. That law, also known as the National Labor Relations Act, gave employees the right to choose collective bargaining as their voice at work. Ordinarily, problems with working conditions, otherwise known as grievances, are negotiated by union representatives.

The union at Lawrenceville Industries, the International Union of Electrical, Radio, and Machine Workers, appears to be no help. The union and company already are deadlocked in a series of cases spread over years. In one recent case, a group of employees petitioned for a vote to decertify the union. In this tangled impasse, Etta and Ruth concluded that being a union member doesn't help.

They approached three lawyers, one a woman, only to be told that the incident and firing were unfortunate but things like this have to be endured. Finally, they read about the work of the Women's Law Center and were referred to the Springfield chapter of the National Organization for Women.

One NOW member recalled a fight to allow a girl to play on a boys' baseball team. The woman who represented the girl was Mary Lee Leahy, who gained fame for representing the renegade Democratic delegation that ousted the Richard J. Daley delegation from the party's 1972 convention in Miami.

Leahy, too, seems ready for the fight. "This case could make Illinois common law for the rights of employees in the workplace," she tells me. "There's no telling how common this kind of thing is, but I imagine it's a lot more common than we'd like to believe."

The Lawrenceville Peephole Incident could, says Leahy, focus attention on an issue bigger than one factory and two sisters. She describes it as one of the five or ten cases she's seen in her career where outrage touched people to their cores.

Ruth, her husband of twenty years and their three sons live in the white house across from the church in the two-tavern village of Russellville, pop. 150. Three of Etta's four children, one of them a girl, are in the U.S. Air Force. The sisters never asked to lead the battle for workplace rights, but that is where they find themselves.

"For all the trouble it's caused, we wish it would go away. But it won't," Ruth says.

Because they refused to suffer in silence, no longer is their humiliation a private burden. Something happened, binding them to a force larger than themselves.

"I was happy with my little factory job and with being a housewife. But we're not quitting," Etta declares, her face radiant with conviction in her cause.

Adds Ruth: "It wouldn't be fair to women to quit here."

Women Who Kill in Self-Defense

*Sandra Brewer's case
captures the complexity of domestic tragedy.*

Sandra Brewer is free. The Beardstown, Illinois woman of Native American heritage who had suffered beatings from her husband has been acquitted of murder charges by a Cass County jury. After three days of testimony, the seven-man, five-woman panel concluded that Sandra Brewer had committed no crime in the early hours of March 6 when she fired a shotgun point blank at the chest of her husband, Michael Brewer. In the words of defense attorney Milton McClure, "the verdict is a new springtime for Sandra Brewer."

The quiet trial in Virginia, Illinois is the latest in a trend of women judged to have killed in self-defense.

On Wednesday, May 17, 1978 Sandra Brewer took the stand in her own defense. She was allowed by Judge Fred W. Reither to affirm or deny events as McClure presented them to her. Her two-hour story was filled in by the testimony of witnesses. Among them was the acting chief of Beardstown police, Michael Dyer, who received Sandra Brewer's phone call minutes after the shooting and stayed with her in the following hours.

That is but a sketch of a tragedy that could demand the judgment of Sherlock Holmes or the insight of Miss Marple to reunite events with their human motives. Along with the crime, lawyers in the trial sought to reconstruct the emotions in the wee hours of March 6. State's Attorney Robert Welch argued that Sandra Brewer triggered the deadly sequence. It was up to McClure, who was Sandra Brewer's court-appointed counsel, to counter Welch by means of a meticulous reconstruction of actions and words in Michael Brewer's last minutes.

Sandra Brewer, 21, is 5 feet 2 inches and weighs 110 pounds. People still call her "a girl." The dark-haired, brown-skinned woman was 5 years old when her parents abandoned her and her seven brothers and sisters. Michael Brewer, who was 5 feet 6 inches and weighed 130 pounds, had grown up in Beardstown, an Illinois River town of 6,800 people. His parents, brothers and sisters still live there. The Beardstown house where Brewer died was the peripatetic couple's fifth home. In the bedroom, two loaded long guns, a rifle and a .20-gauge shotgun hung on the wall.

As a house painter, Michael Brewer was employed six or seven months of the year. The rest of time the couple and their son lived on unemployment checks and on the $65 a week Sandra Brewer earned as a dishwasher in a Beardstown cafe. She finished her last shift at noon on Sunday, March 5, and was picked up by Brewer and their son Luke, born in 1974.

Trouble began during Sandra's pregnancy with Luke. Her physician, Dr. Robert Cox, testified he had found her body bruised in an August 1974 routine examination. Two years later, he stitched a laceration on her scalp. She acknowledged, Cox testified, that in both incidents her husband had hurt her.

McClure told of a decaying marriage that erupted in violence. On two occasions, police had been called to intervene in family fights. In October, 1977, they were summoned to PeeWee's tavern in Beardstown. Officer Michael Dyer, who took Sandra Brewer's March 6 confession, found the Brewers in the street, Michael sitting astride his wife.

Hours before Michael Brewer was to die, Sandra had telephoned the Beardstown police, complaining that "her husband was bothering her and trying to get in the house," police officer Robert Flood testified. He said nothing could be done as long as the two were married.

"If he shot me, could you do something?" Sandra replied.

"A little loud," Flood recalled.

Michael Brewer came home at 3 a.m. to a locked house, his clothes deposited on the doorstep. According to testimony, he broke a pane of glass and reached in to unbolt the door from the inside. Sandra Brewer was awakened.

She confronted her husband in the living room of the single-story, five-room rented house. She declared she wanted a divorce. Michael Brewer slapped her. Minutes later, he lay dead on the couple's bed, his abdomen torn open by a deer slug.

"I'll see you and your son dead before I leave." These are the words of Michael Brewer, as Sandra Brewer testified. She had snatched the .20-gauge Mossberg shotgun off the wall and was holding it on him as he spoke.

"You don't have the guts to shoot," Michael Brewer is alleged to have said.

When the shotgun roared, its barrel was four inches away from him, according to testimony from an Illinois Department of Law Enforcement firearms expert.

McClure built Sandra Brewer's innocent plea on self-defense, asking jurors to embrace the doctrine of reasonable doubt.

"The burden of proof lies with the prosecution," he asserted. "They must prove her version untrue. If there is a reasonable hypothesis besides guilt, take it, for that means reasonable doubt. If her explanation is consistent with her innocence, then it becomes your duty to find her not guilty."

Sandra Brewer is far from alone in having the final say with an abusive husband or boyfriend. But her case is notable, legal experts say, for its emphasis on "reasonable doubt" in a self-defense plea.

McClure was at some pains to establish a history of brutality.

"A man who will beat his wife in pregnancy will beat her anytime," he said. But his main thrust was not what Sandra Brewer had suffered but the quality of that final moment of decision.

Although "in great fear of bodily harm, Sandra Brewer was at that last moment an armed woman who, even so, waited to fire until she had no alternative," he said. "For the first time in their married life that night her husband threatened her son," he argued. "I think that did it. Based on past performance she had ample reason to believe him. She was alone at 3 a.m., deserted, with a drunken man threatening her and her son. If she wanted cold blood, it was simple. She could have shot him from across the room when he came to the door. Bang! She didn't. This girl waited to the very last minute. He could have stopped. He didn't have to die," McClure argued.

Sandra Brewer's lack of passivity could have been viewed as a dangerous break with the well-documented tradition of female submissiveness that has become clear in recent cases. Michael Brewer's close friend and companion that night testified Brewer had stayed away from home because "Sandra was trying to pick a fight... He went home to straighten things out," he said.

In Welch's words, Brewer was the peacemaker. "If he was as violent as she said, then he would have had the gun," Welch said. "Instead, I believe she was advancing on him. He was backed into the far corner of the bed, as far back as he could go, as if he were a cornered animal," and shot, Welch argued.

The norm of female passivity has a double cutting edge. A study of how sex factors affect verdicts in murder trials, published in the *Journal of Psychology*, showed that because females are typically seen as passive, juries assume they will kill only under strong provocation or insanity.

In earlier murder trials, women have chosen to plead insanity. In Lansing, Michigan, Francine Hughes was acquitted of killing her husband although she set fire to the room in which he slept. Jennifer Patri, of Waupaca, Wisconsin, shot her estranged husband and later burned her home. She pleaded innocent by reason of mental defect to arson and innocent by reason of self-defense to murder. She was found guilty of manslaughter.

McClure chose self-defense pure and simple. Arguing that Sandra Brewer's actions "were not the actions of a guilty woman" enabled him to tie his defense to the reasonable-doubt clause. "Self-defense stands unless disproved," he asserted.

Brewer's lawyer hit hard on another ground where many defense attorneys fear to tread.

Research suggests that defenses characterized by hard-edged feminism may prejudice juries against the female defendant. Alan Eisenberg, attorney for Jennifer Patri, who was found guilty of manslaughter, had enlisted help from feminist activists from the University of Wisconsin.

Unlike Eisenberg, McClure's approach on Brewer's behalf was low key. He neither foreshadowed his strategy nor spoke to reporters on the record before or during the trial. "My experience as a lawyer is that hell has no fury like a man whose wife is leaving him," McClure said in the courtroom prior to his victory.

"It's believable that he said 'I will not let you leave.' It hurts his pride. 'You haven't got the guts,' he taunted. She backs. He approaches. At the last moment, the gun nearly against him, his threat to her and the child just having been said, she shoots. He did not have to die. If he had not been so determined, so arrogant, so male, this would not have had to happen," McClure said in his closing statement.

The jury deliberated two hours and fifteen minutes before returning a verdict that speaks to the complexity of domestic tragedy. Jurors concluded, as McClure put it, that they could not "undo the past, but only look to the future and prevent another wrong." Sandra Brewer wept when she heard the verdict. She had sat motionless throughout the four-day trial, her shoulders and jaw squared, "too proud to beg," as her lawyer put it. But on the steps leading into the Cass County courthouse she exulted, lifting her arms skyward in the late afternoon sun, ready for the "new springtime" her lawyer had hoped for her.

Illinois Times

JANUARY 5-11, 1979   25¢

DOWNSTATE ILLINOIS' WEEKLY NEWSPAPER

THE CHRISTMAS SKYJACKING
DRAMA AT THE MARION AIRPORT
P. 4

VOLUME 4, NUMBER 15

Hijacked TWA jetliner with eighty-nine passengers aboard sitting at Williamson County Airport.

A Christmas Skyjacking

A St. Louis suburban teen aimed to finish her dead mother's mission.

MARION, ILL.—On December 21, 1978, the eyes of the nation were cast on this deep southern Illinois community when Robin Oswald hijacked a TWA jetliner and demanded release of a notorious criminal and con man from Marion's federal maximum security prison. The inmate, Garrett Brock Trapnell, is the same man Robin Oswald's mother was attempting to spring a year earlier when she was shot to death over the prison by the pilot of a helicopter she had hijacked in St. Louis.

Barbara Oswald, a mother of five who was finishing a master's degree, had taken up Trapnell's cause after reading a book, *The Fox is Crazy Too: The True Story of Garrett Trapnell, Adventurer, Skyjacker, Bank Robber, Con Man, Lover.* Now, with still another skyjacking underway, an array of federal agents and journalists speed through rural Illinois lands far from the metropolises of Chicago and St. Louis toward a tiny airport where the drama unfolds.

TEN A.M.

Trans World Airlines Flight 541, carrying eighty-seven people from Louisville and St. Louis to Kansas City, was hijacked a short time ago. It's not the typical terrorist or desperado at work.

The hijacker is Robin Oswald, of Richmond Heights, Missouri, a St. Louis suburb. The young woman with curly blonde hair claims to have three sticks of dynamite strapped to her waist beneath her bulky sweater. In her left hand she grasps a doorbell-like device that is wired to the explosives. She demands the release of Trapnell, who was shot and captured at John F. Kennedy International Airport in New York in 1972 while attempting to hijack a TWA flight. Oswald tells the pilot to land at Marion, in southern Illinois, where Trapnell is held in the federal maximum security lock-up that replaced Alcatraz.

From her seat in the nineteenth row, the second-to-last on the left side of the twin-jet McDonnell Douglas DC-9, Oswald commands the attention of law enforcement and the nation's news media for the next ten hours.

For now, her act is a secret between herself and the flight attendant whom she has chosen as her messenger to communicate with the pilot. Seated across the aisle from Oswald is Bud Zaret, 50, a New York businessman headed to a morning meeting in Kansas City.

"We were about forty minutes in the air out of St. Louis," Zaret tells us later, "when I saw the stewardess leaning down over the girl, whispering. She was holding her side; I thought she was sick. Then I saw the stewardess run toward the cockpit saying 'Oh my God.'"

The pilot, James Miller, of Kansas City, takes seriously the young woman's threat to change course or have his plane blown up. Over Kansas City, "he pulled up, squawked the proper ID for a hijacking, and asked for clearance to Carbondale," Joe Frets, a Federal Aviation Administration spokesman, says later.

In these moments, Robin Oswald is at the height of her power. She has taken an irreversible step, setting in motion a chain of lightning-fast responses, mobilizing the awesome focus of a nationwide law enforcement system and taken many lives in her hands.

ELEVEN A.M.

Twelve minutes ago, the hijacked aircraft landed at Williamson County Airport near Marion, a modern facility that serves the major industries of "Little Egypt"—the federal penitentiary and Southern Illinois University, ten miles west.

"The eighty-three passengers and four crew members are doing what the hijacker is telling them to do," Federal Aviation Administration spokesman John Leyden tells reporters.

Meanwhile, the massive machinery for disarming the hijacker with the goal of preventing a tragedy goes into motion. FBI agent Richard McCauley leaves no doubt who is in charge: "As general policy, by agreement with the FAA and the Department of Justice at the very highest level in DC, we have jurisdiction over skyjackings on the ground, and the airline has air jurisdiction. We have a plan of action, but there's no pat way of handling a skyjacking," he says.

Special Weapons and Tactics (SWAT) team snipers and police from federal, state and local agencies head toward the Williamson County Airport, or already are in position. Bernard Thompson, an FBI hostage negotiator, arrives from Louisville. A special phone hook-up with the isolated plane connects Thompson with Oswald. The 17-year-old skyjacker remains in control.

"She was real calm, as if she didn't have a problem in the world," Marine Pvt. John Culberson, 18, says later.

William Werner, 47, of Kansas City, says Oswald kept her composure throughout. "She was just not the type you'd expect to do something like this," he says.

"She was very beautiful," says Army Pvt. Levi King.

Yet some on the plane believed that beneath Oswald's cool lay a death wish.

"I was scared that the FBI was not going to give her what she wanted and that we were all going to become molecules," Steve Vagnino, of Clayton, a tony St. Louis suburb, later relates.

Oswald has an unrelenting demand for the FBI: She wants to speak with Trapnell.

NOON

Garrett Brock Trapnell was 34 in July, 1972, when he boarded a TWA flight from Los Angeles to JFK with a cast on his arm. From under the cast he pulled out a pistol, handing flight attendant Constance Tokarski a note. He demanded freedom for black activist Angela Davis, who faced felony charges after weapons registered to her were used to take over a California courtroom. He wanted $300,000 and change. And he needed an audience with President Richard Nixon.

Trapnell let the ninety-three passengers disembark. But he held the crew at gunpoint, commanding the pilot to take off and circle the airport. The drama concluded when an FBI agent, posing as a ground crew member, shot Trapnell in the arm after being allowed to board the plane.

That would be Trapnell's last moment of freedom.

By then Trapnell, although only in his mid-30s, had orchestrated a career in spectacular crime, aided by good looks and charisma that drew women to him.

He came from an overachieving military family; a cousin was an aviation pioneer; his father a U.S. Naval Academy grad; an uncle a much decorated Army lieutenant general who survived the Bataan Death March in World War II.

Trapnell, too, was a pilot, which figured into his exploits. He and an accomplice would fly to Canada to rob banks. With a credit card stolen from a dancer, he once rented a plane and flew it to the Bahamas, where he robbed a jewelry store. He ditched the plane in Florida but got caught when his driver's license was found on the seat of his rental car.

He'd been arrested nearly two dozen times but often ended up in mental hospitals rather than prison.

On this winter day in 1972, Trapnell is not even at the Marion prison; he's defending himself in U.S. District Court, in Benton, twenty-two miles north, against escape charges stemming from the helicopter death flight of Barbara Oswald, Robin's mother.

The trial has entered its last day when word reaches Benton of yet another air piracy. The courtroom is cleared of observers, its doors locked. Security is such that a reporter has to remove his shoes and be hand-searched.

It is Trapnell's secret if he knows what is happening a half-hour south. Perhaps he does; Robin Oswald had shown up earlier at his trial and had spoken with him. On this day, Trapnell asks U.S. District Judge Harold Baker for a continuance.

"As a result of the type of security measures in force today, I am not in an emotional state to address the jury," Trapnell says. His motion is denied and the jury, sequestered from the news, begins deliberations.

Oswald doesn't get him on the phone as she asks. The FBI tells her he doesn't want to talk to her.

ONE P.M.

By early afternoon, the terminal throngs with more reporters than police. CBS, NBC, AP, UPI, the *New York Times, Los Angeles Times, Washington Post, Washington Star* and *Chicago Tribune* are represented along with reporters and broadcast crews from across Illinois, Missouri, Indiana and Kentucky.

Solid information doesn't come easy. At the airport bar, business booms. Through the long day into the night of the winter solstice, reporters wait for Oswald—or the FBI—to make a move.

"I want Garrett. I want Garrett," she repeats again and again, passengers said.

TWO P.M.

Robin Oswald, a former pompom girl and high school dropout, was deeply disturbed by her mother's death seven months earlier. Posing as a real estate salesperson in a hurry to get down to Cape Girardeau, in the Missouri Bootheel, Barbara Oswald chartered a helicopter in St. Louis. In the air, she produced a .44 revolver and ordered the pilot, Alan Barklage, to land in the Marion prison exercise yard.

Barbara Oswald, 42, had been troubled much of her life, and once told a reporter she'd been a prostitute. She turned around her circumstance by joining the army, and afterward worked toward a master's degree in a program focused on parole. She wrote a paper about Marion, read Trapnell's writings and became involved with him through letters. She visited the magnetic prisoner, taking her daughter along.

Wrestling in the helicopter to keep her gun, Oswald pulled a second gun. But the combat-trained Barklage shot and killed her. The story is that Robin Oswald has set out to finish her mother's mission. KMOX reports that people have seen the dynamite strapped to Robin Oswald's waist; other speculation has it that the dynamite could be in the belly of the plane. Dynamite doesn't set off airport metal detectors.

THREE P.M.

Robin Oswald releases six passengers, three older people who have told her that they've had heart attacks and a mother with two small children. Through the FBI's Thompson, she orders milk and sandwiches. With Trapnell never getting on the phone, her even temperament starts to erode.

Oswald's sister, Catherine, a brother Michael and his wife are flown to Marion. Robin refuses to speak with them. The plane's power supply is exhausted and passengers huddle together in the front section, enduring sweltering heat in darkness.

"The only time I got panicky," Zaret, the New Yorker, says afterward, "was when the pilot said there was only thirty minutes of power left. She wanted to talk to a prisoner and gave them twenty minutes to let her talk to him or she'd push the button."

FIVE P.M.

The airport runway is dark. More than 100 reporters and techies pace the terminal. Lights of an occasional helicopter or small aircraft reveal police of varying sorts scurrying about on the tarmac. A generator has been brought to the plane to power the phone connection. Oswald tells workers bringing the generators to remove their coats and hike up their pants legs.

"She never let a guy behind her," Zaret recalled—meaning the men were unable to use the bathroom throughout the negotiation.

"At first we were scared," said Neil Barker, of St. Louis who, like the skyjacker, had attended Clayton High School. "Later, at four or five o'clock, some of the passengers became light-hearted, talking and smoking in the aisles. Then, after five o'clock when the phone started working again, she ordered everybody down."

Just before six, thirteen more passengers, mostly elderly or children are released. An FBI agent observes later that Oswald was concerned about people.

"Aren't I the nicest hijacker?" she remarks to a flight attendant.

SIX P.M.

Oswald is losing control. While she continues to talk with the FBI, passengers sneak out through the front door. Men block the aisles so she is unable to see what is happening.

One escapee, Army Pvt. Conrad Smith, of Kansas City, ignores a police order not to speak with reporters. Smith, who had taken pains to rescue his two pool cues before leaving the plane, says: "I was scared. She said the plane would blow up at 6:30 if she didn't get a chance to talk to her boyfriend. But nothing happened."

A grim-faced Illinois state trooper pushes through reporters and grabs Smith by the arm, pulling him into a guarded room and chiding him for his disclosures.

Reporters are like restless cats, their faces taut from concentration. Nobody makes small talk except for a CBS pilot from Chicago.

"I can't even have a martini until they decide if we're staying," he complains.

A new reporter arrives to bolster the *New York Times* presence. "Who's coordinating the press on this thing?" he asks. No one, he is told.

SEVEN P.M.

"She's starting to get real jittery," State Police Sgt. Andy Muzzarelli tells a reporter, who shares the words with rivals in line at the terminal's one pay phone.

"There's no way we can possibly take a chance [of rushing her]," Muzzarelli is quoted as saying.

An elderly woman, a mother and baby and then several men— all surrounded by police cordons, are hurried through the crush of reporters. More hostages are escaping.

"What's it like on the plane?" a television reporter asks.

The escapees ignore the questions.

SEVEN-THIRTY P.M.

The terminal is frantic. More passengers are being led through reporters, who grow angrier at the news blackout. A middle-aged man, a recent escapee, drops the bombshell.

"It's all over," he says, the first to break the news. "They took her off the plane. She surrendered."

EIGHT P.M.

FBI Special Agent In Charge Edward Hegarty confirms the news.

"I think she finally came to her senses that she did not want to end her life," Hegarty tells reporters.

Her "explosive device" was made up of three railroad flares. No one was hurt at any time during the ordeal.

Robin Oswald is nowhere to be seen. A photographer from the *Louisville Courier* with the sense to set up outside the terminal manages to snap her picture leaving the plane in manacles. She is moved quickly to the St. Clair County Juvenile Detention Center. Passengers mill about, free to talk. A woman describes the skyjacker as "a sweet-looking girl."

A half-hour after Robin Oswald's surrender, a jury finds Garrett Trapnell and another inmate guilty on all counts of attempted escape in the helicopter skyjacking that ended with Barbara Oswald's death. Not for another day does the teenager's motivation become clear: She believed, mistakenly, that Trapnell was her father.

Wanda Brandstetter Was Wronged

"If you ever go to the State Capitol,
You had better act right
You had better not stumble
You had better not fight...
You'll get in trouble with The Man."
  —Adapted from Leadbelly

Wanda Brandstetter, 55, Chicagoan, wartime riveter, licensed pilot, retired WAC, PhD (in biology), wife, mother of three adopted children (now college age), home remodeler, supporter and erstwhile lobbyist for the proposed Equal Rights Amendment to the Constitution, was declared guilty of bribery by a Sangamon County jury on Friday.

The all-white jury of eight female and four male "plain Americans" deliberated nearly seven hours before concluding that Brandstetter had indeed intended to buy a pro-ERA vote from freshman state representative Nord Swanstrom, a Republican from Pecatonica, Illinois, last May.

In the law's eyes, that verdict transformed Brandstetter from an honest family woman active on behalf of public welfare to a convicted felon. That is one frame in which this episode is viewed. It's also possible that Brandstetter was a scapegoat and a means by the established order to impose punishment on those most rabidly and unremittingly pressing to ratify the Equal Rights Amendment.

Brandstetter is an example, as Sangamon County State's Attorney William Roberts put it, to "serve notice to would-be bribers that the laws of the state of Illinois are not for sale."

More likely, business as usual in the General Assembly's political fundraising game will shift underground temporarily, like a floating crap game. And perhaps, too, smarting from this wrist slap, pro-ERA tacticians will become more strategic when next they seek to win friends and influence people. As far as perception, perhaps some people will wonder if the reason Justice wears a blindfold is that when she slaps one hand she won't see the five or ten or 200 she didn't slap, but should have.

At her trial, each of the dozen witnesses, from cops and lawmakers to Brandstetter herself, had sworn, so help them God, to tell the whole truth and nothing but the truth. But in the wholeness of truth, the law sometimes cuts narrow measures. Again and again in Brandstetter's five-day trial for bribery and solicitation, the defense team of Chicagoan Sheila Murphy, her brother, John Murphy, of Cheyenne Mountain, Colorado, and Michael Costello, of Springfield, pleaded for opportunity to present a wider view, so the jury could consider whether circumstances might make a difference in dispensing justice.

Sangamon County Associate Circuit Judge Jeanne Scott, the first woman to sit on the bench of Lincoln's Seventh Circuit, in Springfield, turned back those initiatives. "I have tried to indulge you by letting you have latitude in this case," she said at one point. "I have asked questions about birthdays and bumper stickers to the jury. I don't care if you bring in the man in the moon if you can tie it to the case. But I cannot chuck the rules of evidence and just wing it."

That ruling cost the defense a vital part of its case. And the jury, like discoverers of a lost culture that had emerged piecemeal amid the corn, put together the parts of the testimony they heard into a picture isolated from its context. Said the convicted Brandstetter, her emotion contained even in defeat: "The truth did not come out in court."

In Springfield, elements of the truth lay waiting for Brandstetter like an iceberg in front of the *Titanic*. In the State Capitol, the long-standing, often brazen, and usually undisturbed political tradition of sweetening legislators' campaign pots with dollars and support was never examined.

Judge Scott did not allow House Parliamentarian David Epstein to address the court as an expert witness. In pleadings before jury selection, attorney Sheila Murphy said what Epstein's testimony would have been, and Epstein, seated at the back of the courtroom, confirmed Murphy's accuracy: "Citizens have the right to offer campaign contributions. Millions of dollars are contributed to state legislators who are still able and expected to vote their consciences."

That, according to Epstein's opinion by proxy, is business as usual in the legislative marketplace.

Campaign pledges and support are not only lawful in Illinois, the Murphys repeatedly insisted, they are a basic right. "If citizens do not have the right to petition their representatives, to express their opinion and offer their support on matters of public policy, if the only lobbies allowed to express their views are sophisticated, professional, non-citizen groups with finesse, then the average citizen has lost the right to make his opinion known," John Murphy said in court. "If so, we've lost our freedom. It's gone."

At three o'clock in the cool morning of May 14, 1980, Wanda Brandstetter arrived in Springfield for a few hours of sleep before ERA's big day. By mid-May, Stop ERA had contributed nearly $100,000 to the warchests of anti-ERA and undecided legislators. Brandstetter knew the nature of the game. A supporter of the ERA since it passed out of the U.S. Congress in March of 1972, she had exercised her right to inspect campaign contribution records of ninety legislators—seventy Republicans and twenty Democrats.

In the twenty-seven months since Rep. Nord Swanstrom had entered the race for a seat in the General Assembly, he had received four checks from the opposing Stop ERA PAC. The checks amounted to a total of $1,900. Such infusions of cash are the life-blood of election campaigns.

In Brandstetter's trial, three months after her early morning arrival for ERA's big day, another of her defense lawyers, Michael Costello, explained that time-honored tradition this way: "The most important qualification for the legislature is getting elected, and that takes money. Most is contributed by the American populace."

By May, 1980 the activists leading the pro-ERA movement were ready to believe that money and support might succeed where idealism had failed. They were, in the words of National Organization for Women president Eleanor Smeal, ready to play "hardball politics." They also were playing from behind. For eight years, the ERA had failed to win in the Illinois General Assembly. ERA won its victories only in public opinion polls. In Springfield, the proposed amendment was dogged both by Phyllis Schlafly and by bad luck.

In 1978, when victory seemed close at hand, a block of African-American legislators from Chicago withheld support to protest an unrelated snub. In May, 1980, rumors of bribery snatched away apparent victory. In August, Brandstetter's attorney John Murphy argued that the rumors of bribery were part of a conspiracy to "damage, sully, and tarnish the efforts to have the state ratify ERA."

All night before the vote was expected, ERA supporters maintained a candlelight vigil in the Capitol rotunda. By 8 a.m. the gallery was filled with red as well as green. Amidst flood-stage emotions, sporadic quarrels between sides broke out. Both sides were determined—"desperate," Sangamon County State's Attorney William Roberts contended in Brandstetter's trial. Many had served in the struggle for years, but as lobbyists most, Brandstetter included, were amateurs.

Lobbying on both sides was fast and furious. Legislators, especially the swing ones whose votes could mean passage or failure, were the targets. Word had filtered down from ERA's old friend, Rep. Giddy Dyer, a Republican moderate from Hinsdale, that her young friend, Rep. Nord Swanstrom, was wavering. Dyer shared a "mother-son" relationship with the inexperienced legislator, who had never before voted on the issue. Although he was known to oppose ratification, in confidence with Dyer he gave "every indication of a person ready to change his mind," she later testified.

Swanstrom was targeted. Two times in the afternoon of May 14 Brandstetter joined groups lobbying him in the halls outside the House chamber. Once, catching his momentary attention, Brandstetter offered verbally to give "a month of my time working for him in his district and raising up to $1,000 for his campaign," she testified. She handed him a business card that identified her as a National Organization for Women field organizer.

"If he saw he had support from both sides, he could vote his conscience," she said.

Later, after Brandstetter had found her card on the floor, she approached Swanstrom a second time. As he prepared to return to the House floor, she quickly wrote a note on the back of a second business card: "Mr. Swanstrom the offer of help in your election + $1,000 for your campaign for pro ERA vote." The Equal Rights Amendment was never called for a vote in the Illinois House on May 14. The sponsor, Rep. John Matijevich, a North Chicago Democrat, took a 4:30 p.m. headcount and came up twos short of the 107 needed for passage.

The next day, bribery charges rocked the capitol. Rep. Thomas Hanahan, D-McHenry, a longtime ERA foe and labor leader whose stand had reportedly cost him the position of secretary-treasurer for the AFL-CIO, trumpeted an experience of a fellow Democrat, Rep. Gary Hannig, of Mt. Olive. Hannig, said Hanahan, had received a promise of $10,000 for a pro-ERA vote. Though loudly sounded and widely reported, those never-substantiated charges faded away. Hannig apologized, saying he might have misheard. Was Hanahan, who once had referred to feminists as "braless, brainless broads," initiating a conspiracy of sorts? Nobody knows. The charge never merited true investigation.

On May 16, Wanda Brandstetter, back home in Chicago, received two visitors. The men claimed association with Swanstrom and demanded $1,000. She sent them away. It would be revealed later that her visitors were agents of the Illinois Department of Law Enforcement.

Swanstrom, a dutiful young man who had written polite notes to Phyllis Schlafly and Stop ERA officers thanking them for the contributions and assuring them he would hear their requests, was disturbed by Brandstetter's second calling card. The day before agents paid Wanda Brandstetter a visit, he had asked the advice of House GOP leader George Ryan, who he referred to as his "leader" and "father-confessor."

Ryan consulted Dan Webb, then director of the state Department of Law Enforcement. Sangamon County State's Attorney Bill Roberts, in whose jurisdiction bribing lawmakers would fall, was called in. In June, a Sangamon County grand jury indicted Brandstetter on two counts, bribery and solicitation of legislative misconduct. Meanwhile, the scandals had effectively torpedoed ERA in 1980. When the roll was finally called on June 18, ERA failed by five votes.

On August 22, Wanda Brandstetter was found guilty of bribery —and innocent of solicitation. Minutes after the verdict, bitter recriminations broke the stunned silence of the courtroom. Jurors were polled about their verdict individually, and asked if they had read the *Illinois Times* editorial that appeared on the stands the day of the trial, "How not to bribe a legislator." They had not.

Sheila Murphy, who had appealed to childhood, motherhood, and the war wounded in her attempt to preserve Brandstetter's innocence, demanded that the verdict be set aside. Murphy contended that Roberts had engaged in "prosecutorial misconduct" for his closing arguments, in which asserted: "We don't want blood, we don't want to send her to prison. We just want a conviction."

Replied Roberts: "I did not feel any animosity toward Wanda. We had this case dumped in our lap."

Emotions ran so high in the trial's closing moments that Scott postponed hearing a motion to set aside the verdict. Brandstetter, free on bond, was swarmed by haggard reporters and Klieg lights. After midnight she joined her husband, Hugo, 58, son Russell, 19, and daughters Ericka and Susan, both 17, at their choice of accommodations, Motel 6.

The following day, ERA supporters across the nation staged walkathons to raise money for the continuing struggle to ratify ERA. Nearly 100 marched in Springfield. Although most said they were "disappointed" or "dismayed" at the verdict, it did not seem to dampen their spirits on the sunny August day.

Author's note: On November 8, 1980, Brandstetter rose to her feet in a Sangamon County courtroom for sentencing, her voice quavering. "I stand here because the men of this nation have betrayed one half the human species, their own mothers included," she said. Associate Circuit Judge Jeanne Scott fined her $500 and 150 hours of public service, either working with mentally ill or tutoring low-income students in biology, in which Brandstetter held a doctorate. She moved shortly after to Indiana, where she founded NOW chapters in three cities. For two years her lawyers filed motions to overturn the verdict. But the Illinois Appellate Court eventually upheld the conviction, and the Illinois Supreme Court declined even to hear the case. Brandstetter passed away peacefully in 2011, at age 86, in Michigan City, Indiana.

PART IX

Welcomes

Sandra's three grandchildren were born in the years *Bay Weekly* dominated Martin-Lambrecht-Knoll family life. Her reflections on the birth of the three, starting in 2000, made their way into her broadly themed weekly Editor's Letters—and into this book.—Editor's Note

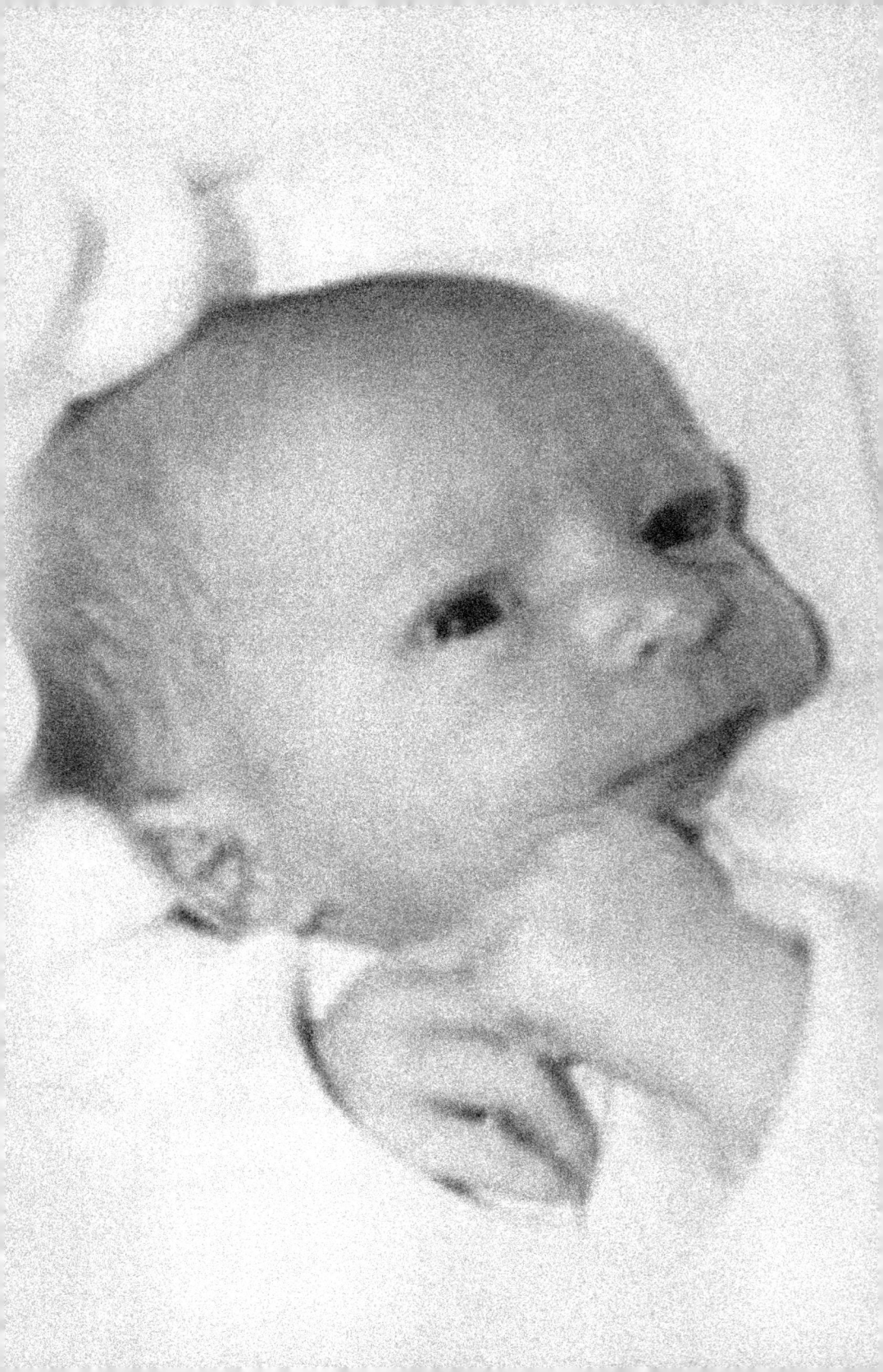

A First: Grandson John Alexander 'Jack' Knoll Jr.

*Holding the child, you touch the far reaches
of the ages, beyond your beginnings,
beyond your end.*

As my daughter-in-law labored and my son sweat, her parents and I haunted the halls and snoozed the couches of Anne Arundel Medical Center's Clatanoff Pavilion. Four thousand babies were born in that well-appointed birthing center this year, but our hopes were pinned on one. A week after his or her August 18, 2000 due date, the first child of Lisa Kate Edler and John Alexander Knoll was keeping its appointment, and none of us could think of any better place in this world to be.

Still, expectation can keep you on the edge of your chair for only so long. One way or another, there were hours we would have to pass. The hours weighed lighter on me than on the others, for I rode them out in the kind of trance of well-being I enjoy in a train. In both passages, there's nothing I can do but wait. Planned waiting is time I've learned to welcome as a friend. In anticipation, I'd brought a bag full of books and newspapers, bottled water, socks and a blanket—and a cell phone to link me to my husband. Bill was at home delivering his own first born, a book, but he was prepared to join us at whatever hour this child demanded.

Between reading—Harry Potter this time, not the terrible choice I'd brought to my own first labor, Jean-Paul Sartre's *No Exit*—

sleeping and going to the mental movies with Marilyn and Howard Edler, I revisited my own births.

What woman doesn't count her births as the epic labors of her life? So I remembered that first labor, giving birth to Alex, the man about to become the father of this child. Lisa is surely enduring now what I experienced then, and what her mother must know as well: the shock of working your way through an unanticipated and often violent seizure of your body. Nobody tells you what labor will be like because labor is not an experience you can put into words. It speaks only the language of the body.

I had grown forgetful by the time I did it all again, giving birth to Nathaniel five and a half years later. Both their births were duly and curiously attended by my first husband, John Knoll, who would become a grandfather at a distance.

(What do men experience at their child's birth? Whatever that might be is far distant from reality of the child's mother. So deep, however, it might take a poet to surface it.)

I traveled back far longer, joining hands across the years with Elsa giving birth to me, and Catherine to Elsa. To Florence giving birth to Gene, my father, and his long-dead brother Jack. To Mary giving birth to John, the grandfather. To Ada Jane giving birth to Bill, whose grandchild by way of Alex and Lisa will be the first newborn he cradles in his arms. And so to Marilyn and her second-born, Lisa, who labors as we wait and dream.

But when each new child squirms and squalls into the world, the stage is his. So I was glad to dwell in those hours with the great chain of mothers, where we are all ageless: all infant, mother, grandmother.

August 24 gave way to August 25 and still Lisa labored. The knife of pain was dulled by epidural anesthetic, but she labored long, through the hours when all the world slept, even those nearest her, though fitfully.

The magical, shifting fogs of a rain-soaked evening gave way to the brilliance of morning light when Dr. Donna Jasper declared this child would be born in the style of Caesar. "Don't worry, we do this all the time," she said. But we worried, and Lisa's parents' hearts iced with fear for their daughter, the child they had made and Marilyn borne while Howard—as was the custom then—slept alone at home.

The next we grandparents knew, all else had given way to joy: all fear and hope and anticipation dissolved by the sight of Jack. For the long-awaited star of this night's drama was a boy, John Alexander Knoll Jr.—Jack—taking life's stage at 8:11 a.m.

What was in his parents' hearts I can only imagine. I know what was in mine as, within the hour of his birth, I cuddled his 7 pounds, 11 ounces. Holding the child, you touch the far reaches of the ages, beyond your beginnings, beyond your end. With Marilyn, Howard, Bill and all our people, I was not alone.

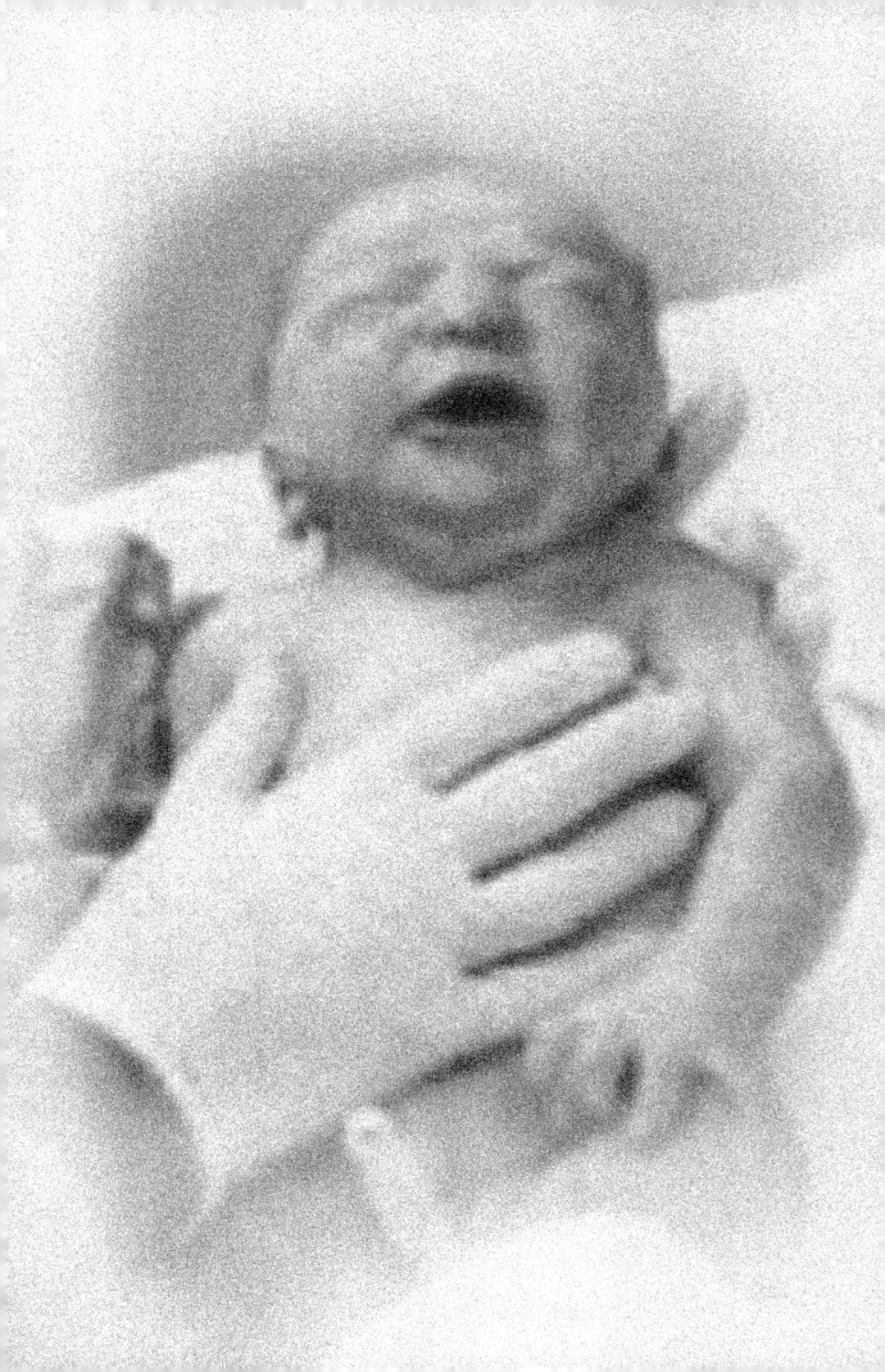

Elsa Leigh Knoll Enters the World

If I am lucky, I will live to see this Elsa redefine my standard of human potential.

In a far corner of the post-9/11 world, people are naming their children Osama. Here in Chesapeake Country, we're expecting a lot of Cals (for Ironman Oriole Cal Ripken, retiring from baseball after twenty-one years). Closest to home, my second grandchild came into the world at 8:21 a.m. on Thursday, October 4, 2001, as Elsa.

Her full moniker is Elsa Leigh Knoll, and each name of it resonates. But it's Elsa I can't get past, for she is the second Elsa in my life. And full well though I know this 7-pound, not-quite-10-ounce infant will grow into her own woman, I can't help believing she gives the first Elsa a second chance.

The first Elsa could use it. If you could navigate this world on natal grace alone, my mother could have had it as her oyster. Elsa Olivetti had, in her own way, the will of Mussolini, the beauty of Marilyn Monroe, the inventiveness of the Wright brothers, the playfulness of a young cat and the work ethic of Cal Ripken. She believed she could do anything, and she just about could. A poor child of immigrant parents, she bought her piece of the American dream by hard work—and the good luck to be working hard in World War II's boom economy. By her 30s, all the hallmarks of 1950s' success were hers: She wore furs and diamonds and drove convertible Cadillacs.

But Elsa Olivetti was not lucky in love. She did without that vital nutrient in her earliest hard-scrabble immigrant days, and for all her life love always proved unreliable. For its lack not all her gifts together could compensate.

For her namesake, fate has opened a different book. Our new little Elsa is born into prosperity if not peace. Loving her with tenderness as well as fierceness, her mother, my daughter-in-law, will be no Catherine Olivetti, as hard on her daughter as fate was on her. Her father, my son, who blooms in her presence and can change diapers too, will share in bringing her up, shining his light on her. Her brother, 13-month-old Jack, will be as blessed as she by love and goods and plenty.

Ringing round that four with love are circles of grandparents, uncles, aunts, cousins and great-grandparents—even to her 90-year-old great-grandfather Leighton, who gives her second name.

Elsa Leigh has been born lucky in love, and in her life I'll see each day the proof of what enough love, enough time and good times can do to nourish the great gifts we are born to. If I am lucky, I will live to see this Elsa redefine my standard of human potential.

For each of us in her adoring circle, Elsa keeps a different promise.

For Lisa Edler, her mother, she brings 'Elsa Ledler' out of the nicknaming society of chanting girls into the flesh. For Alex, her father, she is his own Elsa, as he was Elsa's own Alex. For Bill, she is the closest thing to a daughter. For John, she balances the scale of progeny: two sons and a grandson; two daughters and a granddaughter. For Marilyn and Howard, she mirrors for their daughter the matched set of their own family. She brings a sense of completeness, new love and a bigger family.

For me, a girl in the family will, I hope, allow me to indulge in the womanly arts of grandmothering and mothering I grew up with, adventure and initiation into the rites of girl- and womanhood, rooted in trust.

For herself and for each of us, Elsa has already satisfied her first challenge: how a second child coming so soon can make her own place in a family that seemed complete without her. For she has given each of us something we lacked but never dreamed to count as ours.

Some of us will call her Ellie. Some of us, blessed with an Uncle Elsworth, say they'll call her Els or simply El.

I don't know what I'll call her. Elsa is a big name for a tiny baby, and every time I hear it, I shiver. Whatever I call her, in naming their daughter her parents have given me the gift of hope. My hope is that one of us can complete another. Out of time, out of reason, out of touch—and without becoming less ourselves

So I am enrolled in the sorority of double entendre, whose members hear one name and evoke two people. For Bridget, Tessa is not only daughter but a sister dead too soon. For April, James is not son but a young soldier dead in Vietnam. And for me: Elsa brackets my life.

We all hear echoes every time we hear our new love's name.

Hello There
Ada Olivia Knoll

Grow slowly, sweet babe. We're not finished with the world we're making for you.

In the first sight of just-born life, grandparents see different visions than parents do.

Back when it was our turn to multiply and be fruitful, we gaped in amazement at what we had made. Thrust into our arms, those few pounds weighed us down with the burden of human destiny.

So it is good that having a new baby is "like living with an angel," as my baby said after his first few days with his baby, Ada Olivia Knoll, borne by Elizabeth Weckback Knoll on March 23, 2005. Otherwise, Nathaniel and Liz might join a universe of parents shivering with terror at what they've taken on. In fact, the new family is as happy as if they had good sense, as my grandmother, Florence Bunting Martin, would have said.

For grandparents, it's different. With the birth of my third grandchild—cousin to Jack and Elsa Knoll, who live in Annapolis, not a continent away like Ada—I'm catching on.

For us grandparents, past and future converge in those tiny, wiggling bodies. At the first close encounter, the lineaments of lineage wash over those round cheeks, button noses and rosebud mouths. It's as if you're drowning in genealogy, as all the faces from your past life take their moment upon this little stage.

This phenomenon may explain why each side of the family sees its own images in a newborn.

Cheated of the biological link the rest of the grandparents enjoy, Bill Lambrecht hears the echo of his mother's name as he embraces this second Ada in his life.

That's not the only stage on which we see the past unfolding.

We're also retracing in days the epochal development of brain-driven life. Blessed to have shared all but the birthday of the first ten days of Ada's life, we watch, enraptured, as the brain stem awakens so this infant can fill her lungs and stomach, digest her food and empty her bowels and bladder. Moments later, as Ada squirms and wiggles with life, higher regions of the brain yawn into awareness, her eyes open, and within hours she can focus and follow.

At least as wonderful is the dawning of the great collective unconsciousness. The smooth, miniature features that have combined in this unique way crease now with the ancient expression that will serve her for anguish as well as gas. Now the brow smooths, the lips curve and Ada's parents delight in her smile. So do we grandparents, equally warmed by this preview of all the smiles we hope to share. Finally, she releases into the broad visage of perfect contentment. For my part, I am content to believe that she "by the vision splendid Is [her] way attended." For what parent or grandparent can look on a new baby and not believe that William Wordsworth captured 203 years and four days before this girl's birth.

Our birth is but a sleep and a forgetting:

The Soul that rises with us, our life's Star,

Hath had elsewhere its setting,

And cometh from afar;

Not in entire forgetfulness,

And not in utter nakedness,

But trailing clouds of glory do we come.

As for the future, hope and fear combine as we grandparents look down that tunnel from this fully present convergence. Looking into the future as a new mother, I carried the world on my shoulders. As a grandparent, I know with staggering clarity the world into which Ada will go. What she'll find in that terra incognito has been made by what I've done or left undone.

I want a far better world for my grandchildren and for yours. Getting there from here is the business I must be about, while I have world enough and time.

PART

X

Farewells

Sandra produced elegantly written appreciations for those who have passed, honoring her family, pets and people of her community with whom she'd grown close. These stories proved especially popular to her readers, and more than one asked that Sandra's words see them out of this world and into the other side. Writing these appreciations, she felt like a medium into whom something of her subject's essential character passed so that she captured them, like a portrait painter, not in their whole lives but in moments of truth. For her readers, her goal in each was to bring tears to their eyes.—Editor's Note

Vera's Last Act

As Chesapeake Bay's most glamorous
restaurateur exits the stage,
a new dream takes shape.

If Vera Freeman had been in the movies as she intended, she couldn't have acted her way to a better-scripted ending. But when Effrus Freeman, optometrist to the stars, proposed to the aspiring girl who grew up on the Crow Indian Reservation in Montana, that dream was deferred.

"It can be like this every day," he said. *"We'll have a wonderful time."*

I really didn't do any modeling or dancing. I got a job at the telephone company.

I can't leave my job, I told Dr. Freeman.

"All right," he said. *"I'll take you to work every day."* The first day he said, *"I feel like I'm going on a fishing trip, getting up so early."*

I went into the office and looked around and asked myself, what am I doing here?

And we did have a wonderful time.

TIME'S WINGED CHARIOT

On this June afternoon in 2006, as the sun gilds St. Leonard Creek with a glory that pinches your heart, Vera is watching the end of the dream she lived instead of the one she left in Hollywood those many years ago.

Long the hostess, Vera Freeman takes it all in at a dedication dinner in her honor at Vera's White Sands Beach Club, now open under new ownership.

What was once so utterly familiar has changed, as former homes do, becoming places you no longer belong.

On the White Sands Road exit from Route 2-4 in southern Maryland, the sign is down, and Vera's ageless, exotic effigy no longer beckons. Vera's White Sands, the advertised destination, has been gutted, its signature pink painted over. This weekend, Vera's White Sands Beach Club reopens, recast by neighbors Steve Stanley and Lisa Del Rico.

Pale (sunlight seems never to have touched her skin) and bemused, Vera comes as guest to her former domain, the Calvert County promontory she colonized as Polynesia on the Patuxent.

She is here to be honored. Her gnarled hands, soft from a lifetime of luxury, will be imprinted in wet concrete. Then it will be over, and she will go home, across the compound to her little castle.

Instead of Hollywood, Vera made her home here in Calvert County, where she arrived in the early 1950s as the accidental but willing hostage of two avid and successful real estate speculators, her husband, and legendary 20th-century Maryland politician Louis Goldstein.

> *Dr. Freeman was also into real estate and he always wanted to come to the East. I didn't know why at first. Then I read in the Washington Star that he was the pioneer developer of the club aspect of Virginia and Maryland.*
>
> *This was all trees around here. Louis Goldstein, who owned the property, brought us out on a terrible winter day. "Why do you want to go on a day like this?" I asked Dr. Freeman. "Because I want to see it at its worst," he said. He bought 800 acres and built White Sands. I brought the white sand and the palm trees.*

On this promontory over two creeks, Vera would build the castle of her dreams.

> *Ever since I was a little girl, I wanted a castle. I'd walk to school through the snow—in Montana it snows every day— and I'd see these tumbleweeds, these 10-feet tumbleweeds with snow and ice shining like glitter. They looked like castles. I thought, someday I'll have a castle.*

CARVED GODDESSES
WITH EAGER, BARE BREASTS

Then she and Effrus Freeman built the stage on which Vera would perform an exotic, one-woman show for the next half century.

"I didn't find it like this forty-one years ago. I made it this way," Vera said of her Calvert County Shangri-la.

She cultivated banana palms among the dogwood on her promontory that overlooks St. Leonard and Johns creeks. She decorated it with Asian, especially Pacific Islands, exotica.

On my first trip to the Orient in 1973, we bought all of these things. Always after that we went, Dr. Freeman and I together, traveling and buying and collecting the things that fill this place. After he died, in 1980, I traveled on my own. I'm still traveling.

Much at Vera's was pink: the patio, the napkins and the women's room and, of course, the strawberry, whipped-cream and paper-umbrella-adorned rum concoction that might accompany your sunset.

Everything at Vera's was exotic. Carved goddesses with eager, bare breasts and sparkling nipples girded the dining room. Faux leopard skin covered the bar and its stools. Tropical hats and headgear from deep-sea divers ornamented the bamboo-roofed indoor bar. Beaded curtains draped windows. The embroidered umbrella above your table hid you from effigies of wild animals on the prowl. Leis (usually plastic but real orchids on special nights) carried diners into the realm of the exotic.

Most exotic of all was Vera, gowned in flowing, gold-threaded, Bombay silk, bejeweled with gold and diamonds, diademed in shells. When she visited your table, you basked in the glow of her champagne-sipping celebrity.

After a hectic day, this and that, when I go to my boudoir and I dress for the evening, I forget all of it. I'm in another place. I come in here, and I meet such lovely people from all over the East Coast. There aren't that many from Calvert

County. Sometimes I meet the third generation of people who have come here. And I'm still here.

That was the Vera's I discovered midway through the 1980s. I never saw Vera, slender and gorgeous in her bathing suit and her real orchid lei, swim out to greet arriving yachts, as she recalls.

The white sands had, by the time I met her, washed away. The slot machines were long gone, too, outlawed in the 1960s and carted away by lawmen who refused Vera's plea for just one souvenir. No, those one-armed bandits were deposited in the Chesapeake Bay to create fishing reefs, it was said.

Year by year, the illusion faded by small degrees. Age tinkered with the plumbing and some nights the curtain barely raised. Would the kitchen open? Would you be noticed and served?

Yet we—and many others—continued to visit. Over the years, our trips to Vera's became pilgrimages, as if we were returning to a favorite and long-running play, *Auntie Mame* or *South Pacific*, with its original leading lady.

For her illusionary Polynesian paradise was still a place to forget the cares of the day as the setting sun puddled the creeks glowing lavender-pink. If, that is, you weren't in a hurry, and if you cared less about dinner than watching the show.

Usually we ate—and sometimes quite well, as new blood and new chefs brought upswings—on our visits. But year after year through the late 1990s and into the new century, we believed we had paid our final visit at season's end each autumn. Even the ageless Vera could not outrun time.

But sure enough, every spring, the doors opened and she returned.

YONDER ALL BEFORE US LIE

Each spring, Vera returned...until this year, 2006.

When Vera's White Sands Beach Club opens on June 24, Vera will be present only in name. New owner Steve Stanley has bought her name along with her business and 2.3 acres of prime waterfront real estate, all for over $2 million.

"I was chosen by her for some reason," says Stanley, who met Vera as a regular at her bar.

Stanley, 46, a paving contractor, sees karma in their entwined fates. Like Vera, he has a story, and it is one he likes to tell.

He migrated from College Park after a marital avalanche, lured Solomons-way by the fishing and to affordable property around White Sands. He, too, came in winter, when darkness coupled with loneliness.

"The following spring," he says, "when the time changed, I realized the beauty."

He discovered the bar at Vera's and became a regular, and Vera's martini friend. "I'd plant palm trees and bananas at home, and bring the extras here," he says, "never thinking a place like this could be mine."

Vera made the opening move, he recalls. Vera says he raised the prospect of purchase. From whichever direction, negotiations moved quickly. Before the first week ended, he had permission to begin restorations.

Lisa Del Rico is his partner and restaurant manager. "We're trying to keep her dream alive," he says. "We see a beautiful opportunity to restore this antique to its original beauty."

The footprint is still Vera's; everything else has changed. Two rebuilt piers of slips angle into the waters—one into St. Leonard's Creek, the other into Johns Creek. Marine squatters have been evicted. Eight or ten boats declared derelict have been crushed by the grapple of Stanley's big excavator and trucked to Calvert County Recycling. Next he'll bring back Vera's white sand for a new beach and tiki bar; then he'll reclaim the rundown swimming pool.

Big and ruddy, underdressed for Vera's in near-fluorescent cap and T-shirt, Steve Stanley is a jump-in-and-get-it-done kind of guy, tireless and in command of a staff of seven dozen working men.

"I've cleaned out, fixed up, modernized," he says of his takeover. "It had to be done."

Just as the Freemans were people of an era, so are Stanley and Del Rico. It is a different era. Vera's new White Sands and Beach Club will be a distinctively 21st century destination.

Steve's profession has made its mark, with stamped concrete replacing old slate and growling earth-moving equipment reshaping the landscape as his and Lisa's guests—Vera's friends and White Sands neighbors—gather, a week before their grand opening for Vera's dedication dinner.

Workers swarm like bees around their hive. Outside and in, it is a changed hive.

"It's a new building on top of the old," Stanley says. "Nothing wasn't upgraded."

New palm trees are being planted on newly sodded and landscaped grounds. Vera's old totem pole and Aloha mural catch your eye with an unfamiliar freshness. But pride of place goes to a new fountain, featuring a large frog.

You open the door on a new, wide-open, nearly spartan Vera's. Much of the exotica has been removed, though some old oddities have weathered the change. Upholstery is still leopard print, bamboo and fishnets suspending glass baubles still plentiful. The sea-shell sea-serpent siren still hangs, suspended from the dining room ceiling.

In the entrance, Tony Herrera airbrushes final touches onto the murals he's painted onto three walls. The self-taught artist from Lanham, Maryland, is refining exuberant palm trees over a lovely wavy ocean. Across the large, echoing room, he painted a deep-blue underwater scene dominated by a giant sea turtle.

On the reopened deck, the point of the promontory, stonemasons puddle the concrete sheet where Vera will imprint her hands. Vera adds a lasting impression to the new restaurant as her handprints are cast in concrete with the new owners looking on.

In the midst of the construction, chef Sean McNeely, formerly of Rod 'n' Reel in Chesapeake Beach and Rams Head in Annapolis, presides over four cooks in an all-new kitchen. He's serving a half-dozen dishes on the new menu, with steamed shrimp, cherrystone clams and mussels for appetizers, and Steak Chesapeake (an 8-ounce filet mignon topped with jumbo lump crab imperial and standing on a sheen of lobster sauce), crab cakes and cucumber dill salmon.

The long, hair-pin bar is full for the first time in a long time, with a Passion Bay frozen drink maker working full time and bar manager Denise Rapp keeping drinks flowing. Beer, but not wine, is ordered by brand names.

In the dining room, some two dozen waitresses and waiters anxiously fete the guests. Each table is set with leis, but this is not the old Vera's.

For this last day, the old Vera still gets star billing, and she is still dressed for her part. She has traded Indian silks and peacock feathers for a burgundy velvet caftan, fringed and cuffed in faux leopard. Rings—one a lion's head with gem eyes, another a diamond burst like you see in the sky on the Fourth of July—still bejewel her fingers. Today's necklace is a chain of gold and onyx from which dangles an idol. She no longer wears a hibiscus in her long, platinum hair.

She may have to ask who you are as you pay your regards, but she knows what's going on.

"It's a shame they couldn't keep the peacock feathers," she remarks. She'd gathered them from her own flock. From another molting, she had a dress sewn.

She's leaving on her own terms and, though the novelty of it all may disorient her, she knows what to do.

She's drinking a martini and holding court.

"I'll just have a small steak," she says, when the waitress takes her order.

This business of sticking her hands into concrete, she is not certain about. But friends and family reassure her, gather her rings and roll up her cuffs. She gets through it, a bit tremulously, rebounding into radiance once the photos are snapped.

After Steve and Lisa hug and kiss her, Steve says Vera is to make a speech.

"Where is my martini?" she quips, in a thin voice.

Vera is frail, and she is tired. "I can't believe how old I am," she whispers to me. People still think I can go twenty-four hours a day, but I can't."

Any minute now she will leave her party. Her name will still head the marquee, as Vera's White Sands Beach Club perhaps enchants a new generation.

She will lean on the arm of her latest escort, Selvin Kumar, and cross the new pavement, skirting the earth movers, to her home on Johns Creek, a white marble villa with a swimming pool in the living room and a Rolls Royce in the garage.

But she lingers a bit longer to take me to the museum—a favorite side room where she gave private interviews—where mementos from her life have been exiled. Here is the suit of armor, the diver's head-gear, idols and statues of demons, the wooden Kenyan giraffe—a recent acquisition. Framed and mounted, here is the library of articles written about here, mine among them. Here, too, are the paintings of Vera and her alter egos, including the prone nude that hung over the bar, and the portrait of her crowned and adorned in those peacock feathers. Here is the gong that announced her nightly entrance for her one-woman show.

She wanders through the room reverently until her energy is spent. Her last exit is silent, without the reverberations of the gong. Perhaps in her soft round bed this long June night she will see it all from the ninety-plus years of her life, as though it had happened on the silver screen.

Coda:
Vera Freeman

FEBRUARY 12, 1914-JANUARY 23, 2007

Empress of Glamor

If sunsets glow a little showier this year, flashing brighter pinks amidst glistening gold, I won't be surprised. That's how I next expect to see Vera Freeman, Calvert County's empress of glamor, who died January 23, three weeks short of her ninety-third birthday.

It's the stuff of legend, how this sparkling blonde exotic came to illuminate Calvert's waterfront.

In this mid-20th century American girl's alternate success story, a shapely, strong-willed half-Indian from the frontier wilds of Montana finds glamor, wealth, pleasure and (if not complete, a full measure of) happiness.

"She did everything she wanted, several times over," says stepson Lee Freeman.

Vera's dream directed her to Hollywood. But she found her starring role not in the movies but on the arm of Effrus Freeman, eye doctor to the stars and a speculator in real estate. Business opportunities led the doctor and his glamorous wife to a man whose imagination matched their own: Calvert County's homegrown icon of wealth, political power, Louis Goldstein. Under his guidance, the fur-coated Vera tip-toed in high heels through the snow onto the promontory where she would create her own legend.

Thus the stage on which she acted out her life's story became St. Leonard's Creek in deep Calvert County. There she decreed a pleasure dome be built above a beach of imported white sand. For over half a century at Vera's White Sands Restaurant and Marina, her Polynesian paradise above the Patuxent, she entertained her public.

Appreciation was much of what Vera wanted. Vera's was never so much a business venture as a stage arranged to show her at her exotic best. From her annual 'round-the-world travels, she collected baubles, bangles and expensive exotica—a Polynesian boat, a Kenyan giraffe, a marble Romanesque Venus—to furnish her stage.

As sunset approached during the warm months that she spent in Calvert, a minion would strike a great brass gong. Then—in diaphanous sari silk, platinum hair bound American Indian-style with a precious headband, her fingers and wrists heavy with gems—Vera would appear. Completing her entrance, the setting sun would flame the western sky.

Throughout the evening, drinkers and diners would pay their regards to Vera, the queen of it all, as she sipped champagne or a martini. We, her public, arrived by land or water, would have leis slipped around our necks and think ourselves lucky to have stumbled into the show in such an unlikely setting.

When, over the years, the service was slow, the food less than scrumptious, the set tarnished at the edges, Vera persevered. How long, we wondered, could she last? What would become of her, and her kingdom?

For we had glimpsed, behind the glamor girl, the woman who got past losses as real as yours or mine by her sheer determination to live the life she liked.

Vera's luck held. When she was ready to retire, too weary to sustain the show, a successor appeared—as admirers and aides always had in this enchanted life. She sold her business last June and retired to her adjacent home, a Roman villa by way of Hollywood, swimming pool in her living room, overlooking sunrises on Johns Creek.

From there, she watched a new, beach club version of Vera's White Sands face the future.

For ordinary mortals, it's ashes to ashes, dust to dust. But Vera's particles surely will revert to the spectrum of light from which they were borrowed.

Sue Eslinger

JUNE 11, 1938-MAY 13, 1996

Celebrating the last stands of anachronisms

In the early days of the weekly newspaper *Illinois Times*, you might have seen the world through photographer Sue Eslinger's eyes. Wide, hungry eyes they were, focused on an Illinois easily overlooked.

Enchanted is how we felt in those days, Sue and I—eager photographer and newspaper freelancer—setting forth as correspondents to explore the pleasant plains, sleepy towns, and bloody battlefields.

May 1978 to August 1981: Those were our times. As our day dawned, Springfield was picking up the pieces after 1978's Good Friday ice storm. Sue's photos in *Illinois Times*, her first published anywhere, showed tons of splintered wood being turned into mulch.

Sue was 39 when those pictures appeared. Before that moment, she had been one more central Illinois wife and mother metamorphosed by Sangamon State University, (now part of the University of Illinois) into a woman with a degree in search of a purpose. At that new university's Learning Center, where Sue and I worked by day—she as a math tutor as I taught writing—she'd found part of that purpose.

Then Sue discovered photography. For the first time, she felt something akin to what her husband must have felt flying those F 4 Phantom IIs into the wild blue yonder. Sue Eslinger was on a roll.

In our next collaboration, we followed an act of God with an act of woman. In a small Illinois town, Sandra Brewer, a 21-year-old Native-American woman, was on trial for murdering her husband. Sue and I covered the May week Brewer was tried and acquitted. Sue, who'd Sandra Brewer was tried and acquitted, spelling each other in the courtroom. Sue, who'd grown up in Illinois River country, had her camera in hand when Brewer emerged from the Cass County Courthouse a free woman.

The ebb and flow of life in small towns fascinated us as much as the drama. Together we traveled Illinois, finding stories as abundant as roadside blackberries. Roses in Pana, soda fountains in Virginia, apple orchards in Carlinville, home-made pies in Ellis Grove, mineral springs in Okawville, ferries in Calhoun County, and the only hotel in deep southern Illinois' Pope County. Celebrating the last stands of anachronisms was our cup of tea.

What we liked best was tracking down the old storytellers, men who had seen life and knew its secrets. Up in Brimfield, Bill Notzke told us how he transformed trouble into the stone whimsies of his Jubilee Rock Garden. Down in Calhoun County, George Carpenter recalled steamboat days and Carl Wittmond, wearing the 17-carat diamond ring given him by the notorious Paul Powell, told us how he brought a ferry to Brussels.

We struck gold in Chester, where newspaper editor Joe Akers charmed us with his stories. On our second visit, in 1979, Joe took us to meet his old friend Irv Piethmann. The farmer archaeologist-Indian lore expert, who was dying of cancer, spread before us the treasures of "the best life I've ever lived."

Small towns, old men, and wild women: Those were our stories.

Early in 1979, we jumped into battle over home birth. A long-haired nonconformist named Cat Feral, who'd studied midwifery on the West Coast, was under attack by Illinois Attorney General William J. Scott. While we covered the story, Feral had occasion to practice what she preached. As we witnessed the March 1980, home birth of Feral's daughter, Celeste, Sue caught some of the most dramatic pictures *Illinois Times* had ever printed.

The ecstasy and exhaustion of childbirth fascinated Sue. She attended birth after birth, snapping her automatic shutter as another child was pushed slithering into the world. In exchange for the privilege of shooting a childbirth, Sue gave each new set of parents a copy of her prints. Unlike the photos Sue shot for IT, these photos—none of which has ever been published—were in color.

Soon, our partnership spanned an even more defiant campaign: the Equal Rights Amendment. We witnessed great marches in

Chicago and a conscience-driven guerrilla struggle in the Statehouse, where women chained themselves to pillars, poured pig blood on marble floors, and fasted to life's edge.

"Choice is what ERA is about," Sue told me. "It means I don't have to be like her. I can make my own way."

Make her own way Sue did. By August 1981, other interests—genealogy, the stock market, Macintosh computers—had displaced photography. Our last story together compared the virtues of Springfield's competing Popeye's and Queen Bee's barbecue.

Sue retired from the university in May 1985 and moved to Florida, vowing she'd never be cold again. There she began a more momentous battle. Her decade-long fight against breast cancer was Sue's most triumphant story. On that battleground she discovered a depth of resources whose surface she had only scratched.

As we met during that final decade, Sue would chronicle her gains and setbacks with the clear, accurate eye I knew and loved so well. The ease with which she accepted this invader, even as it was winning the war, awed me. She felt no terror, she told me, nor any certain hope, but she was inclined to believe in reincarnation as there was a lot she still had to do. She wanted, for example, to play more golf. And she especially wanted to see the new baby, due in February to her son, Steve, and his wife. Sue. She got that wish: Megan Rhea, her first grandchild, lay on the bed between Sue and me as we talked far into the evening of March 11.

"When the cancer appeared, I cried for three days," she told me. "Then Dick [Sue's husband] and I went to Abe Lincoln's New Salem. Walking through the village, I understood that people live and die—many with far less comfort than I've enjoyed.

"I saw," my friend the mathematician told me in our last conversation, "myself in that equation."

On Monday, May 13, 1996, at 4:30 a.m., Sue Eslinger died, surrounded by her husband and their children, Steve, David and Joan.

That's when, I hope, dear Sue made her own flight into the wild blue yonder.

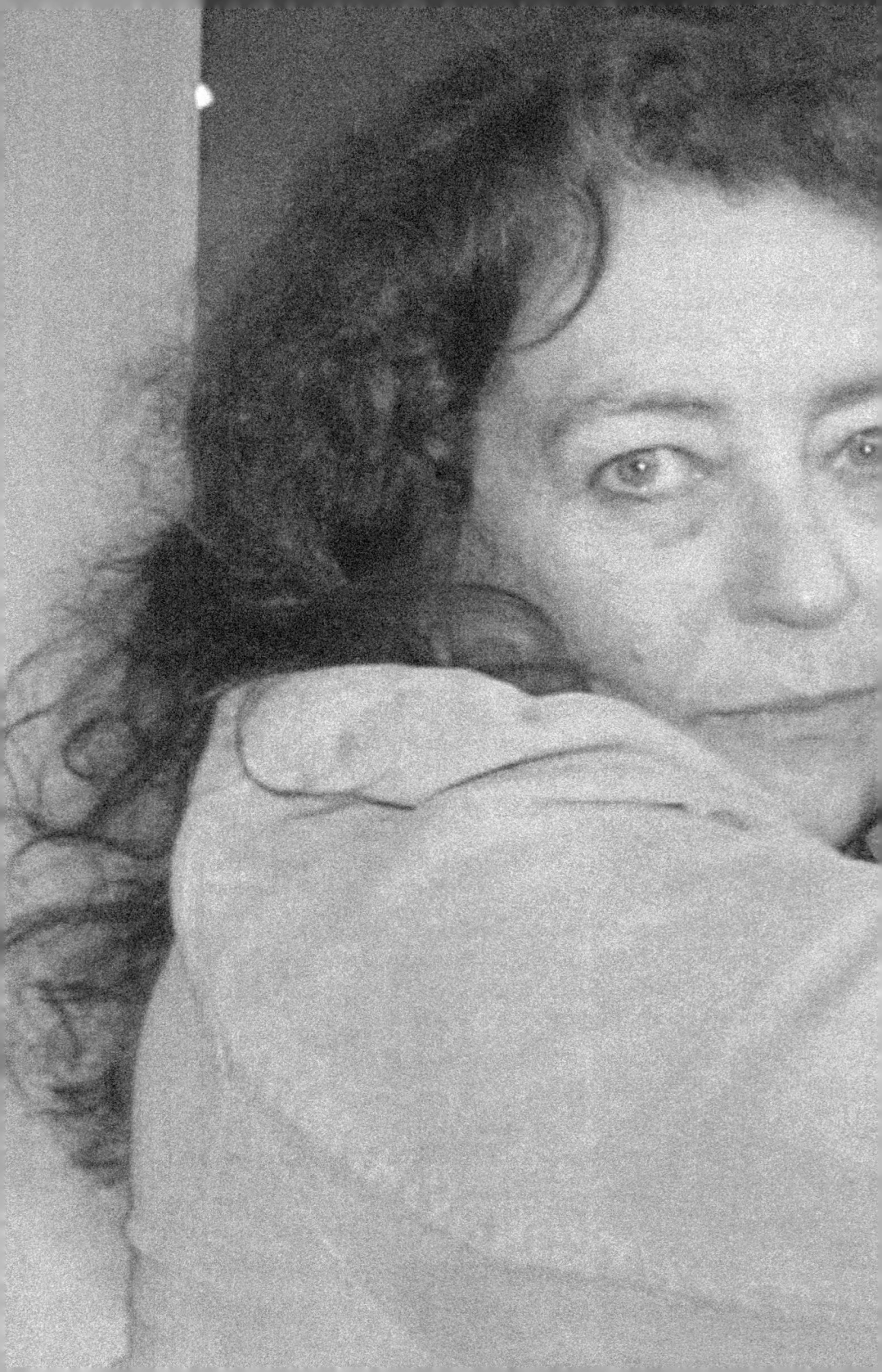

Sherryl Kirkpatrick

OCTOBER 17, 1949–JUNE 11, 2018

In our Eden, she was Eve.

Sherryl Lynn Shiflett Kirkpatrick died June 11, 2018, a shock-attack victim of stomach cancer.

Over the sixty-eight years, seven months and twenty-five days of her life, Sherryl created a world whose inhabitants could count themselves deeply loved and well entertained. In her universe, there was always time for the good times we all say we value but may neglect without a Sherryl to set our values straight.

Don't see just one side of her. Sherryl was a hard-working woman any boss would be lucky to have on their side. She could manage an office—as she did for lawyer J.J. Smith in Upper Marlboro, Maryland, and Hospice of the Piedmont in Charlottesville, Virginia. She could take a complex process from beginning to end, as she did at Maximum Title, in Camp Springs, Maryland. She could sell a product or service, convincing you you'd be so well served by Sprint or Alltel phone service. She could ingratiate a staff of odd ducks into working like a team. She could step out on her own, creating Home Town Title in Solomons Island, Maryland, with another Cheryl as her partner.

But when Sherryl came home, she left work in the office and locked that door behind her. For then she opened the door to the time that was her lifetime. If you knew Sherryl, you know what I mean.

We all have our stories about how Sherryl Kirkpatrick lived well and fully.

In one of those stories—and this is a real human story, no fiction—Sherryl and Michael and Jennifer and Zac and their damn, dumb dingo dog, Jake, live in a ramshackle cottage on the shore of the great big wide Chesapeake Bay. The house is never quite warm enough when winter's wind blows right through it, and often too hot when summer steams Chesapeake Country in its big crab pot. But that's no matter because life here spills out onto the green lawn that connects a community of mismatched neighbors: Mark and Becky Ladley, John and Laura Cody, Bill Lambrecht and me. Here, summer is sweet and endless as we sit in the gazebo of our White House, steal out onto a forbidden private pier, share our moveable picnics. The guys drink beer and kick back, the women share secrets and stories over wine and the kids play like the school bell will never ring on their time. Jake guards it all, and, for entertainment, there are kittens.

In that Eden, Sherryl was Eve. Curly-haired, casually voluptuous, accepting of all (even when we might not be accepting of one another—or of ourselves) she emanated the energy that inspired us all to live in our lives' time. Sherryl was permissive of life.

With husband Michael, whose name she took and children she bore, she forged an exquisitely balanced partnership. Perfectly paired in the art of letting go, they delighted in one another's virtues and forgave each other the ingrained habits that set every partner's teeth on edge. Sherryl and Michael were famous for their speechless marathons, living in the same house, sleeping in the same bed wordlessly for weeks until somehow the ice broke.

Sherryl and Michael raised children Jennifer and Zachary with mostly minimal interference—though it may not have seemed so to Jennifer, in those school-war adolescent years when how-dare-mother-know best.

Look what they got for that method of childrearing: independent, self-directed adult children who—now that the tables are turned and the kids have gotten to be the boss—still want their parents as partners in their lives. Jennifer and Zac have gratefully inherited the habit of living well, keeping their independence while satisfying life's demands. Sherryl lived in full, blessed awareness that her kids not only loved her but also craved her company.

Her grandchildren—three big boys and two little girls—shared an even-more expansive Sherryl who, as Grandma, could be all good times and no discipline. Grandsons Taylor, Colin and Ethan Phipps had a lacrosse rooter in sports-loving Sherryl, a Washington pro-football devotee, as well as a confidant, family historian and travel guide who opened the world to them. Granddaughter Annie Kirkpatrick was Grandma Sherryl's city walking pal and story-time companion. A welcome second granddaughter, Ellie Kirkpatrick, arrived in the nick of time, thus sharing the last three month's of her grandma's life.

Family for Sherryl extended backwards as well as forwards. A daughter who lost her mother, Claudine Virginia Shiflett, too soon—Sherryl was only starting her own life when her mother died—she adopted Michael's mother Kathryn 'Kassy' Crown with a bonded love that could make many a mother-in-law jealous. Even Michael must now and again have been jealous of their female intimacy, for they could be on their own without him and certainly knew all about the ways their son and husband could improve.

In turn, Kassy gave Sherryl the early means and impetus to continue on another path begun in her earliest days. Sherryl's father, Elbert 'John' Owen Shiflett, was a military man. Their many postings—including Fairbanks, Alaska, where she and her adored little brother Mackie went to school by dogsled—made Sherryl itch to travel. Sherryl, Michael and often the kids and grandkids traveled throughout Europe to Croatia, England, Germany, Greece, Ireland, Italy, the Netherlands, Portugal, Scotland, Spain and Wales, with Paris her favorite world city; and to Morocco in North Africa. In the Americas, they visited Belize, Costa Rica, Mexico and Puerto Rico.

Even her diagnosis with cancer didn't keep Sherryl from a last trip with Michael, a cruise in November of 2017 up the Mississippi on the *Delta Queen* from New Orleans to Memphis.

It must have been that military lifestyle—plus who knows what factors on Michael's side—that made it easy for Sherryl to give up a home she loved for another she might love better and would certainly love differently. She and Michael hopscotched from a "garden apartment" on Washington DC's east outskirts to a Camden, Ohio farmhouse in Michael's student years at Miami University of Ohio to that Bayfront cottage to a mansion overlooking Virginia Rt. 29. All those were rentals as Michael, the architect, prepared to design the house planned just for them and the first house they would own. They gloried in that Madison, Virginia, home, and upscaled their hippie ways to do it justice. Shoes remained in the entrance, the cleaner was admonished to remember the picture frames and the habit of keeping dogs—the wolf-dog Zeus having moved onto greener pastures—forsaken.

For all that, when the urge hit them, when Zac and family were making a go of urban-homesteading in Pittsburgh, they abandoned Michael's masterpiece for city life in a four-story rehabbed 1850s' rowhouse. Sherryl had country roots in Buchanan, Virginia, population 1,300 in 1950. Her libertarian spirit thrived in country open spaces. Yet Sherryl adapted to the city, delighting in her life's new teeming opportunities.

Even cancer couldn't tie her down. After her diagnosis, Sherryl, Michael and their children's families bought a home outside Deep Creek in western Maryland where three generations could all be together and have the best of both worlds.

In all those places, everywhere she lived and traveled, Sherryl made friends who felt as close as sisters, each thinking she was Sherryl's BFF.

Sherryl created a family, a community and a legend for her always-open-to-more experiences and odysseys. Her adventures and misadventures all became stories that we tell and retell in paroxysms of laughter and tears that open our hearts—as she did.

The love our dear wife, mother, grandmother, in-law and friend made was equal to the love she gave. That love lives beyond her end, which bonds us all in grief and sorrow.

Dr. Francis Gouin
The Bay Gardener

JUNE 3, 1938–AUGUST 2, 2018

*His spirit lives on in gardens
across the Western world.*

We all knew the Bay Gardener, who died August 2, 2018, of cancer, younger than he had hoped, at 80.

Frank Gouin was Chesapeake Country's fountain of gardening wisdom, known globally for his scientific innovations. He was so generous with his time, so giving, that he'd answer any question readers could think of and maybe show up at your house to talk about your problem.

In his *Bay Weekly* columns since February 24, 2005, you learned a strategy each week for encouraging your patch of earth to become its most fruitful.

There more to the extraordinary man behind the column, Dr. Francis Gouin, the University of Maryland professor emeritus, liked his title; he worked hard to earn it, taking each step along the way by trial, error and revision. His specialty was practical, results-producing science, as befits a man who held his pants up with suspenders and told you to call him Frank. To me, he was always Dr. G.

The flinty New Hampshireman, who grew up speaking New England French alongside English, had a path laid out for him. Romeo Gouin, a master plumber, taught both his sons his trade. Maurice stuck to it; Francis struck out on his own, making what he needed out of every resource that came his way.

"Dad bought us tools, not toys," he wrote for *Bay Weekly* this Father's Day, noting his "appreciation of a father who greatly influenced my life."

401

Dr. G spent his life with one or another tool in his hands. Whatever a job needed, he had or could make, and in his spare time he set about building anything that captured his fancy: violins, guitars and banjos; boats; parade floats that took the prize every year.

Thrift was another family lesson, and he couldn't let any old thing go to waste. He restored not one but three vintage tractors, starting with a 1949 John Deere B. When finally he had both the John Deere and an Allis-Chalmers B in operating condition, he found himself a Farmall B and started on it.

"This will make for a colorful collection of green, orange and red for the Shady Side Fourth of July parade," he wrote about his prize-winning fleet.

Then he took on a 1930 Ford Model A, restoring it from the wheels up. With its shiny black body and summer squash-yellow wheels, it was a beauty. It ran pretty well, too, rattling through Southern Anne Arundel County at 45 miles per hour so that passengers got the authentic ride, shaking and rattling even as they rolled on 21st century roads.

Between tractors, he restored a 24-foot MacGregor swing-keel sailboat, finishing its red hull to the exacting standards of Garry Williams of Osprey Marine Composites.

"Frank was pretty good at it—and dedicated," Williams said. "When I'd tell him it wasn't quite right, he'd go at it again and again, until he got it."

"I was never afraid to tackle something different because it was a challenge," Dr. G told me not long ago—the first year since he was a child in which he didn't plant a garden.

OFF TO COLLEGE

Under young Frank's care, the family's 30-by-12-foot New Hampshire garden produced bountifully, and with it his ambitions.

When Romeo bought a small 25-acre vegetable farm with a roadside market, Frank figured out how to increase productivity. First, he built a cold-frame to extend the New England growing season. Then he planned a greenhouse, working with his vocational education teacher to erect and figure out how to heat a torn-down one on a foundation Frank designed.

Working the farm and selling plants, vegetables and his mother's pies at the roadside stand, "I earned enough money," he said, "that I decided to go to a two-year college, New Hampshire's Thompson School of Agriculture in Durham." Living and working in the school greenhouses on weekends earned him 65 cents an hour. He saved the cost of a meal ticket by cooking for himself, putting to use skills ingrained by his mother, Theresa, who feared her son would marry a woman who couldn't cook.

That should have been that. Frank would have earned his two-year degree and gone back home to Gilford to start his own nursery and greenhouse operation. Except that fate, his teachers and Providence intervened.

The scientists he worked with told him "you're wasting your time at the two-year college." Others said the same. The local doctor offered room and board in return for his help.

Over a week of rain that kept him from his nursery work, he made up his mind. "I sat at the end of the bed and thought, and I went." He shook his head in wonder at the paths taken and untaken. "It was the hand of God."

Enrolled at the University of New Hampshire, he met his wife-to-be, Clara Olesniewicz, a Polish Catholic girl, at the ice-skating rink. They courted on snowshoes.

"He was different," she says, "and when you don't have money, you do things you can afford to do."

On one date, that meant gigging frogs. On another, grilling hot dogs over a fire that melted the snow. Others, walks in the woods—a good thing, because Clara had determined she'd only marry a man who would walk in the woods with her.

At the university, Dr. G began a lifetime habit of practical research, developing methods still in use. Research on rooting mountain laurel earned him a National Science Foundation Scholarship of $250 that paid two-thirds of his senior year tuition and took him, and Clara, to Harvard to present his first academic paper.

In gratitude for the boost that scholarship gave him, he's endowed an annual University of Maryland scholarship to help students do research. Between his writing—including for *Bay Weekly*—and consulting, "We have $53,000 in trust," he told me last month.

He learned as much in the field as in the classroom. His college advisor, William Smith, knew a capable young man when he saw one. Smith hired his new student for $1 an hour to manage Triple Trouble Blueberry Farm, a 500-acre operation.

Three acres of high-bush berries were cultivated as pick-your-own. From the 53 acres of wild low-bush berries, Frank oversaw shipment of 125 to 150 tons of frozen berries a year to Boston, to the Tabletop Pie Company, Boston Frozen Food and local bakers.

"I had sixty people working for me, including kids raking the wild berries, sorters, packagers and drivers. We'd load 7 tons a day onto 16-ton freezer trucks," he recalled. "At 5 a.m., I'd call Boston and argue with buyers over the price of fresh and frozen berries."

Married, Frank and Clara would have headed cross-country to graduate school in Texas if acceptance from the University of Maryland had not arrived first. In College Park he earned his Master's degree and, as the family grew to four and the department quadrupled his grad student salary to $8,500, his PhD.

"I was curious," he said of his advantage over others.. "My research was unique. Nobody had done work like I was doing."

"Frank was always one to see a need and do something about it," said Clara, his wife of fifty-six years and a landscape architect working for Howard County Parks. "He was not theoretical, always practically oriented."

The University of Maryland kept its bright, ambitious graduate, hiring him for its practice-improving Agricultural Extension Service. There he climbed the academic ladder to full professor and department chair.

In those years, 1962 to 1995, he gave "120 percent of his time to horticulture," he said. Ninety percent went to the University of Maryland Cooperative Extension Service, solving practical problems for horticulture professionals, from farmers to landscape architects, and for home gardeners statewide, expanding his reach with a radio program and informational bulletins, often illustrated by Clara.

Managing his research by "begging, borrowing or stealing," Dr. G transformed the way plants are grown for us—and the way we grow them ourselves.

BESTOWING WISDOM

When readers asked *Bay Weekly*'s Bay Gardener a question, they got the real goods.

If you wanted to know about blueberries—which plants to choose, how to fertilize and prune them, their demand for soil with a pH no higher than 5.0—he'd tell you. He had to learn those answers for himself almost sixty years ago at the Triple Trouble Blueberry Farm.

You wanted to know how to pot plants? Research for his master's degree resulted in a new fertilizer, Osmocote, a slow-release fertilizer for container production.

"There was no product like it," he said. "First we made mass-application formulas for the nursery industry. Then we worked out concentrations for a gallon container, so you can use it at home."

Before Dr. G's formulation, 85 percent of the plants sold by nurseries had been grown in the ground. Now, 85 percent are grown in containers, so you buy them with roots intact and carry them home conveniently. His PhD research advanced the nursery industry from southern climes as far north as Canada and Norway.

"The most critical work was root hardiness, because we knew nothing about how much cold roots would take," the Bay Gardener explained. "The Kennedy Center is a good example. They were losing all their stuff shortly after Thanksgiving. I told them that was because they'd planted boxwoods, which die at 21 degrees. We replaced it with Japanese holly, which looks like boxwood and can survive down to 14 degrees below zero. It's still there."

From that research, he says, came the whole list of plants by hardiness used by landscape architecture. What that means to you is cheaper, hardier plants that grew up in the same climate where you buy and raise them.

"Frank Gouin knows more about plants than anybody," said Tony Dove, the former chief horticulturist at Smithsonian Environmental Research Center, one of Dr. G's many students.

You probably didn't want to have your soil tested. But Dr. G would say you had to have your soil tested. That was his refrain, part of the answer to most every question. That's because—and here he might show his impatience for science doubters and know-nothings—plant vitality depends on soil chemistry: on the make-up of organic matter; on the presence of nitrogen, potassium, phosphorus along trace elements including iron and boron; on pH, soil acidity or alkalinity, for which every plant has a very particular taste.

So Dr. G told you how to take your sample and where to send it, and when you did, he'd translate the science into practical advice for your garden.

If you wonder whether it all made a difference, Sheila Brady attests that it does. "He's alive in our gardens, in projects all around DC and as far as Boston, Denver and Portland," said the principal partner of the renowned Washington, DC, landscape architecture firm of Oehme, van Sweden and Associates.

"He'd read all of our soil test reports and recommend what nutrients were deficient or okay, so we could amend our soils. Our gardens would be prolific and beautiful because the soil chemistry was right," she said.

Compost, you ask?

Dr. G was the guru of composting; he invented the science of it. Since the early 1970s, he's made compost from every kind of waste, from sewage sludge to dead chickens on Eastern Shore poultry farms to crab and lobster waste, working with stuff so stinky "it made me lose my breakfast."

Those years of work explain his excitement about Bloom, the soil conditioner produced from sewage sludge at the Blue Plains Wastewater Treatment Plant in DC.

He's taught composting throughout the state, country and world, including to Master Gardeners, a program he pioneered throughout Maryland.

Christmas time, you could buy or cut your own Maryland-grown tree because of Dr. G's first big project. Western Maryland Christmas trees were dying. He discovered they were poisoned by fly ash from power plants in Pennsylvania, Virginia and West Virginia. With bipartisan help from U.S. Sen. Charles 'Mac' Mathias, R-Md., and Democratic U.S. Rep. Steny Hoyer in the years before the Environmental Protection Agency, he helped us—and the trees—breathe easier by providing the scientific basis for forcing down plant emissions and the sulfur content of the coal they burned.

"I did so many things," he said. "I've had a hell of a lot of experience," adding his strongest profanity for emphasis. "Can't is not in my vocabulary. Dad would be proud."

UPAKRIK FARM

If you couldn't find Frank in the garden, you'd likely find him in his workshop. Unless he was at the Farmers Market, selling products, from persimmons to pine boughs, of Upakrik Farm. That's the way it's been since 1995, when he retired as the chairman of the University of Maryland Department of Horticulture and Landscape Architecture. He retired early, worn out by the hassles of campus bureaucracy.

On Rockhold Creek in Deale, he and Clara found a place so right for them that they didn't need to confer before surprising the real estate agent with their simultaneous *we'll take this*. At 11 acres, it was just big enough for small-scale farming: tending a big garden; reviving the Christmas tree farm; planting a peach orchard and a half dozen generous persimmon trees.

Its big barn included a workshop, with an office, woodworking and machine shops and big, open spaces for building and rebuilding. That's where he made his stringed instruments, played them and then gave them away. Built and restored boats, then paddled and sailed them. Restored his three tractors and his Model A Ford.

Dr. G drove the John Deere tractor to *Bay Weekly* to convince me to drop the Cooperative Extension Service's Ask a Gardener column in favor of one he proposed writing. That visit—or maybe it was an earlier one—led to hundreds of Bay Gardener columns, written exclusively for *Bay Weekly*.

Upakrik Farm is where his dogs romped and his cats luxuriated, where he cooked and pickled and canned and made kielbasa from Clara's father's recipe. That's where he and Clara were, she said, "so happy."

This time of year, I'd be bringing our soft-necked garlic crop to Dr. G, asking his help in making it into braids, a skill he'd watched and learned as a boy. *Would you like some onions,* he'd ask, and send me home with them—and later tomatoes, squash, cabbage, kohlrabi and, of course, a load of compost. No matter the season, you didn't leave Upakrik Farm empty-handed.

In spring he bestowed pussy willows on me; in fall, all the persimmons I could eat; in winter, wreaths and roping he'd made himself. We'd get those the Sunday after Thanksgiving, the day we cut our Christmas tree from his fields. Not this year.

The Bay Gardener has left us, but he did not leave us bereft. He shared his knowledge with us. He is alive in our gardens—our hearts and our minds.

Bay Gardener

by Dr. Francis Gouin

Mother Nature has taken centuries to convert subsoil to topsoil. With quality compost readily available, you can make high-quality topsoil in days.

Never cover a sandy soil with a clay or silt soil or cover silt soil with a sandy one. Importing the wrong soil will cause drainage problems. Have the soil in your yard tested to determine the amount of sand and silt and classify your soil as loam, sandy loam, loamy sand, silt loam or clay loam.

Sonia Linebaugh

FEBRUARY 23, 1946-OCTOBER 12, 2018

*Her pilgrim soul tarried with us
to make a newspaper.*

One of the days between April 22 and 29, 1993, Sonia Linebaugh dropped in to see how we were doing in the adventure of *New Bay Times*. She stayed for four and a-half years.

What Sonia did to nourish our start-up newspaper for the next 192 weeks is recorded in black-and-while history. Those faded pages, preserved in *New Bay Times, New Bay Times~Weekly* and *Bay Weekly* volume books, tell a long story but an incomplete one.

Books preserve what was done, the finished act of journalism. Like documenting a baseball team's season by its statistics, a print-only record misses the spirit of the team and the freely, fully given genius of each of its players. The sustaining spirit Sonia poured into our family newspaper lives in human memory.

It was Alex Knoll who dated Sonia's surprise appearance in our shoebox office then, at Tri-State Marine in Deale, Maryland, to those days between the first and second editions of our prototype, fortnightly issue. We hadn't printed enough of the first to make all the introductions that had to be made between *New Bay Times* Vol. 1 No. 1 and Vol. 1 No. 2 two weeks later.

Those were among the hardest weeks in our now 25-year history, for going in we'd figured out the first issue—but not the second.

We've gotten through all our weeks by our prevailing power to draw to us, if not always exactly what we needed, then repeated tidal flushes of creative energy. Sonia filled both bills.

Joining *New Bay Times* was a logical next step for Sonia as well as a lifesaving step for us.

411

Sonia and I had discovered each other very shortly after her move to Fairhaven Cliffs in the late 1980s. We were brought together by our polymath neighbor Lee Summerall, whose creative energy added its own buoyancy to our early efforts in flight. Both artists in search of our medium, Sonia, who was then the visual artist, and I, a word-maker, turned to each other for inspiration and collaboration.

New Bay Times would devour all I had to give—all any of us had to give—and still be unsatisfied. It drew Sonia—and over the twenty-five years, hundreds more—like a magnet exerting its irresistible force on iron filings.

When the reprinted Vol. 1, No. 1 appeared April 29, 1993, Sonia's name was on the masthead, with Alex, under the heading Production. That meant she and Alex stood together at Lee's donated light table, mounted on a desk-high flat file cabinet, to cut and paste column widths of printed text onto cardboard flats the size of a full double-truck sheet of *New Bay Times* pages. Using the proportion wheel, she'd size photos to the blanks to be filled pre-production by our printer, in Waldorf, Maryland. She'd paste tiny corrected words over misspellings, rolling it all smooth with brayers. In the early months, even fortnightly production took us long into the night, sometimes beyond into the early morning.

Sonia gave us all that and way more.

In Vol. 1, No. 1, she shot and assembled the photomontage for my first *New Bay Times* environmental story, Trashing Our Beaches. Vol. 1, No. 2, she wrote Dandelions Abound for what would become the feature Who's Here. Her first personal essay, the reflection Calm and Storm, appeared on June 17, in Vol. 1 No. 5. By that same issue, she'd taken over Not Just for Kids, then our center spread.

Week by week, Sonia shaped every page, becoming Page Editor by our second year, 1994. Week by week—pasting, writing, drawing, photographing, imagining, creating—she lifted us on her shoulders. By our third year, 1995, she had earned the title Associate Editor.

Sonia's genius was spinning art from everyday life. She was a universalist, drawing in every aspect of experience.

If you met Sonia, you were likely to find yourself written about—or writing; drawn or drawing. Neighborhood kids posed for cover shots with hollyhocks—that's Maureen Carr, who grew up to graduate as a Marine from the U.S. Naval Academy—or kittens needing homes. She lured the Carrs, the Veiths, the Hines, the Kellys, the Swaggerts, the Smiths, the Brewers, the Brumbaughs and every child of every staffer into reading and reviewing books and writing poems and stories.

No safer were own kids, Stephanie and Darin, who modeled for her drawings and shared and recorded their adventures, from enduring the imprinting of the pet goose Sir William to learning to windsurf to motoring a sailboat down the intercoastal waterway. All our young interns—even Betsy Kehne, way back then—came under her spell and found themselves transformed into fluent writers, easy storytellers, amazing fabulists.

A remembered Halloween encounter with a costumed tree to her backyard birds and flowers to her sacred places—most every sight that swept into Sonia's ken turned up in those early pages. Much of what she experienced—from a doomed baby bird to USNA football to her beloved Mother Meera, who she believed was an avatar of the divine mother—we experienced through her eyes, words and pictures.

For us, she threw herself deeply into the world of Chesapeake Country, encountering, reporting, writing. Her specialty was illuminating the human angle of environmental stewardship, with stories on controlling mosquitoes, managing your own backyard sewage treatment plant and community affairs. Just as comfortably, she got to know troubled rivers, ancient mariners and opera seamstresses.

From that first week, Sonia stayed with *New Bay Times* through July 31, 1997. In *Bay Weekly*, she popped back in.

There was more than newspapering in her life. A pilgrim soul, Sonia searched for realms beyond what we can see and touch and hear and taste and feel. She explored those realms, and now it may well be that her soul is exploding, expanding into the vast energy field beyond the dynamic tapestry woven of time.

M.L. Faunce

MAY 27, 1944–OCTOBER 31, 2021

What we said before she died

M.L. Faunce won't sit at a Thanksgiving table this year. But she'll be the centerpiece of many hearts and thoughts. Many of us will say all the good things we hesitate to say when their recipient is able to hear our compliments.

M.L. and I were lucky. We talked about all we'd done together and meant to each other, especially intensely over the months in the first half of this year when we were putting together her book of stories from *New Bay Times* and *Bay Weekly*, *My Date With an Oyster and Other Tales of a DC Girl Discovering Chesapeake Country*, for publication by New Bay Books. By then we knew she was advancing toward her death (a terrible cancer called primary peritoneal took her), so we stayed pretty much at the heart of things. The book was timely. I was grateful for the renewed connection, and grateful—plus a little envious—of the pictures she sent me of sights, often avian, along her tropical morning walks.

Sent when she was still able to walk. Little and tough, with a body frame that fit the $E = mc^2$ equation, she ran the streets of DC she knew well as a fifth generation woman of the city, and a deeply entrenched congressional staffer. When her job sent her to live in Alaska, she added skiing to her regimen, often with dachshunds Kenai and Sitka.

We were extraordinarily lucky, M.L. and I, for we got to relive the pleasures—without the stresses—that came with working in journalism together as writer and editor from 1995 to 2006. We had the extra gift of hindsight, knowing what we knew now and didn't know then. Plus, we were living out Shakespeare's words "to love that well which thou must leave ere long."

Over those months, we told each other our gratitude. There are so many levels of my gratitude to M.L.

First—and this she knew because of the electricity more than the words—I am grateful to M.L. because she felt the magnetism of our newspaper, where almost everybody was trying their absolute best to make a living document of those times, this place.

M.L. writes in the introduction to her book: "Intrigued by the stories in *New Bay Times*, I thought: Maybe I can write about Bay life, too. I sent a first piece to Editor Sandra Martin—and she accepted it!"

I would find, over the years, that M.L. matched our absolute best with her own. How grateful I am for that rare gift! Soon, she was seeing stories under every bush. She dove into Bay Country, where she was living out her childhood dreams, writing about "the nature, culture, history, community, news and activities and all the seasonal changes, where the fish were biting, what's happened to the once-prolific oyster that filtered the Bay for centuries, the lives of watermen and future of skipjacks that sailed the Bay," she recalled.

There's another point of gratitude: M.L. was bringing me stories fired by pure love of what she saw and was doing. She gave me not only quality but also quantity. It takes a lot of stories to fill a paper week by week.

Add on many more points of gratitude because M.L. wrote by assignment as well as inspiration. "M.L., we need a story on the state of oysters," I'd say, and she'd give me a story and more. She gave *Bay Weekly* our one and only Best of Show story, beating out all the *Washington Post* and all the big dogs in the science & environment category in the newspaper competition.

For twelve years, "I had the pleasure of writing by whim and assignment," M.L. wrote.

Farewell, M.L., my gratitude for those twelve years will last as long as I do.

My Date
With an Oyster

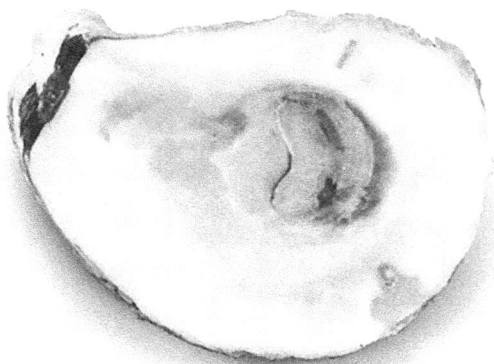

*and Other Stories
of a D.C. Girl Discovering
Chesapeake Country*

M.L. Faunce

 New Bay Books

Philip Tinsley

OCTOBER 17, 1939–JULY 23, 2022

He lived and died with all he wanted.

We always believed Philip Tinsley could do anything. Now, again we see that confidence was well placed, for Philip did the best thing a person can do with this one, rare life—find a companion-lover to see him through to its end.

That's the end of a well-lived story. Along the way, there are an infinity of other stories. In one of them, we—that's my small family of Bill Lambrecht, here with me today, and sons Alex and Nathaniel Knoll, here is spirit—fell under Philip's care.

What would we have done without him!

In 1974, Bill and I each came to forks in the road. As with Janice and Philip, strong forces were drawing us together. Rather than seek his fortune in the wider world of journalism, he signed on as a State-house reporter with the *Alton Telegraph*—half time, at first, at $80 a week. Rather than return to my roots in St. Louis after a divorce had left me homeless and income-less, I managed to get a $13,500 mortgage for a bungalow in Springfield.

Editor's Note: Sandra wrote this story on deadline at a coffee shop in Springfield, Illinois en route to Philip Tinsley's memorial held in his deep woods homestead near Athens, Illinois, around a fire, with a shaman conducting.

1429 South Second Street was a cute little house in a bushy surround, but oh it needed help. Philip stepped in and, with his brother, Virgil, made me a workable kitchen. He and Janice then gave me the stove to cook on—a Quick Meal Magic Chef from the American Stove Company—an early gas enamel beauty, adorned with a chick hopping out of its shell.

My family lived in that house for a decade. Philip and Janice married in my living room, with Judge Ben Miller officiating and 6-year-old Nathaniel and his friends as witnesses. Over the years, Philip solved the problems of that 1908 bungalow and enhanced its charms. One of these enhancements, still rotating in Nat's mind, is a lazy-Susan Scrabble board.

For both Alex and Nat, he was the model of manly mastery of material elements. Alex, himself now a respectable home maintainer, watched Philip and thanked him for all he taught. Nat remembers Philip's patience with a small wild boy.

"He walked me around their 12 acres," Nat asked me to say in his stead, "and when a bee stung me he took the sting away."

As we rescued and re-rescued our little bungalow, the magazine-production class I devised and taught at Sangamon State University created the *Homesteading Armchair Reader*. Philip—ever so able, ever so undaunted—took the principles of homesteading home. My family watched with awe and applause as Philip, Virgil and their father built a road into their land, and at its end erected Janice and Philip's homestead. With its passive solar wall, compost privy and wood stove, it was, for us lesser mortals, the epitome of a virtue we all needed and sought in those revolutionary days: self-sufficiency.

We visited their home many times over our years in Springfield, and celebrated memorable Thanksgivings there, with the family of friends we shared. Once Bill's work took us to Washington, DC, and the family deployed Phil's derring-do bravery in starting a weekly newspaper on Maryland's western shore of Chesapeake Bay, the friendships endured. But the visits which had been so common and casual were rare.

When I returned to Springfield—I still call it home—in 2019, I begged an invitation to Philip and Janice's place, longing to see it one more time.

In the warmth of the June sun and renewed friendship, Janice and I spoke of what we had made of our lives. Then I turned that question on Philip.

"I live on land that I own in a house that I built with the woman I love," he said. "What more could I want?"

Gene Martin

NOVEMBER 26, 1907–NOVEMBER 6, 1993

A Toast to My Father

It's not the Bay's oyster famine that will stop him.

No, even though a 250-acre farm in Washington State now produces more oysters than the whole Chesapeake, we'd find oysters. We'd hound Bootie Collins till he handed over a freshly tonged bushel. Then we'd array them out front on the picnic table and hose them down, washing away Chesapeake bottom mud and thin, wiggly oyster worms. Finally we'd scrub them with a brush for good measure. Only then could they come indoors for Bill and Alex to shuck, me to wash and jar, and everybody to eat—raw, steamed, stewed, fried, and, with jars in the freezer, in even more creative ways.

When we drove back to the Midwest for Thanksgiving and my father's birthday, our cooler would hold Mason jars of frozen oysters, the world's best-traveled seafood. Dad's house in St. Louis was the end of the line. We wouldn't be in his and Violet's warm, lived-in kitchen for much more than a minute when I would unpack a jar of the cold but now unfrozen oysters and Dad would say, "Let's see how they taste." He'd eat a whole pint jar out of a bowl until I made him an oyster plate so he could enjoy them in style.

Gene Martin had been swallowing oysters with gusto for most of eighty-five years. When he was a boy in Chicago, though Chesapeake oysters were just a little down from their 1880s' peak, iced oysters in the shell traveled by freight to the Midwest, where they were a darn sight more popular than prairie oysters. Everybody ate them, from childhood on. Everybody of Dad's generation still did, though their children and grandchildren might gag to see them do so.

I grew up eating oysters as naturally as I ate ice cream. I'd probably just seen Dad eat one when I swallowed my first one back in the early 1950s. (As Mother used to say, "Gene Martin could serve you **** on a shingle and make it look good." In my personal memory is the day he sliced himself an onion and made it into a sandwich with mustard. He carried it to the bar to eat and every customer in the place wanted one, too.)

I can tell you just where we were when I ate my first oyster: The oysters rested in chipped ice back in the hot kitchen of our St. Louis restaurant, the Stymie Club, and when anybody ordered a half dozen or a dozen, the salad man would shuck them to order. When he wasn't busy, he'd shuck them one at a time for me until I'd eaten my fill. That was usually closer to a dozen than a half dozen.

So I was proud when it became my turn to bring oysters to Dad, and I wanted to serve them in style and abundance.

Style and abundance: Those are the qualities I was proudest of in my father.

As a restaurateur, he was a professional host, and I've never met a man better suited to his calling. Of all my million memories of him, the stereotype is Gene Martin behind a bar pouring a drink, taking a bet, smiling a little cynically, telling a story, riveting you with his cool blue eyes and the symmetry of his narration. "Everybody loved Gene Martin," my mother, Elsa, would say. From the early 1940s to the early '60s, she was Gene's straight man, as well as business partner and wife, in that order. "He could shoot a man in front of a full house and everybody would swear Elsa did it," Elsa insisted.

No wonder the bar at the Stymie Club was always full. At Gene's place, you always felt at home. Looking back, I have to think most of our customers felt better at the Stymie than they did at home, because they spent a lot more time at our bar and in our booths than they did in their living rooms.

The years I was his little girl, the Stymie Club was Gene's home, too. He wasn't much of a family man in those years, and when Mother and I moved to a house a mile away, he didn't join us, though he did, even after Gene and Elsa divorced, continue to eat his Sunday meals at our house. That Elsa could surely cook.

But Gene couldn't stay home, even when home was a supper club and cocktail lounge. He liked to go, and I loved to go with him. Eating out at friends' restaurants...celebrating summer with extended-family picnics...visiting race tracks and once the great racing country around Lexington and Louisville, Kentucky...touring his home city, Chicago, and the city's hot spots...night clubbing: Dad introduced me to the world and made me comfortable there. Like a good date, he never left you uncertain or on your own.

In his mid-50s, Gene married Violet, the love of his life, and slowly settled into the family routine. He even cut the grass. I've had fewer shocks in my life greater than finding my father in his kitchen pasting in green stamps. For those thirty years, his and Violet's house was open to me and my friends and my children. We'd appear out of the blue carrying gifts and all of us, no matter how many, would crowd around the table, eat a meal and drink the sweet, forbidden wine that Dad loved but reserved for holidays because, after all those years of drinking, alcohol made him sick as a dog.

But that would be the day after. Now, we'd exchange news and—if college football wasn't on television—soon we'd be after Gene Martin to tell stories. Sometimes, when he was sick or grouchy, he'd shrug off our pleas, scolding, "How can you expect me to remember that? That was seventy-five [or fifty or twenty-five] years ago!" But more often, he'd agree, and moments later, after he'd arrayed the facts and composed the structure in his own mind, he'd begin:

"When I was a little boy"—sometimes it was as a "little girl" that he'd say he'd been a firefighter or a hobo or drove a car. That's how Dad's stories often began when I was a little girl.

But in later years it was truth, not fantasy, we craved, and Dad was famous for it. He might take us back to Chicago, in the century's teens, to show us how and at what Lakefront beach his brother Jack had sustained the freak injury that would kill him just as he reached manhood. Or with him we might tour the campus of the University of Illinois in the 1920s, watching Dad and his pals swallow goldfish as casually as we did oysters. A few years later, we might ride the rails with him—that was Alex's favorite, and in college he wrote a short story recounting how his grandfather learned first hand the rules of Jim Crow.

Each decade of his long life had its stories: St. Louis gambling in the 1930s; wartime Key West—a wide open place where you lived hard and fast and loved it—in the 1940s; prosperity, dice and diamonds in the 1950s.

Once he settled down, toward the end of the '60s, news and observation replaced adventure in his stories. Nothing got by Gene Martin: no new business, sports statistic, nor bit of city, state, regional or national news. Though I've not yet ridden St. Louis' new light rail commuter train, I can tell you all about it because Dad—months after the joints in both his knees had been replaced—rode the route from start to finish. His disappointments—whatever they were—never made his stories.

Yes, Elsa said, "Gene Martin had kissed the Blarney Stone." Listening, I drank in the stories and the art of storytelling. Rule 1, I observed, was the storyteller's absolute confidence in his tale. Though Gene made barely a gesture—nothing more than the arc of a hand—he set the stage. Underway, he never hesitated nor faltered: relentlessly and artfully the logic unfolded. Nobody whispered when Gene Martin told stories.

Rule 2 insisted that a story be chock full of facts, and accurate ones, at that. The storyteller must recall and recreate times, places and people, even to the numbers on the street and the clothes the characters wore. Dad showed that same startling memory in giving directions or going out for rides. You never got lost following his directions. Long demolished city neighborhoods came back to life on his tours.

Hence Rule 3: Revere your story's structure. My father's stories followed their own map, and you could, too. No helter-skelter in his storytelling. Facts flowed in neat order so that you always knew Who was who, did What, When, Where and How—though Why you had to be smart enough to figure out on your own.

Rule 4: Quit when your story's over. "That's the way things were back then," Dad would simply end—and all would believe him. Then he'd say, "Come on, let's have another glass of wine." Or we'd all pile in the car and drive to the latest ice cream parlor for a cone.

His last rule is why—after I swallowed the news of Gene Martin's quiet death from heart failure, in his bed, Saturday morning November 6, 20 days short of his eighty-sixth birthday—I ate a dozen Chesapeake Bay oysters in his honor.

Reminder for My Mother: Elsa Olivetti Martin

JANUARY 1, 1921–AUGUST 6, 1988

On Your Daughter's 73rd Birthday

This is life.

The breeze that touches me is dancing in the trees. Reeds sway. Temperature is palpable as pleasure.

Colors are saturated with sun and muted in cast shadow. Greengreengreengreen hueing a full palette. Thin blue sky, puffy white clouds, streaks of the ones you called buttermilk.

My ears buzz with sound, but I think I'm just one point of reception of the hum of life, amplified by electricity flowing through our wires, radio waves through our atmosphere, blood through our veins. Cars whizz unseen on the road beyond. The crow caws. The osprey whistles. The cardinal tweet tweet tweet-a-tweet tweets. Voices—a man's dominant—rise from neighbors visiting in the hollow. Our neighborhood's new young Alex cries *maaa...*

I am crying mother, too, on June 30, 2016, the seventy-third anniversary of the day you bore me.

Do you hear me?

I was thinking probably not when the sun radiated its streaming medallion right into my heart. From its center Holy Mary Mother of God stepped out to me. Her face was yours.

This is what I then understood.

I am in the middle of the short descent I can count. On my lap sit Alex and Nat (no daughters born to me). Elsa and Ada sit on their laps. I sit on your lap. You sit on Catharine's lap. We are out of one another's wombs.

Even my short vision spans 120 years. But my imagination can multiply. If I say a rosary of mothers—five decades of ten mothers each—I touch beads for fifty mothers. In depth, together we fifty stretch back 1,250 years. All the way to the year 766 AD. In width, together we blanket Earth.

For all those mothers through years and years and years, I am the point of consciousness.

Life thrills through me. Heaven and Earth throb with life. Beneath us, pregnant Mother Earth creates, silently, and all that is dead will be alive. We are the atoms spinning.

This is life.

Remember.

PHOTO CREDITS

ACKNOWLEDGMENTS

As a retrospective on five decades of a life in journalism, *Fire at the Stymie Club: Stories from the Mississippi River to Chesapeake Bay*, encompasses the contributions of many people. So my gratitude is wide and deep.

To begin at the beginning, credit is due my parents and grand-mother—Gene, Elsa Olivetti and Florence Bunting Martin—for setting me on my story-telling ways as well as enmeshing me in a life full of good material. My family extended to the staff of the Stymie, who shared their love and inspired me with their human stories that deserve more telling than they get in this book. My grandmother's first cousin Cora Smith gave me the raw material to make deeply satisfying stories out of two lives whose letters were preserved in her legacy of papers.

How I wish I could thank in person the shoe-leather, un-bylined reporters of the *St. Louis Post-Dispatch* and *Alton Telegraph* for sharing with me (oh so conveniently preserved on newspapers.com) the story behind the story of my unconventional father and life at the Stymie. In wonderful synchronicity, my husband wrote for both papers a couple generation later.

For my induction into journalism, I thank Fletcher 'Bud' Farrar, who—though he spared encouraging words—allowed me pages of his newspaper, *Illinois Times*, to fill with stories during the late 1970s and early 1980s and occasionally beyond. A selection of the stories I wrote way back then proved fit, by editor Bill Lambrecht's stan-dards, to reappear in this book.

My photographer-partner during those times, Sue Eslinger, compounded the pleasures of discovery. Lifelong thanks to her—and to Judy Shereikis, our friend and colleague, who nudged us together into our heady adventures.

The three decades of my ownership of *New Bay Times-Bay Weekly* opened the floodgates of inspiration and tasked me in the discipline of mastery of my craft. Among the hundreds of people who collaborated in that enterprise, first thanks are due to my son and partner John Alexander Knoll, who was our Atlas, and to husband Bill Lambrecht, who was our rock.

Extraordinary help was generously given by investors Elsa Olivetti Martin, Cora Smith, Ada Lambrecht and Don Richardson—as well as the many people who contributed to the safe-landing campaign organized by P. Sue Kullen in our final months.

Among so many contributors who gave us their hearts and soul, special thanks to Sonia Linebaugh, Bill Burton, M.L. Faunce, Lisa Edler, and the Bay Gardener, Dr. Francis Gouin—and to Betsy Kehne, who gave her youth as well as her heart and soul. For keeping all our stories, mine included, on the up and up, thanks to proofreaders Richard Wilson and Martha Lee Benz.

Each of our readers has earned my endless thanks for completing the circle, for a writer without a reader, without you, is a voice crying in the wilderness.

Each of the subjects of these stories is owed my appreciation as well, for allowing me to broadcast their experiences to thousands of readers. Among those are my three grandchildren, Jack, Elsa and Ada Knoll, who had no right of refusal on their birth stories.

The making of this book is the gift of my husband, who recognized I could not be torn away from telling the stories of others to bring my own book to life. Contributing their eyes along the way were Alex Knoll, who once again pulled rabbits out of his hat; Linda Kulla, my oldest friend; Nathaniel Martin Knoll, my younger son; and Ruth Knack, whose generosity I have appreciated over the years. I also thank our early readers and hope they have been compensated by good stories.

The last word, as always, goes to Suzanne Shelden of Shelden Studios, whose genius and generosity, patience and perseverance brought this book forth for you, it is my sincere hope, to enjoy.

Sandra Olivetti Martin

Sandra Olivetti Martin